The Online Journ@list

Using the Internet and Other Electronic Resources

Third Edition

Randy Reddick

FACS Los Angeles & London

Elliot King

Loyola College

Harcourt College Publishers

Fort Worth Philadelphia San Diego New York Orlando Austin San Antonio
Toronto Montreal London Sydney Tokyo

070,4
R 313

Publisher	Earl McPeek
Acquisitions Editor	Stephen Dalphin
Market Strategist	Adrienne Krysiuk
Developmental Editor	Jill Johnson
Project Editor	Jon Davies
Art Director	Garry Harman
Production Manager	Serena Barnett

Cover illustration: Cluzy design

ISBN: 0-15-506752-4

Library of Congress Catalog Card Number: 00-26101
Copyright © 2001, 1997, 1995 by Harcourt, Inc.

Address for Domestic Orders
Harcourt College Publishers, 6277 Sea Harbor Drive, Orlando, FL 32887-6777
800-782-4479

Address for International Orders
International Customer Service
Harcourt, Inc., 6277 Sea Harbor Drive, Orlando, FL 32887-6777
407-345-3800
(fax) 407-345-4060
(e-mail) hbintl@harcourtbrace.com.

Address for Editorial Correspondence
Harcourt College Publishers, 301 Commerce Street, Suite 3700, Fort Worth, TX 76102

Web Site Address
http://www.harcourtcollege.com

Printed in the United States of America

0 1 2 3 4 5 6 7 8 9   066   9 8 7 6 5 4 3 2 1
Harcourt College Publishers

Preface

In the early 1990s, widespread computer-based communications networks, most prominently the Internet, came online. This innovation has changed the practice of journalism forever. The impact of the Internet on journalism promises to be more encompassing and pervasive than any other revolution in communications technology.

Pat Stith, Pultizer Prize–winning computer-assisted reporting specialist for the Raleigh (North Carolina) *News & Observer* has said, "Those who use these tools will be ahead. Those who don't will be left behind—and may not survive."

Nora Paul of the Poynter Institute for Media Studies has told journalists, "By taking advantage of the access to information and people available to you by using a computer, your research and interviewing can have a range and immediacy that is simply impossible without a computer's assistance."

In the three years since the second edition of *The Online Journalist* appeared, the Internet and other computer-based communications networks have been transformed from dynamic, widespread, accessible new channels of communication to arguably the dominant channels of communication. On January 10, 2000, America Online and Time Warner announced a merger to create a fully-integrated Internet-age media and communications company. The hosts of television shows routinely urge viewers to get more information from their Web site. In fact, it seems as if every self-respecting 14-year-old has a personal home page. Movies are made about romancing conducted via e-mail.

Moreover, nearly all college students have access to the Web, and newsrooms now provide reporters with Internet access at their desks. This edition of the book reflects and incorporates these trends.

The third edition of *The Online Journalist* describes and demonstrates the resources available to journalists and how reporters can use the Internet and other online resources to do their jobs more efficiently and effectively. It also discusses the impact this exploding technology is having and will have on journalism, the pitfalls reporters and editors must avoid as they enter cyberspace, and the legal and ethical issues raised by online journalism. It takes an in-depth look at the Web as a publishing medium for news and makes an early assessment of the overall impact these changes have had on journalists and news media.

Jargon-free and intended for both students and professional journalists, this book is a valuable resource for those beginning to apply the Internet to journalism and experienced Net surfers. It helps readers maximize their use of this new technology and capitalize on the opportunities the Web offers journalists.

In addition to introducing the range of online resources and clearly explaining how to use all the major applications on the Internet, *The Online Journalist* includes a glossary of terms, as well as appendixes that describe useful online resources for journalists and give guidance for selecting an Internet provider.

As in the first and second editions, we feel grateful to many people. We would like to thank our families—our wives Anita and Nancy; our children Aliza, Marcie, and Jordan (Elliot's own new third edition), Laura, Ben, Roxanne, Jennifer, Heather, and Jacob.

We would also like to thank the following professors for their reviews and feedback on the second and first editions: Virginia Bachelor, State University of New York College at Brockport; Jacqueline Lambiase, University of North Texas; Franklin Parks, Frostburg State University; Mike Cowling, University of Wisconsin—Oshkosh; Nancy Roberts, University of Minnesota; Paul Adams, California State University—Fresno; Kim Walsh-Childers, University of Florida; and Jim Ross, Northeastern University.

Loyola College continues to be a supportive environment for experimenting with online resources. Since the second edition, Elliot has established the New Media Center of Loyola College as a high-end research and development facility for Web-based content. We would like to give special thanks to Elliot's associates at the New Media Center, Barney Kirby, Megan Sapnar, and Tina Lariviere. We appreciate the support and encouragement provided by Neil Alperstein and Andy Ciofalo for this project and for seeing the contribution the Internet can make to the Department of Writing and Media.

FACS, now with offices in San Jose (Silicon Valley) and Pasadena, California, and in London, continues to support and encourage the efforts of Randy to help journalists and journalism students to use these new technologies for doing better reporting. Special thanks go to Jack Cox, Peter McCarty, Chris Gardner, and Mary Jacobson.

Elliot King: eking2@prodigy.net
Randy Reddick: reddick@facsnet.org

Contents

Chapter **1**   **An Introduction**   1

    The Mission of This Book   2
    Technology, Access, and Journalism   3
        The Payoff of Increased Access   4
    For Whom This Book Is Intended   6
    Between the Second and Third Editions   8
    How to Use This Book   10
        When Something Doesn't Work   10
    A Last Word   10

Chapter **2**   **The World Online**   11

    The Emergence of Computer Networks   13
    Understanding Client-Server Computing   14
    Host, Client, and Server   14
    Client Location Governs Functionality   16
    Network Connection Type Affects Functionality   16
    Cyberspace Is the Networking of Networks   16
    Defining the Internet   17
        A Set of Rules: The Internet as Agreement   18
        Network Control   19
        Cost Structure   20
    A History of the Internet   21
        Military Origins   21
        Supercomputing Centers Established   22
    Internet Applications   23
        Electronic Mail   24
        The World Wide Web   24
        FTP   24
        Usenet News   25
        Chat   25
        Telnet and Gopher   25
    The Convergence of Cyberspace   26
    The Growth of Portals and Hybrid Services   26
    What's Available Online   27
        Government Information   28
    Human Sources   28
        Libraries and Special Depositories   29
        Books and Magazines   30
    Other Good Stuff   30

The Future of the Infrastructure   31

Chapter **3**   **Working the World Wide Web**   33

    History, Development, and Structure of the Web   34
      The Popularity of the Web   36
      The Structure of the Web   38
    Web Transfer Protocols   38
    The Anatomy of an URL   39
    What You Can Learn from the URL   40
    The Essentials of HTML   42
    Your Browser   42
      Browsers and File Types   43
    Working the Web   45
    Here and Back Again   47
    Enhanced Reporting   48
    Finding What You Need   48
      Using Subject Directories   51
    When You Find What You Want   53
      Sourcing Cyberspace Material   54
    A New Medium   54
    When the Web Goes Wrong   56
    Conclusion   58

Chapter **4**   **Contacting People by E-mail**   61

    The Basics of E-mail   62
      Getting Started   63
    Anatomy of an E-mail Address   64
      E-mail Software Comes in Different Flavors 65
    Creating and Sending an E-mail Message   66
      Editing Messages   67
      Sending E-mail   68
      Including a Signature File   69
      Addressing Your Mail   69
      Getting to the Destination   70
    Receiving and Responding to E-mail   71
      Receiving Attachments   71
      Managing Incoming Mail   72
      Responding to E-mail   72
      Saving Your Information   74
    Viruses   74
    Finding People   75
    The Law and E-mail   77
    Netiquette and E-mail   78
    E-mail Is a Tool for Reporters   78
      E-mail Produces Story Leads   80
      E-mail and the Public Record   80

Conclusion   81

Chapter 5   Online Communities   83

Discussion Lists and Listservs   84
Subscribing and Unsubscribing to a List   85
Setting Your List Parameters   86
Two-Way versus One-Way Lists   88
Finding Relevant Lists   89
Posting Messages and Using Lists   89
To Quote or Not to Quote   91
Discussion List Archives   92
Usenet Newsgroups   94
Network News Hierarchies   95
Configuring Your News Reader   96
Organizing Your Newsgroups   96
Navigating Usenet Levels   98
        Reading and Responding   98
Finding the Right Newsgroups   98
Archived Usenet Information   100
Proper Usenet Behavior   100
Using Chat   101
Chat and News   102
Instant Messaging   102
Webcasts   103
Conclusion   104

Chapter 6   Search Strategies   105

How Search Sites Work   106
A Comprehensive Strategy   107
Using Online Tutorials   107
Learn from Other Journalists   109
Using Subject Catalogs and Directories   110
        Not All Indices Are Created Equal   110
        Some Representative Directory and Catalog Sites   111
Scout Sites Focus on a Single Topic   112
Specialized Search Tools   113
        Match the Tool to the Job   115
Constructing Productive Searches   116
        Using Boolean Logic and Literals   117
        Other Search Refinements   119
        What the Search Engines Miss   121
Meta-Searches and Agents   122
Managing Bookmarks Wisely   124
Keeping Current   125
Common Sense and Naming Conventions   127
Conclusion   128

Chapter **7**   **The Internet beyond the Web**   129

    What Telnet Offers   130
    How Telnet Works   131
        Closing Telnet Connections   132
    A Sample Telnet Session   132
    Capturing a Telnet Session with Log Utilities   135
    Getting Help   135
    Moving Files with FTP (File Transfer Protocol)   135
        Anonymous FTP   136
        Navigating FTP Server Directories   137
        Handling and Using Files   137
    Finding Files Using Archie   140
    Words of Caution   141
    Jewels in Gopherspace   141
        Working Gopher   143
    Conclusion   144

Chapter **8**   **Evaluating Net Information**   145

    Understanding the Problem   146
    Production Qualities   146
    Domain Checks   148
    Measuring Confidence in Site Ownership   148
    Using the Whois Database   152
    Weigh Data Integrity Using MIDIS   154
    Protocol Weight and Other Internal Checks   155
        Less-Used Protocols Add Credibility   156
        Newsgroups versus Discussion Lists   157
    Traditional Approaches   158
    Conclusion   159

Chapter **9**   **Network News–Web Publishing**   161

    Why Online Publishing Has Exploded   162
        Economic Incentives   164
    People Are Reading Online   166
    Publishing Parameters   167
    Newspaper Ventures: Large, Medium, and Small   168
        Broadened Coverage   171
    Magazines Climb Online   171
        Developing Unique Style   173
    Television, Radio, and the Web   174
    New Journalism on the Web   176
    New Media Challenges   176
    Conclusion   179

Chapter **10**   **Law, Ethics, and the Internet**   181

Free Speech and the Internet   183
Libel Considerations   184
What Is a Public Figure?   185
Does Net Culture Encourage Libel?   186
Service Providers and Libel   186
Copyright   187
Using Information Found Online   188
Misappropriation   189
Implied License   189
Fair Use   190
A Work's Market Value   191
Copyright and Web Sites   192
Copyright Protects Creators   193
E-mail   193
Confidentiality   194
Erased Files—Not   196
Speech Codes   196
Open Meetings and Freedom of Information   197
Access for Online Journalists   198
Obscenity and Other Free Speech Issues   199
Online Ethics   200
Three Rules Hold   200
Beyond the Rules   201
Conclusion   201

Chapter **11**   **Getting More out of Your Browser**   203

Personalizing Your Software   204
Choosing a Home Page   205
Setting Your Mail Identity   206
Remembering Your Password, Automatic E-mail Checks   209
Automatic E-mail Signature   210
Managing Bookmarks Wisely   210
Bookmarks and Their Folders   213
Edit Site Titles and Descriptions   215
Multiple Bookmark Files   216
Save Time with Keyboard Shortcuts   217
Searching within a Document   218
Copying Text   218
Navigating by Keyboard   219
Staying Connected on the Road   219
Web-Based Mail Services   221
Configuring Public Browsers   222
Wireless Access   222
Extending Browsers with Plug-Ins   222
Streaming Media   223

Portable Document Format (.pdf)   223
Alexa, the Research Assistant   224
Plug-In Cautions   227
Selecting the Best Software   227
Distinctions among Browsers   228
Distinctions among E-mail Clients   231
Managing Attachments   232
Stationery and Mail Themes   232
Concerning AOL and CompuServe Browsers   233
Using Generic Browsers under CompuServe and AOL
Accounts   233
Conclusion   234

Chapter 12   Net Impact on Journalism   235

How Television Changed Journalism   236
The Web's Challenge to Television   239
Liberation of Content and Its Presentation   240
Rise of the Multimedia Journalist   241
Increasing Debate and Press Accountability   243
The Economics of Journalism   245
The Impact of the Internet on Journalism   246
Conclusion   246

Appendix A   Starting Places for Journalists   247

Keyword Search Sites   247
General Directories   248
Hotlists and Other Journalists' Resources   248
Professional Organizations   249
Other Useful Sites   251

Appendix B   Choosing an Access Provider   253

Commercial Hybrids versus ISPs   253
Shell Accounts, SLIP, and PPP   254
Price, Features, and Free Access   255
Internet Service Providers   256
Commercial Hybrid Providers   256

Glossary   257

Credits   264

Index   265

Chapter **1**

An Introduction

When he was working for the Halifax *Daily News*, Tom Regan was doing a story on Canada's troubling national debt. "Several politicians and right-wing business groups were running around yelling 'The sky is falling!' and demanding that the government make enormous cuts in Canada's social programs," Regan wrote. "I wanted to find out if there was any substance to these dire predictions."

What Regan did was to post some messages to Usenet news groups and to electronic discussion lists related to Canadian politics. In his postings he asked "for anyone with real information to reply to my query." Then he used an Internet program named Gopher (the first Internet browsing program) to find documents on the Canadian economy. All this took him about a half hour, he reported.

"When I checked an hour later, responses to my queries abounded," he wrote. He had notes from a professor in Montreal and the names of "three international economists from major U.S. financial firms who said Canada's debt crisis was being overblown." Another note led him to an expert on Canadian economics living in Australia.

"Without the Internet, it would have taken weeks to research the story, and I would have been limited to 'experts' in and around Nova Scotia," Regan concluded.

During the past five years, an increasing number of journalists have joined pioneers like Regan to use the Internet as a means of communicating with other people and of accessing information stored throughout the world. In fact, the Internet is becoming as fundamental a tool for reporting as the interview and the telephone.

For example, Sergio Charlab, special projects editor at *Jornal do Brasil*, had a challenging assignment. An important book about computers and the human mind had been translated into Portuguese. Charlab said that *The Emperor's New Mind* by British mathematician Roger Penrose "is interesting, but it was not easy for a non-technical person to analyze its thesis." By posting messages to what he felt were appropriate Usenet news groups, Charlab found others who had not only read the book but had written papers critical of some shortcomings in Professor Penrose's theory. Ultimately, Charlab obtained the e-mail address of Professor Penrose and "interviewed" him. He did all this without one telephone call.

In the fall of 1996, Silicon Graphics, a major computer manufacturer released a new line of equipment ranging from workstations to supercomputers. The announcement revealed the technological direction of the company for the next several years. For months, company officials had stumped the country, alerting key journalists and analysts of their plans.

But for the announcement itself, Silicon Graphics organized a real-time press conference on the World Wide Web. Journalists and others accessed the Silicon Graphics Web site, where they obtained background briefing papers, biographies of senior executives and press releases describing the new products in detail. They also could listen to a live audio feed of company officials outlining their plans. And they could submit questions via e-mail to which the executives could respond.

For its last set of major announcements the year before, Silicon Graphics had asked about 75 journalists to fly to company headquarters in northern California. By moving their press conference to the Web, they were able to attract more participants at less cost. And the journalists themselves received a superior briefing about the key issues.

This chapter will

- describe the mission of this book,
- discuss the relationship of technology, access, and journalism,
- characterize the target audience for the book,
- point out the differences between the second and third editions of *The Online Journalist*, and
- suggest a sequence for using the book to master online skills.

The Mission of This Book

This book is about empowerment. It is about the empowerment of individual journalists, the empowerment of entire organizations, and the empowerment of other information providers. Its aim is to give journalists and students of journalism the skills they need to flourish in the years to come.

This book describes a group of information-gathering tools that make some types of high-level reporting less dependent on company resources than on a journalist's initiative. The objective of this book is to teach good journalists and students of journalism how to practice better journalism.

In the past, elite media with enormous news budgets have sent out correspondents to centers of power and to locations of history-making events at home and abroad. They have had access to the inaccessible.

Today, "ordinary" reporters and student reporters using global computer network resources such as the Internet have instant electronic access to important documents, government data, privately held information, the world's greatest libraries, and expert sources and government officials without ever leaving their desks. Instead of going to Washington, Ottawa, London, or Cairo, New Delhi, Beijing, Taipei, Tokyo, or Cape Town, today's journalists may bring to their own desks resources from important centers of the world. And the same tools that reach around the world work down the block and around the corner.

Moreover, a reporter "fishing" for people who have firsthand knowledge of newsworthy events can reach tens of thousands of potential sources in just a couple of hours. A carefully worded query posted in the proper news groups, entered into online forums, and sent out to the right electronic mail lists can quickly net a bountiful harvest of eyewitnesses to some event, of victims to some plot or oversight, or of people with other firsthand knowledge that qualifies them as a news source.

Finally, every reporter who has held a beat has had to interview somebody on topics about which the reporter has had little background or expertise. Aside from being uncomfortable, the reporter is likely to ask ill-informed questions. Such questions elicit answers that do little to inform readers or audience members. Many news sources make it policy not to waste time with poorly informed journalists.

Again, through Internet resources the journalist can quickly locate and download "white papers" on just about any topic imaginable. Tucked away on sites on the World Wide Web, in news-group cubbyholes, listserv archives, and various specialized computer directories are storehouses of information that can provide journalists with answers to basic questions. More important, with that information in hand, journalists can ask more penetrating and probing questions than they could in the past.

Technology, Access, and Journalism

Interesting, timely, and accurate information is fundamental fodder for good journalism. For the last century, access to information has primarily defined the work that reporters do. Beats and specialization revolve around access. Police reporters work with information from the police. Court reporters become experts in understanding legal information. Sports reporters traffic in batting averages and zone defenses.

For years, the White House beat was considered the most prestigious in U.S. journalism. At the bottom line, the role of a White House reporter was defined by access to information from the White House. The first White House reporters hovered close outside the Executive Mansion itself, monitoring who entered and left for meetings with the chief executive. In the early 1900s, Theodore Roosevelt began meeting formally with reporters on a regular basis. His actions granted a certain status to those reporters. From then on, White House reporters were privy to information that reporters working in Philadelphia, Chicago, or Los Angeles just could not get on a timely basis.

That situation is rapidly changing. With the development of commercial databases, computer bulletin boards, and the Internet, journalists working anywhere can have the same access to much of the information once restricted to White House reporters. Today, any reporter with access to the Internet can visit the White House briefing room at http://http:// www.whitehouse.gov/WH/html/briefroom.html and obtain White House press releases, transcripts of press conferences and speeches, summaries of reports generated by federal agencies, and a host of other material.

Along the same lines, business reporters can now obtain Securities and Exchange Commission filings electronically. Science reporters can explore the databases of the National Institutes of Health, the National Science Foundation and the National Library of Medicine among other resources. Court reporters can access court filings and decisions. In almost every area of interest to journalists, reporters dramatically increase their access to information through the Internet.

In the same way that telephones allowed reporters to interview people around the country, Internet applications allow people to locate and obtain information from locations around the world. In short, online information allows reporters to do their jobs better no matter where they are physically located.

The Payoff of Increased Access

The question is, "Do reporters need access to more information?" After all, isn't there already a glut of information? Moreover, with so much information available, will reporters be reduced to simply sifting through information produced by others to pass on to busy readers?

The answer is complex but clear. The more access to information reporters have, the better reporters will be able to fulfill their mission to inform the public about key issues and interests of the day. More access to more information can only lead to better journalism.

The late investigative reporter I. F. Stone demonstrated in the1960s and early 1970s the power of exploring public sources of information ignored by other people. Relying exclusively on not-so-obscure, but little-publicized public documents, he revealed how the U.S. government misled the American people about its policies in Vietnam. To review most of those documents, Stone had to be in Washington. Increasingly, a reporter anywhere in the country has that ability.

Increased access to documents can also reduce reporters' reliance on specific sources, allowing them to be more independent and objective and making it more difficult for politicians and handlers to put a specific "spin" on events. For example, early in his administration, President Bill Clinton pushed for passage of a $30 billion crime bill. Some Republican senators charged that the bill was filled with pork-barrel projects. Most of the reporting about the bill consisted of charges being hurled back and forth in Washington and the potential political repercussions for President Clinton if the bill was defeated.

But with that bill accessible online, reporters from Altoona to Anchorage could have downloaded and analyzed what kind of impact the proposals would have had in their communities. They could have then interviewed local sources to get their readings on the measures. Local officials could have reflected on the impact of the bill—not on inside-the-beltway politics but in their own communities. Using online access, reporters can make national and international news more relevant to their own communities. Should they wish, reporters anywhere can now analyze the federal budget according to their own criteria rather than the criteria of politicians in Washington.

Far from reducing reporters to sifters of information, the explosion of access to a wider range of sources of information will make the role of reporters much more valuable. Reporters will be able to develop more authoritative stories more quickly. More important, reporters will be the only ones in position to synthesize information from disparate sources into stories that are relevant to their readers.

For example, let's say a legal reporter wants to investigate the performance of the local court system. Among the key questions: "How long does it take civil suits to be resolved?"; "How many judges does the civil court have and what is the total budget?"; and "How satisfied are the litigants who use civil court to resolve their dispute?"

In addition to surveying local court records and interviewing local, self-interested participants, the reporter with online access could compare the local court performance to court performance in other similar cities. The reporter could identify experts, key players and knowledgeable observers around the country to provide insight and perspective. If there were appropriate federal information, that could be identified and located as well. The reporter could network with other reporters working on like topics, drawing on their expertise and experience. And all this research could be conducted without traveling and within the normal daily work routine.

Reporters craft useful, interesting stories. Online access to wider sources of information means that more reporters can pursue more stories of greater interest to specific readers or viewers. More fact-filled and broader in scope, those stories should be of greater value than ever before.

For Whom This Book Is Intended

You do not have to be a Macintosh maven, a Windows whiz, a UNIX virtuoso, or any other kind of computer savant to be proficient at harvesting online information. This book tells journalists what buttons to push to find the information they are seeking. It does so using plain English. It also describes strategies for how to think about gathering information online. *The Online Journalist* assumes that most journalists have little desire to become computer programmers or to learn computer languages.

Instead, *The Online Journalist* assumes that most reporters have in mind certain information they need and that they want the information in a hurry. If they get the information quickly, they can spend their deadline time crafting the best story possible rather than wrestling with inflexible machines. Not only will journalists proficient with these tools have more time to write, their reports can be more thorough and comprehensive. It is the aim of this book to enable journalists to get quickly and easily the information they need in their work.

At the same time, this book assesses the impact of the Internet on journalism. It looks at the Internet not only as a tool for reporters but as a new medium for news. It looks at the efforts of news organizations to reach audiences via the Web and discusses legal and ethical ramifications of the use of the Internet in journalism.

To use online sources of information, journalists have to have access to the Internet and the World Wide Web. There are several different ways to get access to the Web. Almost all colleges and universities in America are now connected to the Internet and the Web. Students and faculty should consult their information-services support team to arrange e-mail accounts and get an overview of the online services on campus.

Off campus, many media companies provide online access to all of their reporters. Many already have at least a couple of computers networked to the Internet. In the not too distant future, Internet access in media companies should be as ubiquitous as telephone access.

Moreover, millions of people have arranged their own Internet access either through services such as CompuServe and America Online or through Internet service providers. MindSpring Communication, the Microsoft Network (MSN) and other major companies provide Internet access as do many small providers around the country. Moreover, some cable television companies offer high speed Internet access via either Excite@Home or Roadrunner. And local telephone companies, in conjunction with third-party providers offer higher speed access via telephone lines using Digital Subscriber Line (DSL) technology.

Although many people use Internet service providers primarily to gain access to the World Wide Web, in most cases these providers also offer the full range of Internet tools such as e-mail, Telnet, and FTP. In 2000, the prices Internet Services Providers in the United States charge ranged from around $50 a month for DSL service to zero, for people who were willing to have advertising continually running across their screen. Most analysts anticipate that access will be less expensive in the future.

In addition to having online access, this book assumes that the reader has some familiarity with computers and uses a computer for word processing. This book describes the process of finding information online and bringing that information to your computer. The assumption is that at least in terms of text files you find online, you will be incorporating material from those files into your work on computer.

Although this book describes how to make use of computer-based tools to do better research for stories and projects, this book is NOT a computer book. It is written in English, generally speaking, the "newsroom variety" of English, cleaned up a little.

There is no attempt in this book to be all-inclusive or encyclopedic. Instead, we have focused on a limited selection of network tools that are

- easily accessible through the Internet or, if commercially based, priced for the common person
- either indispensable tools (like e-mail) or ones that provide a high rate of return for the time invested in learning to use them

The Online Journalist teaches how to use online tools and how to get further help for each tool. This is especially important when we are describing a moving target like the Internet, which changes shape from week to week. Each tool is described in a setting that illustrates how the tool may be (or has been) used by journalists.

As with other tools, the user becomes more proficient and skilled with frequent use. *The Online Journalist* describes the tools and provides electronic addresses of computer sites housing information or providing services of particular value to journalists. It is hoped that you will test the tools and hone your skills by employing them at many sites. Appendix A contains a focused list of electronic addresses for online resources that will serve as starting points for online journalists.

The Online Journalist assumes that most readers will be accessing online resources from a personal computer of the Macintosh or Windows compatible variety. With some more basic tools, you may connect to distant computers and talk to those computers through a program with a plain, text-based, command-line interface. But most often, particularly using the World Wide Web, you will enjoy the benefits of the graphical user interface associated with Windows and the Macintosh.

Between the Second and Third Editions

This is the third edition of *The Online Journalist* to appear in five years. Three developments have led to this new edition. First, as noted in the prior two editions, the Internet is a moving target. New services are coming online and existing services are improving rapidly or dropping out. For example, during the past two years, Instant Messaging, once a backwater of Internet use for real aficionados, has been picked up by tens of millions of users around the world.

When this book first appeared, there were only a few thousand Web sites worldwide. One of the most popular sites was at a community college in Hawaii—because it was one of the only sites available to visit. Now almost every college professor, student, and anyone else owning an account with an Internet Service Provider may create a home page. Most large companies have extensive presences on the Web that they advertise routinely on television. Government agencies are scrambling to make information available on the Web. Small companies, nonprofit agencies, local governments and untold numbers of others who provide information to the public either have Web sites or are considering their use.

The use of the Web has grown accordingly. By 2000, it was not uncommon for middle school students to regularly use the Web to conduct research for reports, to chat with their friends, and to play online games at all hours of the day and night.

The second reason for this edition of *The Online Journalist* is that the software used for Internet applications has improved dramatically. Many new features have been added. Driven by the competition between Netscape and Microsoft, Web browsers (the software used for navigating the Web) are emerging as the umbrella tool for all Internet services. In addition to navigating Web sites, Web browsers often can be used to survey Usenet news groups, connect to Telnet servers, manage File Transfer Protocol operations and stand in as the interface for e-mail, chat and other Internet tools.

Finally, the Internet is less of a novelty in journalism and society at large. At the time of the first edition, it seemed that only pioneering journalists and those with an affinity for computers were using the Internet. Like database reporting, the Internet was the domain of a few specialists in newsrooms or on campuses.

That is no longer the case. The Internet has now become more familiar to thousands of journalists and millions of people.

The increasing, regular use of the Internet has raised the stakes for journalists. Being the first to use the Net is no longer enough. The goal now is to use these resources effectively.

With these three developments in mind, the third edition of *The Online Journalist* has been reorganized and much new information has been included. The book now follows this plan:

- Chapter 2 offers an introduction to the Internet and a review of the landscape in cyberspace.
- Chapter 3 provides an introduction to the World Wide Web. This chapter alone is sufficient for journalists and students of journalism to begin using the Web as a reporting tool
- Chapter 4 looks at developments in the use of e-mail. In addition to reviewing the mechanics of e-mail and how it can be applied in journalism, it reviews e-mail services provided via the Web.
- Chapter 5 explores other kinds of interpersonal communication via the Internet including chat room and discussion lists. These services are among the most important the Internet offers to journalists.
- Chapter 6 lays outs search strategies for using the Web and the Internet. Reporters work on deadline. They must have techniques in place to find the information they need quickly and efficiently.
- Chapter 7 describes the legacy tools of the Internet such as Gopher and Telnet. Although many journalists and journalism students ignore these services, they can still access valuable information using them.
- Chapter 8 studies the issue of credibility and the information on the Internet. Because information is so easily accessible, journalists and journalism students must work hard to make sure the information they find is credible.
- Chapter 9 reviews the legal and ethical issues associated with the Internet. The more the Internet is used, the more complicated the issues.
- Chapter 10 surveys the use of the Web as a publishing medium for news. In fact, Web-based publications represent some of the best opportunities for new and veteran journalists.
- Chapter 11 offers an in-depth look at the major software applications used with the Internet. Though many people now use the Internet, few use all the features available in their software.
- Chapter 12 makes an initial assessment of the impact of the Internet on journalism. Television, the last major new communication technology, radically altered the practice of journalism. The Internet promises to do the same.

In writing this major revision of *The Online Journalist*, emphasis has been placed on approaches to using online time wisely. Rather than just giving lists of sites to visit, *The Online Journalist* suggests strategies for building those lists and keeping them up to date.

How to Use This Book

There are two ways to use this book. You can follow the chapters in the sequence in which they are offered. If you do, you will start with the basics and learn to be increasingly sophisticated in your application of the Internet to journalism.

Alternatively, the chapters can be conceptually grouped. Chapters 3, 6, 8 and 11 focus to a large degree on the use of the World Wide Web in journalism. Chapters 4, 5, 8, and 11 explore the use of the Internet for interpersonal (one-to-one, one-to-many, and many-to-many) communications and its application to journalism. Chapters 2, 9, 10, and 12 look at the larger issues associated with journalism and the Internet. Chapter 7 opens the door to using legacy Internet services efficiently.

When Something Doesn't Work

The Internet is not yet an "Information Superhighway." In fact, portions of the Internet seem perpetually under construction. You will encounter delays. You will find roads closed. Files you want will no longer be available. You will not have the right version of the right viewer to access information you want. In fact, Chapter 3 has a chart containing common error messages from the Web.

When you encounter barriers, move on to other resources. You will find some delays are only temporary; try them again some other time. Changes and facelifts are daily occurrences on the Internet.

Often, you will have to be patient and persistent. But patience and persistence are keys to good journalism.

A Last Word

This is a hands-on book. You will be introduced to a new set of tools. The only way to become skillful with them is to use them as often as possible. We suggest that you read this book with a Net-connected computer at your side, trying out the tools and tips that the book describes as you go.

But a hammer and a saw and a nail do not make a great carpenter. As you master these tools, you will also want to think about the way you practice journalism. Even if you are familiar with the Internet, this book should help you figure out how to best apply the Internet to the tasks of journalism.

The Internet potentially allows journalists to practice their craft in new ways. The real payoff comes when you realize that potential.

Chapter **2**

The World Online

In January 1994, Albert Gore, Jr., vice president of the United States, subjected himself to a question and answer session in which more than 300 people participated. In the space of 90 minutes, Gore faced a battery of questions about problems ranging from educating children with special needs to ending the civil war in the Balkans.

This was neither a press conference nor a speaking engagement organized by a specific organization. It was the first live, online conference with a United States vice president. The questions were provided by people who had signed up to participate in a forum on CompuServe, a commercial information service. Gore was stationed at a personal computer in the West Wing of the White House. The questioners and the questions were completely unscreened. The people who asked their questions first received answers. Others watched the interaction on screen. (See Fig. 2-1.)

Once the domain of journalists from elite media companies, the questioning of prominent people is now an everyday occurrence online. Journalists and journalism students online have quizzed everybody from hip-hop artist Smoothe Da Hustler to racecar driver Janet Guthrie. Business reporters have questioned executives at Bell & Howell's annual corporate meeting and monitored conference calls with financial analysts explaining companies' corporate results. After NASA launched its solar telescope, journalists, along with thousands of students, could interact directly with the lead scientists involved in the project as they watched virtually real-time images from the telescope on their computer screens.

When Kristin Leutwyler, senior editor at *Scientific American*, was writing a personality profile, she needed to interview Nicholas Negroponte, director of the Media Lab at the Massachusetts Institute of Technology and author of the book *Being Digital*. Told by the press office at MIT that Negroponte was too busy for telephone calls, faxes or face-to-face meetings with journalists, she asked for weekly electronic mail exchanges, and met her deadline.

And journalism students are taking full advantage of online resources as well. For example, when Douglas Brown, then a junior at Loyola College in Maryland, was assigned to do an in-depth report on environmental problems and proposed solutions for the Chesapeake Bay region, he used the World Wide Web to access every piece of legislation pending in the U.S. Congress concerning Chesapeake Bay.

The use of the World Wide Web, the Internet and other online information resources have become important tools for journalists for a simple reason — they allow journalists to do their jobs better. Using the Internet, reporters can find information quickly, information that was once quite difficult to obtain. They can also communicate with people in new, convenient and efficient ways.

Fig. 2-1: Part of the transcript from Vice President Al Gore's first online conference on CompuServe.

```
% Moderator recognizes question #6
  glen Falkenstein (102)


(#102,glen Falkenstein) What do you think is goiong to end the problem in
bosnia?
(#196,Vice President Gore) We (the US) have believed for some time
(#196,Vice President Gore)  that the Bosnian government forces should
(#196,Vice President Gore) not be subject to the internation
(#196,Vice President Gore) embargo on the arms they
(#196,Vice President Gore) need to even the odds. And we have proposed
airstrikes
(#196,Vice President Gore) to prevent the agressors form taking
(#196,Vice President Gore)  advantage of the situation
(#196,Vice President Gore) while the arms are delivered.
(#196,Vice President Gore) But our allies, whose votes we need in
(#196,Vice President Gore) the Security Council, don't
(#196,Vice President Gore) agree. We will continue to work for peace, though,
(#196,Vice President Gore) in other ways — including maintenance of the
toughest sanctions against
(#196,Vice President Gore) Serbia in history. And the biggest airlift of
(#196,Vice President Gore) humanitarian supplies since the Berlin
(#196,Vice President Gore) airlift. And if a real agreement
(#196,Vice President Gore) can be reached, we will help enforce it.


% Moderator recognizes question #8
  David Rogers (26)


(#26,David Rogers) Mr. Vice President...
(#26,David Rogers) Hello from a Houston, Texas student...
(#26,David Rogers) What effect will the information highway...
(#26,David Rogers) have on our health care system...
(#26,David Rogers) in our future?
(#196,Vice President Gore) It will make it possible to conduct remote
(#196,Vice President Gore) diagnostics with much higher accuracy,
(#196,Vice President Gore) and to link patients to the right specialist
(#196,Vice President Gore) regardless of geographic location...
(#196,Vice President Gore) And by making the transfer of·large
```

As with all tools, however, online resources are used more skillfully by some than by others. In this chapter, you will

- learn the basics of the computer infrastructure, which makes the online world possible,
- receive an overview of the Internet,
- be introduced to several common Internet applications,
- review other online information services,
- survey some of the diverse information available online, and
- get insight into the direction in which the technology is headed.

The Emergence of Computer Networks

Negotiating the online world is as important a skill for journalists as good interviewing techniques and a smooth style of writing. But the world online is complex. Not only is it relatively new, it is still under development. It is changing rapidly.

To be able to understand those changes, it is important both to be familiar with key terms and to have a basic understanding of the infrastructure itself. In the same way that it is important to understand generally what happens when you dial a telephone, it is important to understand generally what is happening when you send and retrieve information via computers.

The key technology underpinning all computer-based communication has been the development of computer networks, the physical linking of two or more computers. The computers can be linked through telephone lines, through other types of cables (including high-speed fiber-optic cable), and through wireless technology.

The number of computers in a network can vary considerably. At one level, all the computers in a workgroup can be linked. The workgroup-level network can then be attached to a department-wide network and then to a company-wide network. The company-wide network can then be joined to other company networks and so on.

As companies, government agencies, and universities have expanded the number of computers they operate, they have created networks to allow people to easily share information and application programs. These networks are known as local area networks (LANs). In a local area network, one or more computers may function as a central resource for several other computers. The central computer is known as a server and frequently contains files that many people on the network use. It also contains the software that allows each of the computers on the network to share information with each other. One type of computer network design is called client-server computing.

Understanding Client-Server Computing

With client-server computing, one computer does not perform every task that is needed to complete a given activity. Instead, different computers on the network perform different parts of the job. In this way, the job can be completed more efficiently and computer resources are used more economically.

Most client-server tasks—particularly Internet applications—consist of at least two steps. In the first, you request a specific piece of information or a specific job to be completed. In the second step, the request is fulfilled and the results are returned to you for display.

The software that makes the request or issues the instructions for what is to be done is called the "client." The software that fulfills the request and returns the results is called the "server." The same client-server terminology applies to the computers on which the respective software resides.

To put it in more familiar terms, think about a client and an accountant. The client asks the accountant to prepare her income tax return. The accountant performs the work and returns the results.

With the Internet, which is a network of computer networks and will be more fully described shortly, you use the client software to make requests of a server. For example, World Wide Web browsers (browsers will be explained in Chapter 3) make requests to Web servers for information. So, in order to surf the Web, you need access to a Web client and a Web server.

This client-server relationship is crucial to understanding the Internet and what happens among computers on the Internet. If you understand this client-server relationship and two other network concepts, you will be better able to understand the capabilities of the Internet. You will understand why some things work on the network under one set of circumstances and not under others. When the unexpected occurs on the Net, you will have at your disposal the principles to explain the event. You will understand whether the problem is with the client, which is under your control, or the server, which usually is not.

Host, Client, and Server

Beyond the client-server relationship, the other two critical concepts are those of the network host and of the different ways of connecting to the network. In simple terms, a computer is performing host duties when it controls computer terminals (or other computers that act like terminals) which are attached to it by some form of cabling.

The concept of host computing is drawn from the 1960s and 1970s. At that time, many companies and organizations invested in large, mainframe computers. To increase the number of people who could use the large computers, terminals were developed that could send information to the main computer and receive responses. The terminals could not process or store any information themselves. Consequently, they were called "dumb" terminals. The main computer was called the "host." The host processed and stored all the information.

As the use of computing spread in the 1980s and 1990s, many universities and large businesses began to assign students, faculty, or employees accounts on a central computing facility. Some universities still use this approach. When you get an account on a central computer, you are given a user name and a password. With your account comes an e-mail address. You may be allocated a certain amount of disk storage space on the central computer. That computer, which is a host, runs all day and all night. It receives mail for you and stores it until you read the mail and dispose of it. You interact with the host computer through the use of a terminal or a personal computer that is acting like a terminal. All the action in this case, however, takes place through the host.

A host is different from a server. When a server works with client software to perform a task, both the server and the client do some of the processing or management of the information. A host does all the processing and management. The terminal only handles input and output.

For people who access the online world through commercial service providers such as America Online or one of the hundreds of Internet service providers (ISPs), the ISP's computer generally acts as the host. The service provider's computer will, for example, send, receive and store mail for you. Your personal computer acts primarily as a way for you to send commands via your keyboard or mouse to the service provider's computer.

Client-server and host-terminal computing have their strengths. Client-server computing puts more functionality on the individual desktop. Host-terminal computing is usually less expensive to manage. Consequently, a new approach to computing, in which the client has less functionality than a desktop personal computer and more of the processing takes place at the server level, is emerging. This approach is called thin-client, or network, computing. As this network computing develops, television sets, cellular telephones and a range of other devices or "information appliances" will emerge to provide access to the Internet. Processing will take place on remote computers attached to the network.

Along these lines, many Web sites now offer e-mail services. The interface to manage the mail and all the processing reside on the remote computers, not on your desktop.

Client Location Governs Functionality

The distinction between local and remote hosts has an important impact on the functionality of the client software to which you have access. All files and information on the Internet are maintained and communicated in client-server relationships. The server makes files available to other machines (clients) in a format recognized by client software running on the client machine. Where the client software is located and how it is accessed determines what features of the client are available to you as a user and how efficiently the client software operates from the user's point of view.

In terms of where the software resides, a client may be said to be local or remote, just as a host is local or remote. You have a local client if the client software you are using to go out and get information resides on a computer at your desk and you have disk space available on it. With remote clients, you sit at a "dumb" terminal—or an intelligent computer running terminal emulation software—connected to a distant host computer on which you have no disk space allotted.

Network Connection Type Affects Functionality

Basically, you connect to the rest of the world on the Net in one of two ways. In the first scenario, your computer has a network card and network cable coming into your computer through the card. This is known as a "hard wired" connection or a "direct" connection. Such a connection is desirable because it frees the user from reliance on host computers for client software and, to some extent, for access. Instead, one is free to select one's own client software for Internet access and avoid slowdowns brought on by overworked, bogged-down hosts. Data files move quickly across the network, free from slow modem bottlenecks.

In the second scenario, you use telephone lines and a modem to reach a host computer that then gives you Internet access. This is known as a "dial-up" connection. Most dial-up services offer SLIP (Serial Line Internet Protocol) or PPP (Point-to-Point Protocol) access. Such access permits the network navigator (you) to use local clients specially configured for such access.

Cyberspace Is the Networking of Networks

Over time, servers in different locations have been connected to one another, often using dedicated data lines and specialized computer network hardware called routers. In addition, computers are sometimes networked using fiber-optic lines and other technology that allows digital information to move at much higher speed than it does on voice telephone lines. The development and implementation of high-speed data transmission lines has made the "Information Superhighway" possible.

Internetworking represents the connecting of smaller computer networks to form yet larger networks. The development of large networks of networks has depended on two factors. First, physical links among computers had to be installed. Second, computers had to "speak the same language"—to use similar rules or communication protocols for identifying, transmitting and handling information.

In practice, internetworking currently functions in the following way. A university or private concern provides individuals with personal computers. The personal computers are then networked with other personal computers, work stations, minicomputers and mainframe computers, depending on the specific location. The network is then connected with other networks. Using a personal computer working through a server (called a gateway, in this context), individuals can access information residing on computers in more distant networks. The key is having a computer that can access a network, which can, in turn, access information on other computers on other networks. Computers in the internetwork are usually linked by higher speed, dedicated data transmission lines rather than voice telephone lines.

Conceptually, accessing information in this way can be compared to entering a large building with many rooms. Each room you enter has several other doors. You keep opening doors until you find the information you want. High-speed lines allow you to move from room to room quite quickly.

Defining the Internet

The most famous collection of internetworked computers is the Internet. Rapid development of the Internet has made online skills indispensable for journalists. Some veteran users of the Internet like to argue that it defies definition. One old-timer once defined the Internet by describing what it wasn't. Quickly others shortened his definition to "The Internet—not."

The Internet is not an organization. It is not an institution. It is not a club. You cannot become a member. Nobody owns the Internet; and strictly speaking, nobody controls it, governs it, or takes responsibility for it. Still, the Internet can be defined in terms of a physical structure as well as a set of rules.

While complex, the structure of the Internet is understandable. "Internet" is a term used to describe the interconnection of many computer networks in a way that allows them to communicate with each other. Consider this extended metaphor. In the United States, you can drive a car from Los Angeles to New York. You can do this for two reasons. First, there are physical links called roads. These roads take many different forms from single-lane neighborhood streets to 12-lane, limited access interstate highways. If you were to take a cross-country trip, you would be likely to travel on many types of roads.

In addition to the physical links, however, to make the trip from Los Angeles to New York safely, you need to have a set of rules that governs the way all the travelers use the roads. You must know that you cannot cross a double line in the middle of a road; that you must stop at red lights; and that you must travel within certain speed limits, depending on the type of road and weather conditions.

The Internet is the same kind of network as the road and highway system, but instead of moving vehicles occupied by people, it moves packets filled with data. The Internet is comprised of physical links, but in the same sense that no one road connects a home in Los Angeles directly to a home in New York, no single link connects all the computers on the Internet. In the automotive world, different neighborhoods are linked by larger streets. In the Internet world, these larger streets create regional networks. Regional (mid-level) networks connect the computers at different universities, companies, and other institutions. Like larger streets, these mid-level networks enable data to travel faster than data on local area networks.

The specialized computers that control the flow of information on the mid-level networks are also physically linked to what are termed national backbones. The national backbones use lines that transmit data at yet higher speeds and use higher capacity computers to handle information traffic. Telephone companies, cable television operations, and other communication specialists are vigorously competing to install high-speed networks throughout the country. The same process is underway in countries around the world.

"Internet" is the word used to describe the interconnection of these successive levels of networks. As such, the Internet is the series of physical links that serves as the road system for computer-based information sharing. It encompasses the local networks within organizations through which information moves slowly, but only for short distances; the mid-level networks linking universities, large companies, and other organizations; and the national backbones, which allow a lot of information to travel long distances at very high speeds.

A Set of Rules: The Internet as Agreement

The physical links are only one aspect of the Internet. One way to define the Internet is that it is an agreement. This agreement encompasses sets of rules or protocols that allow the information to travel from computer to computer on the Internet "highway system." If a computer or computer network does not support that set of rules, it is not part of the Internet. In other words, to send and receive information via the Internet, computers must package information in the same way. If a computer cannot do that, even if it has a physical link to a network, it is not part of the Internet.

Think of it this way. Motor vehicles and airplanes are both forms of transportation but airplanes cannot use the road system. There are many types of networks and ways to send information between computers. But only computers that follow the specific rules associated with the Internet can use the Internet.

The overarching protocol or set of rules used on the Internet is called the Transmission Control Protocol/Internet Protocol (TCP/IP). The IP part of the protocol is the address for every computer that is physically linked to the Internet. Each computer has a unique address. The IP part of the protocol identifies the sender and destination of information.

The TCP element of the protocol controls the way information is sent through the Internet network. It is according to the TCP protocol requirements that the ability to log on to remote computers, transfer files and perform other operations on the Internet have been developed. TCP allows Internet applications to interact on computers that, themselves, have different operating systems such as UNIX, Windows, or Macintosh OS. Many companies are now using the TCP/IP protocols to send and receive information internally. Internal computer networks using Internet technology but not open to the public are called Intranets. In fact, TCP/IP is emerging as the dominant network protocol in a wide variety of applications and is a driving force in reshaping the nature of computing in many organizations large and small.

In summary, the growth of the Internet has stemmed from two factors. Physical links consisting of high-speed data lines have been established connecting the computer networks—or internetworking—of universities, government agencies, businesses, and other organizations. These links have created a de facto national network. Second, the widespread acceptance of TCP/IP protocols allows information to travel transparently through the linked networks that comprise the Internet, even though different computers have different hardware architectures and different operating systems.

Network Control

Understanding the structure of the Internet sheds light on several important questions. Foremost is, "Who controls the Internet?" The answer is that no one entity controls the Internet. Instead, there is a layer of control at every network level. For example, the people responsible for the administration of your local network may choose to block access to certain Web sites deemed undesirable. For example, Chinese authorities have decided to block information they deem inappropriate from entering China via the Internet. Some commercial Internet providers screen out pornographic material. And some providers do not support the full range of Internet services described below. Many companies and some colleges and universities, for example, do not support Usenet news groups (Chapter 5).

Cost Structure

The lack of a centralized management organization has also had an impact on the cost of using the Internet. Building, maintaining and developing the Internet is an ambitious and costly undertaking. Currently, universities, business enterprises and organizations generally pay a flat monthly or annual fee to connect either to a regional network or a national backbone. Once connected, however, organizations are usually not charged on a usage basis. Consequently, most do not charge individual users for using the Internet. Some commercial service providers, however, do charge by the hour for usage.

Viewed another way, the cost of accessing the Internet is similar to the cost of cable television. With cable, you pay a monthly fee and then you can watch as many programs on as many different channels as you like. With the Internet, once the monthly charge is paid, users can employ as many services as often as they like without additional charges.

This current pricing structure is significant for journalists. It means that you can search the Internet as diligently as you like for relevant information and can communicate with as many people as you can identify via e-mail without worrying about receiving a huge bill at the end of the month. Moreover, it means the Internet can open sources of information—both archival and human—that would be too expensive or difficult to access in any other way.

For example, an editor of a specialized science magazine was looking for someone to write articles about new developments in laboratory automation. Working through the Internet, he came in contact with scientists in St. Petersburg, Russia, who were active in that topic area. Over the course of several months, the editor and the scientists collaborated to develop two articles. At one point in the editing process, the editor was exchanging information with the scientists on an almost daily basis. He did not have to worry about accruing huge costs. Also, the time differential between the United States and Russia was not a problem.

The cost structure of the Internet has also led to a scramble to provide new services via the network. For example, many companies provide a form of Internet telephone service. Others allow for video conferencing over the Internet. Though the quality of these services is still not as good as could be expected, many people believe that ultimately all communications services will be provided via the Internet network.

A History of the Internet

While the Internet is clearly the largest computer network of its kind, it was not the first. In the 1970s and 1980s, similar networks such as Bitnet, which links universities, and FidoNet, which links thousands of bulletin boards, and Usenet, which was created to facilitate online discussions, all thrived. Nevertheless, the Internet has emerged as by far the dominant network of its type and has, to a large degree, subsumed the earlier networks.

The growth of the Internet can be measured in three ways: the number of host computers connected to the Internet, the number of users connected to those host computers, and the amount of information or traffic carried on the Internet. Because of its decentralized structure, precise usage figures are hard to determine. But, by all measures, the Internet is rapidly growing. The number of registered Internet domains in July of 1997 was 26,053,000. In 1998 the number had grown to 36,739,000, and in July of 1999 it was 56,218,000 (source: Internet Software Consortium [http://www.isc.org/]).

On an individual scale, some people projected that by late 1999, more than 100 million people in the United States alone had access to the Internet. In 1996, officials at Sun Microsystems, a leading provider of World Wide Web servers and creator of the Java programming language, predicted that, eventually, all people will have a Web server. If those projections prove accurate, the Internet will eventually represent a communications network that will rival or surpass the telephone system in its importance and usefulness to journalists. Many believe that eventually Internet services will be fully integrated into both the telephone network and the cable television network. Indeed, Internet information, television programming and voice will converge into a single network.

Military Origins

Ironically, the Internet was not originally conceived as a global communications system. Like some other useful technologies, the Internet has its roots, in part, in the need for military preparedness. In the 1960s, the Advanced Research Projects Agency of the United States Department of

Defense began funding projects to develop an experimental computer network to support military research by allowing people spread across the country to more easily share their computer files and send messages to each other.

The Department of Defense wanted the network to be able to function even if parts of it had been disrupted, presumably in a war. The researchers conceived of sending messages by breaking up the message information into discrete packets that would be reassembled at the destination address. They established an addressing system through which the communicating computers themselves could ensure that the information was successfully transmitted or received. These Internet Protocol (IP) addresses are expressed in a series of four numbers between 1 and 255 separated by periods (dots), such as 171.206.72.1. The plan was to have every computer on the network able to communicate with every other computer on the network. In other words, they wanted a peer-to-peer network.

In 1969, an experimental network called ARPAnet was launched with four nodes. The participants were University of California at Los Angeles, the Stanford Research Institute, University of California at Santa Barbara, and the University of Utah. By 1971, there were 19 nodes shared by 30 universities. Developing ARPAnet was complicated because different sites used different types of computers, and the protocols that were developed had to work on many different computer architectures and operating systems. The challenge was to develop rules of communication that would allow information to be sent over many different kinds of networks without regard to the underlying network technology. These protocols began to appear in the mid-1970s and were known as the Transmission Control Protocol, or TCP. By the early 1980s all the systems associated with ARPAnet standardized on TCP/IP.

Supercomputing Centers Established

The next impetus for the Internet came in 1987, when the National Science Foundation decided to establish five supercomputing centers around the country and link them through its own high-speed network known as NSFnet. Because the cost to connect researchers directly to the supercomputing centers with dedicated high-speed data lines would have been prohibitive, NSF encouraged research institutions to form regional networks, which, in turn, were linked to the supercomputing centers. That strategy has led to the basic structure of the Internet, with its multiple layers of networks.

Exponential growth in the use of the Internet began with the launch of NSFnet in the late 1980s as researchers in academic and governmental settings took advantage of the new opportunity to collaborate. In 1990, an effort was undertaken to include commercial and non-profit organizations as well. By the middle of 1993, by some estimates there were more than three million commercial Internet users and that number was growing at a rate of 10 to 20 percent a month. Commercial organizations have the fastest rate of connection to the Internet of any single type of user community. In 1994, the number of Internet sites registered with commercial domains surpassed the number of educational institutions. Since the mid-1990s, most major companies and tens of thousands of smaller ones have connected to the Internet.

The final technological breakthrough also came in the early 1990s. First, researchers led by Tim Berners Lee at CERN, the European particle physics laboratory, created a protocol for hyperlinking information residing on different computers. They called the system the World Wide Web. Shortly thereafter, students and researchers led by Marc Andreesen at the National Center for Supercomputing Applications at the University of Illinois developed a client program named *Mosaic* that is characterized by a graphical user interface. And the online revolution moved into full gear.

Internet Applications

Describing the programs associated with the Internet and applying them to the tasks of journalism will be explored in depth in the next several chapters. This section will provide a brief overview of the different types of software tools available and briefly describe their differences. In a sense, it will survey what's available in your Internet toolbox before you go to work and choose the ones to use.

Internet software applications combine the client-server and host-terminal models of computing for nearly all the applications described in the pages that follow. When you use an Internet software application, the client software will be either on your personal computer, the computer you log on to for access to the Internet (your host), or on yet another computer to which you connect in order to use client software you may not have yourself. As you navigate through the Internet, you will find yourself logged on to different host computers, sometimes gaining access to different client programs and also accessing different servers. It can be complicated. Fortunately, the purpose of advanced Internet software is to hide this complexity from you; and to a large degree it succeeds.

The Internet has six widespread application protocols: Electronic Mail (e-mail), World Wide Web (Hypertext Transfer Protocol or HTTP), File Transfer Protocol (FTP), Chat, Usenet (news), Telnet and Gopher. Each has specialty client software, and Web browsers such as *Navigator* from Netscape Communications and the *Internet Explorer* from Microsoft, are capable of reading and displaying data from all the applications except

Telnet. Browser software needs to be told which client you are using for Telnet, and the browser hands off to that application when you enter a Telnet address into the location window.

Electronic Mail

Electronic mail is one of the most useful features of the Internet and is often the application with which people begin. Electronic mail is a method to send messages back and forth among people with Internet addresses as well as people on other networks with mail connections to the Internet.

The Internet supports both person-to-person communication that is delivered to the electronic address of the intended recipient and one-to-many transmissions in which information is automatically sent to lists of people. Electronic mail and ways to locate people's e-mail addresses will be discussed in Chapter 4. E-mail discussion groups, a method of communicating with many people at once using e-mail, will be discussed in Chapter 5.

The World Wide Web

The World Wide Web is the most exciting new tool for the Internet and is the reason for the enthusiasm that has engulfed the Internet since the mid-1990s. It is based on a hypermedia technology. With hypermedia, information in one document can be linked to other, related documents. For example, let's say you have found a bill in the U.S. Senate in which you are interested. The names of each of the authors of the bill can be linked to brief biographical sketches that are actually stored on a completely different computer. Let's say the biographical sketches include the amount of money senators raised for their reelection campaigns. That information could be linked to a document that lists all of their campaign contributors.

Moreover, linked information can consist of not only text and graphics, but audio and video information as well. The World Wide Web is an ambitious, exciting and powerful attempt to link connected information wherever it may be located on the Internet, allowing the user to easily access and retrieve related files. The Web will be discussed in Chapter 3.

FTP

FTP stands for "File Transfer Protocol." As the name implies, it facilitates moving files from one computer to another. It has become the common language for sharing data. Unlike Telnet, in which you often must know a specific password to successfully log on to the remote computer, anonymous FTP has become commonplace. With anonymous FTP, anyone on the Internet may transfer files from (and sometimes to) a remote system using the word "anonymous" as the user name and your e-mail address as a password. *Archie* is a program that locates files which can be transferred via FTP. The Archie program reads an index of more than 1,000 FTP sites. It is updated constantly and its "what is" command describes the files you have found. Once you have located files via Archie, you can transfer them via FTP. FTP and Archie will be discussed in Chapter 7.

Usenet News

Usenet is a network of several thousand online bulletin boards organized into topic-oriented "news groups." Within these news groups, people read and post (as if to a paper bulletin board) messages related to the topic for which the news group site is home. There are already more than 10,000 news groups with participants ranging from Elvis Presley fans to political activists, from computer enthusiasts to music composers. Usenet is one of many networks connected to and accessible via the Internet. Usenet news is described in Chapter 5.

Chat

Internet Relay Chat (IRC) turns the Internet into something like an international CB radio network. IRC works in text-only environments, and many Web sites host chat rooms in which people exchange messages in real time with whoever is in the chat room at the time. Moreover, client software like *ICQ*, Microsoft *NetMeeting* and *AOL Instant Messenger* allow you to chat with your friends and people of your choosing. Chat is discussed in Chapter 5.

Telnet and Gopher

Telnet and Gopher are older Internet protocols that have been largely superseded by the World Wide Web. Nonetheless, there may be legacy information that can be accessed using those services. Telnet allows you to log on to a remote computer on the Internet. Once you are logged on to a remote computer, it is as if your keyboard were attached to that computer, which then serves as your host. Gopher was the first Internet browsing program and the first program to integrate the information search and retrieval process on the Internet. Like other Internet applications, Gopher consists of server and client software.

More than 2,000 Gopher servers remain linked in that portion of the Internet called "GopherSpace." When you find something you want, the Gopher client software retrieves it for you through menu-based commands. With Gopher it does not matter exactly where the information you want is located. It does not matter what kind of information you want to retrieve. Nor does it matter what tool you need to use to retrieve that information. You use tools from a menu to perform each operation. Telnet and Gopher will be discussed in Chapter 7.

As sophisticated as the application tools get, the basic operation and purpose of the Internet remains the same. At its core, the Internet is a communications network among computers. It allows you to locate and retrieve information on other computers linked to the Internet as well as send and receive messages electronically to and from other people on the Internet and elsewhere.

The Convergence of Cyberspace

From the early 1980s through the early 1990s, online computer-based communication was dominated by proprietary commercial services such as CompuServe, Prodigy and America Online. These services allowed users to dial in and access information that was available only to their members. Until the middle 1980s, people could only send e-mail, for example, to people who subscribed to a similar service.

Many of the services are still in business. But they have reacted to the explosive growth of the World Wide Web, commercial service providers and have integrated their services with the Web. Microsoft, for example, repositioned the Microsoft Network, (originally launched in 1995 as a new commercial information service) as a super-Web site. America Online, CompuServe and Prodigy act as access providers or gateways to the Web for their subscribers. For example, once you dial into AOL, with just a few clicks of the mouse you can access information on the Web.

Conversely, large Internet access providers such as AT&T and Pacific Bell have indicated they will allow users dialing into the Internet to automatically connect to AOL or CompuServe directly. Of course, to access the information stored on the CompuServe or AOL computers, you will still need to be a subscriber to those services.

The Growth of Portals and Hybrid Services

As the amount of information available via the Web has grown, many companies have tried to establish what they call "portal" sites. A portal is a site intended to be a user's first stop when a user goes online. As you will learn in Chapter 3, when you open your browser and go online you are taken to an initial home page. Portal sites are competing to be that page.

Portal sites generally contain a range of services including search engines to help find Web sites of interest, Web-based e-mail (described in Chapter 4), directories of people and business, shopping guides, health information and links to software. Many general interest portal sites also allow you to customize a home page with exactly the information you want. Among the most popular general interest portals are *Yahoo!*, http://www.yahoo.com/; Netscape *Netcenter*, http://www.netscape.com/; *Lycos*, http://www.lycos.com/; and *Excite*, http://www.excite.com/.

While most information on the Web is free, many commercial information services that still require payment are now accessible via the Web. To attract users, many of these subscription or fee-based information providers now offer some basic information for free and charge for more in-depth material. For example, Lexis-Nexis, a primary database of popular news and articles, is now accessible via the Web at http://www.lexisnexis.com/. But you still must subscribe to be able to use its databases.

What's Available Online

Asking what kind of information is available online is a little like asking what's in the Library of Congress. One might as well ask what's available from agencies of the federal government; from leading universities, research centers and think tanks; from large companies, publishing houses and organizations in the business of collecting and disseminating information; or from tens of thousands of entrepreneurs who collect and offer information in areas of their own interests. What's available also comes from hundreds of thousands of people who use computer networks to communicate with each other every day through discussion lists, news groups, postings to bulletin boards, and in a variety of different ways.

And remember, the sources are not limited only to the United States. International information links are strong in many areas. Clearly, there is a lot of information out there—too much to catalog. In fact, nobody knows exactly what is available online and where it is. The growth represents both an opportunity and a hazard for journalists. The opportunity is that, sitting at your desk, you can access information that you may not have even known existed. The hazard is that you will waste a lot of time looking at information that is not relevant to the projects on which you are working.

With that in mind, the following is a partial list of information and services accessible online through computer bulletin boards, commercial databases, and networks such as the Internet that are relevant to journalism. All of these categories of information will be more fully explored in subsequent chapters, and a catalog of these sources is in Appendix A.

Government Information

The federal, state and local governments are the largest producers of public information, and reporting on the activities of government is the biggest single area of concern to journalists. At the federal level, nearly all executive branch agencies, including the White House, the Food and Drug Administration, the National Institutes of Health, Department of Agriculture, National Science Foundation, Environmental Protection Agency, Social Security Administration, National Archives, Securities and Exchange Commission, Department of Defense, military bases around the world, and scores of others now provide access to their information via computer bulletin boards or through the Internet. The Fedworld Web site at http://www.fedworld.gov/ allows you to search scores of federal government Web sites and provides access to many federal government databases. Some of the databases, such as the WorldTec Foreign Technology Alert Service at http://worldtec.fedworld.gov/ are fee-based. Many state court systems have begun to offer electronic access to some of their records. All U.S. federal court decisions are available online. One federal government site (http://www.fedstats.gov/) specializes in dispensing statistics collected by U.S. federal agencies.

The range of information these agencies provides varies. Some, such as the National Archives, primarily offer access to their catalogs and directories, allowing users to identify information they will then have to get using more traditional methods. More important to journalists, many agencies now distribute their press releases and major reports online. Online access represents a vehicle to get both timely information and background material quickly.

Human Sources

In general, most people develop online techniques to access documents. For journalists, however, electronic communication also offers a new way to identify and communicate with people. Communicating with people who have relevant information will continue to be one of the fundamental ways journalism distinguishes itself from other types of fact-finding activities.

Online access to people is provided in several different ways. First, there is electronic mail in which individuals can send private messages back and forth to each other. Sometimes people who refuse to accept a telephone call from a journalist may be willing to respond to an electronic mail message. Electronic mail is a very convenient and efficient method of communication.

Beyond e-mail are news groups and discussion lists. Although technologically they operate differently, in practice, both discussion lists and news groups are like conversations among numbers (sometimes hundreds) of people who are interested in a specific topic. For reporters, these online conversations can serve as windows into the concerns of the people involved in those issues as well a source of e-mail addresses to communicate directly with individuals later. Currently tens of thousands of discussion lists and news groups operate, covering topics from United Nations activities concerning global warming to sadomasochism.

Third, public relations agencies and others now frequently use online communications specifically to reach reporters with potential sources for their stories. For example, public information officers in colleges and universities have assembled lists of university-based experts in different fields, which they forward to reporters upon request.

"Chatting" has emerged as a very popular online activity. Chat is the functional equivalent of the telephone. People who are online at the same time can communicate with each other simultaneously. At times, chat conversations can appear like telephone calls on a party line. A lot of people can participate at the same time.

Finally, many people have created personal home pages on the World Wide Web. These pages are often filled with solid information about the person.

Libraries and Special Depositories

The revolution in electronic communication has transformed the image of librarians from that of custodians of dusty monuments to learning to that of front-line warriors in the information age. Librarians have played a leading role in making information accessible to journalists and others. In one dramatic example, the catalogs of the Library of Congress are now accessible online. The Library of Congress is a powerful tool for journalists.

In addition to the Library of Congress, major public libraries, including federal depository libraries in many cities, college and university libraries, and many specialized libraries are now online as well. For example, the catalog of the French National Institute for Research in Information and Automation (INRIA) is accessible online, as is the U.S. Environmental Protection Agency Library, the Columbia University Law Library, and the Australian Asian Religions Bibliography. Clearly, the range of special repository and library-based information is enormous. In addition to the libraries themselves, very helpful reference material can be found as well. The *CIA World Factbook,* which contains dossiers on 249 nations, can be accessed online, as well as the CIA World Map and the USGS Geological Fault Maps.

Books and Magazines

Not surprisingly, publishers have developed online versions of their publications. All the major national news media, most daily newspapers and hundreds of magazines have gone online. From time to time, drafts of books (particularly books about the Internet) circulate electronically before they are published. And there are many magazine-like publications called e-zines that have gone online as the Web has developed.

In addition to current publications, newspaper and magazine archives are available online. Often, receiving the full text of an article involves a cost; however, several places permit you to identify useful articles online for free. For example, the Montgomery County Public Library has an index of the *New York Times*, the *Washington Post* and the *Wall Street Journal*.

Other Good Stuff

While government data, access to human sources of information, libraries, special collections, and other publications are probably the types of information available online most useful to journalists, there is a wealth of additional information as well. Public domain software and shareware is readily available online. Public domain software is software for which the copyright is no longer enforced (or doesn't exist), so anybody can legally use it. A lot of software developed at research laboratories and other government-funded sites is released directly to the public domain. Shareware is a way to distribute software in which a user pays a license fee only after he or she has tried the program and decided he or she is actually going to use it. Some of this software can help journalists become more productive.

In addition to software, there is an ever-expanding array of information available online. There are many providers of financial services, including tracking and trading on the stock market as well as access to the *Official Airline Guide*, Zagat's *Restaurant Guide* and much more. Hobbyists reflecting a wide range of human interests have set up shop online. Basically, if you look long enough and hard enough, you can probably find information on just about any topic you could imagine as well as the e-mail addresses of people with expertise in those areas.

Finally, people like to play games with computers and there are many different types of games available. One of the more interesting aspects of the Internet is the ability to play elaborate fantasy role-playing games in virtual locations called Multiple User Dungeons, or MUDs.

The Future of the Infrastructure

Distinctions among the different components of the online infrastructure have blurred over time. Nevertheless, for the foreseeable future, the online world will be segmented in several different ways. The first is cost. Large amounts of information, particularly information developed by libraries and universities, will continue to be free. But commercial enterprises are in the business to make money. Many will support their online efforts by advertising and e-commerce, or the buying and selling of goods online. Some online publications also charge subscription fees. The subscription fee approach has worked best for highly specialized information valued by a defined audience. Journalists will have to be very careful to understand the quality of information provided by companies whose bills are paid by e-commerce activities.

One of the most important questions for journalists that is currently being debated is whether government information should be available electronically without cost or at low cost. In the past, from time to time, the federal government has sold its information to a third-party supplier, which then resold that information to the public at a fairly high cost. The Securities and Exchange Commission, however, backed off a plan to sell exclusive rights to the electronic records of the information it gathers to a commercial information service, which would then resell that information. Instead, it began to test electronic access to the public at a nominal cost.

Maintaining low-cost public access to government records in an electronic form will be a key priority for reporters and editors. Ironically, media companies, including newspapers, can find themselves in a complex situation concerning the low-cost availability of government-generated information in electronic formats. Some consider adding value to government information and then reselling it as a potential new source of revenue.

Cost of access is a significant issue as well. Currently, companies charge a monthly flat fee for a connection to the Internet. After the fee is paid, you can use the Internet as often as you like without additional charges. You can send electronic mail to Russia or Israel at no additional charge. This makes the Internet extremely cost effective for journalists and others with limited budgets. Over time, the cost of access to the Internet has gone down. Moreover, in Europe, several companies have experimented with free access to the Internet. In the United States, some companies have experimented with giving away a free computer to users of their Internet service, while others have offered free Internet service to people who buy their computers. As the Internet becomes more tightly integrated with commerce, the cost barriers to access will continue to come down.

The third area in which the different components of the online infra-structure will continue to be distinguished will be the speed at which the lines themselves can carry information. As high-speed lines are installed, new kinds of information, particularly audio, video and graphics-based information, will move freely from computer to computer. Three approaches to providing high-speed access to the Internet have emerged. The first method uses the cable television network for Internet access. The second technology employs the telephone network running a protocol called DSL or digital subscriber lines. DSL allows digital information to move 30 to 50 times faster through standard telephone lines. Finally, wireless commu-nication technology can also deliver high speed Internet access.

In the early 1900s, Lincoln Steffens traveled from city to city docu-menting municipal corruption. His book *Shame of the Cities* is a classic of muckraking. Its power came from the information he collected. The online infrastructure will give you access to more information more efficiently than ever before in the history of journalism. The result should be better stories with more information which better serve the needs of readers and viewers. The challenge for journalists is twofold. They need to learn how to access the necessary information. And they have to be able to fashion that information into compelling stories.

3

Working the World Wide Web

In April 1996, leaders of the seven major industrialized nations of the world—known as the G-7—met in Moscow with Russia, Ukraine and Belarus to review progress in nuclear power safety and the security of nuclear weapons in the former Soviet Union. Traditionally, two types of reporters would cover an event like this—correspondents who cover the top leaders of their countries and those who specialize in nuclear issues.

Those reporters would have access to the briefing documents prepared for the summit. They would have access to the experts whose views could make a difference so they could analyze and assess what took place. And it would be those reporters who would shape the public's perception of the success and significance of the meeting.

Since the birth of mass newspapers, reporting on major international summits has been the domain of a select group of correspondents. But no longer. Prior to the summit, the Center for War, Peace and the News Media posted extensive briefing documents about the meeting on the World Wide Web. The briefing paper was written by Mark Hibbs, the European editor of *Nucleonics Week*. Hibbs also posted a listing of ten sites on the World Wide Web with information on nuclear weapons issues. He included the names and contact information, including e-mail addresses of 14 experts on the subjects. He pointed interested people to two Usenet newsgroups that discussed nuclear issues.

In short, Hibbs provided reporters virtually anywhere in the world the opportunity to conduct original reporting on the summit. The only tool they would need to access all the information Hibbs provided was a well-configured Web browser.

But was Mark Hibbs himself a trustworthy source? In addition to the brief background bio provided on the summit briefing, a quick search of the Web revealed that he had received an M.A. in international affairs from Columbia University and had reported on nuclear security issues concerning Iraq, South Africa and Central Europe. The Web search showed that Hibbs at least had respectable credentials in this area.

The World Wide Web has emerged as the most important new medium to distribute information since television. It allows reporters to access information from around the world instantaneously. It also allows reporters to find information from sources that they previously would never have found. It allows journalists to be more thorough, more accurate, and more complete. And it allows people to publish information for an international audience in a cost-effective, efficient way. The World Wide Web is profoundly changing the practice of journalism.

Moreover, Web browsers such as Netscape and Microsoft Internet Explorer have become the preferred interface for many Internet applications. Properly configured, a Web browser can not only surf the Web, it can access a wide range of other Internet-based services, including e-mail and chat (Chapter 4) and FTP, Gopher and Telnet (Chapter 7). The Web and the Web browser is so dynamic that Chapter 11 is devoted to exploring the advanced features in Web browsers.

In this chapter you will:

- learn the basic structure of the Web, including its history and development,
- be introduced to the software you need to use the Web,
- survey the ways that the Web can be used to enhance reporting,
- explore the possibilities of the Web as a publishing medium, and
- receive tips about how to avoid common pitfalls and resolve basic problems that occur when people use the Web.

History, Development, and Structure of the Web

The World Wide Web was launched when Tim Berners-Lee, then a researcher with CERN, the European Particle Physics Laboratory in Geneva, Switzerland, developed what he called a hypermedia initiative for global information sharing. Since the mid-1970s, CERN had been a leader in developing and using computer networks. In 1988, CERN researchers had collaborated with scientists from the Amsterdam Mathematics Center to establish the European Internet—that is, a network of European computer networks all running the TCP/IP protocol described in Chapter 2.

As a result of their activity in developing networks over the course of nearly 20 years, researchers at CERN had developed a culture based on distributed computing. In a distributed computing environment, tasks are divided among many computers and researchers, who then swap and share needed information.

There were many problems inherent in a distributed computing environment. As Berners-Lee saw it, because different computers and software tools were not compatible with one another, it was difficult, time consuming and frustrating to share information among scientists. Moreover, it was virtually impossible to easily move through related information stored on different types of computers. For example, Berners-Lee wrote in the original proposal for the World Wide Web that, if a researcher found an incomplete piece of software online with the name of Joe Bloggs on it, it would be difficult to find Bloggs' e-mail address. "Usually," he wrote, "you will have to use a different look-up method on a different computer with a different user interface."

The World Wide Web was Berners-Lee's solution to that problem. The objective was to provide a single user interface to large classes of information stored on different computers on the Internet. To achieve that objective, several elements had to be developed, including a simple protocol for requesting information that could be read by people (as opposed to information that can be read only by computers) using various computers; a protocol to convert the information into a format that both the sending computer and the receiving computer could understand; and a method for reading the information on-screen.

To achieve those goals, Berners-Lee proposed a system based on the concept of hypertext. With hypertext, information can be organized and accessed in a non-linear fashion. In other words, you can easily skip around to different sections of a document. For example, imagine you have a book and there is a footnote, labeled number three on page five. With hypertext, you can move from the footnote number on the page to the footnote itself.

In Berners-Lee's vision, page three could be stored on one computer and the footnote on another. The development of hypertext links connecting information located on different computers became known as hypermedia.

Finally, the Web, as Berners-Lee outlined it, would use client/server architecture. As you know from the previous chapter, within a client/server setup, client software running on one computer sends a request to a server computer, which then fulfills the request. Because, in most cases, any computer on a network can serve as either a client or a server, depending on the software that is being run, the number of Web servers could proliferate dramatically. Indeed, any computer with an IP (Internet Protocol) address, the right software, and an Internet connection potentially can be a Web server. And it is for this reason that the Web is so powerful for accessing and distributing information.

Linking all kinds of stored information on all kinds of computers in all kinds of different places, Berners-Lee suggested, would create a web of information. No single document would have links to all other related documents, but users could follow linked documents to find the information wanted.

Moreover, users could assemble their own collections of information stored locally and link to other computers on the Internet running Web server software. That information could then be accessed with Web client software. Those collections of locally stored information, which can include text, images, audio, video, and other types of data, have come to be called home pages, Web pages, or Web sites. A Web page is a collection of information available from a specific Web server, including links to other home pages running on other Web servers. The specific relationship of a home page to a server will be more fully explained in the section in this chapter about publishing on the Web.

Although Berners-Lee clearly laid out the structure of the Web and the strategy, the piece of the puzzle that turned it into a worldwide phenomenon was the development of Web browser software with a graphical interface. The browser is the client software the user employs to navigate the Web and display information.

While he was still an undergraduate at the University of Illinois Urbana Champaign, Marc Andreesen developed a browser, named *Mosaic* that allowed users to navigate the Web simply by clicking the mouse button on text, icons, and buttons. Because Mosaic was developed under the auspices of the National Center for Supercomputing Applications at the University of Illinois, it was distributed for free and rapidly spread through the academic and research communities.

Andreesen went on to help start the company Netscape Communications to publish a commercial Web browser, which was called Netscape *Navigator*. Netscape was ultimately bought by America Online. Realizing the exploding popularity of the Web, software giant Microsoft responded by offering its own browser, *Internet Explorer*. Netscape *Navigator* and *Internet Explorer* are the most frequently used browsers.

The Popularity of the Web

After the emergence of *Mosaic*, Web traffic exploded. At the close of 1993, there were fewer than 1,000 Web pages in the world. Propelled by explosive growth in the World Wide Web, and opening of the Internet to commercial enterprise in 1993, the number of Internet hosts grew dramatically. In October of 1993, as the Clinton-Gore administration opened the Internet to commercial traffic and *Mosaic* was being released to the public, 2,056,000 Internet host sites existed. A year later the number had nearly doubled to 3,864,000, and by the end of 1996, there were more than 20 million. In July of 1999, the number of host domains had grown to 56,218,000 (source: Internet Software Consortium, http://www.isc.org/).

In September, 1995, there were 118,000 registered names for home pages. By 1996, Web servers were being measured in terms of servers per thousands of people in a given site. In Santa Clara, California, the heart of Silicon Valley, in January 1996 there were 554,967 Web servers, according to Matrix Information and Directory Services.

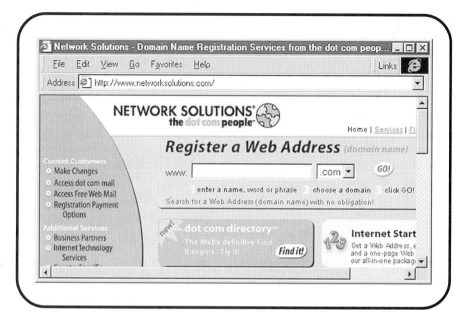

Fig. 3-1: Network Solutions administers domain name registrations for .com, .net, and .org top-level domains through a Web interface at http://www.networksolutions.com.

The popularity of the Web can be attributed to four factors. First, as noted earlier, it provides the first seamless interface to the entire Internet. The Web provides an umbrella for other Internet applications you will learn about in subsequent chapters. Not only are graphical Web browsers easy to use, they are free.

The second reason the Web has become so popular is the vast amount of information available. All sorts of companies, agencies, and institutions, from the White House to local Pizza Hut stores, from Time Warner, the publishers of *Time* and *Entertainment Weekly* magazines, to elementary school students, are distributing information via the Web. Major companies such as IBM have more than one million Web pages.

Third, many companies both large and small believe that the Web and the Internet are important mechanisms for conducting their business. Consequently, they are making huge and well-publicized investments in Web presences. In addition to gathering information, the Web has emerged as an important channel for commerce, for listening to music, for maintaining your personal calendar and other activities.

Finally, the Web is both fun and efficient to use. You can find all sorts of interesting information, from academic research to city guides to directories and descriptions of microbreweries. Not only do many major libraries have a presence on the Web, so do most of the major movie studios. Not only can you find advanced scientific studies, law journals, state-of-the-art literary criticism and reams of census data, you can buy CDs, play advanced computer games, tour foreign countries, and download public domain software from the Web. For many people, the Web is useful both at work and play.

For example, in the mid-1990s, Stefani Manowski was writing an analysis of a war in Bosnia, once a part of the former Yugoslavia. She normally would have done the background research by reading newspaper articles. Using the Web, she was able to download a daily English language news service from Croatia, one of the front-line states in the conflict. Later, she was able to track the activities of some of her favorite music bands, also using the Web.

The Structure of the Web

To successfully navigate the Web, it helps to understand the Web's basic structure. The Web is built on a three-part foundation: a scheme to identify and locate documents; protocols for retrieving documents; and a method for supporting hypermedia links for information stored in different files on different computers. The scheme for identifying and locating documents on the Web is called the Uniform (or Universal) Resource Locator—URL. The primary Web protocol is named the Hypertext Transfer Protocol (HTTP). The method for supporting hypermedia links is known as the Hypertext Markup Language (HTML). For moving among pages on the Web, understanding the URL is critical. For preparing information for distribution through the Web, knowing the basics of HTML is key. But, to understand the reach of the Web, having a grasp of the notion of transport protocols is essential.

Web Transfer Protocols

The main distinction between the Web and other ways to move information around the Internet is the model of data they use. On the Web, all data are treated as potentially part of a hypermedia document linked to other parts of the document residing on other computers. Consequently, on the Web, all data are potentially searchable.

Because of this generic data model, the Web can provide access to servers with information intended to be used with other transport protocols such as Telnet, FTP, Gopher, and Usenet (which will be described in Chapter 7). Nevertheless, a specific transport protocol—HTTP—has also been developed for the Web itself.

The HTTP protocol has several significant attributes. First, it is what is called stateless and generic—that means it can communicate with different computers running different operating systems. Second, it is object-oriented. Object-oriented software allows complex information to be treated as a single unit or object. Third, it can recognize and represent different types of data. That means the mechanisms to transport data can be built independently from the data itself. Fourth, it is not persistent. That means that HTTP does not create an ongoing connection with another computer. Instead, it requests information and once it receives the information, the connection to the second computer is ended. Finally, HTTP communicates with other Internet protocols and gateways.

You can think of it this way: HTTP treats all data like shipping containers. A container can be transported on a ship, truck, train or airplane. It doesn't matter what is inside the container; that will be revealed when the container is opened at its final destination. In addition to sending the containers, HTTP also handles all the paperwork needed to travel from port to port.

You really don't have to understand the mechanics of HTTP. But you must keep in mind that HTTP is designed to move data such as text, graphics, audio and video around the Web. Other tools are needed to actually see or hear the information when it arrive at its destination. Those tools will be more fully explained on the section about browsers later in this chapter.

Second, although HTTP was developed for the Web, it also can communicate with other transport protocols. Unlike other Internet protocols, which can only work with the cyberspace equals of, let's say, ocean freight, HTTP can manage all the Internet methods of transportation. In many ways, the Web is the umbrella application for the entire Internet.

The Anatomy of an URL

To move information to and from a location, the information must have a unique address. The Uniform (or Universal) Resource Locator is an addressing system for locating resources on the Web. In its most basic formulation, an URL (usually pronounced like the man's name, Earl) has two parts: the scheme or protocol used to access the information and an identifier of the information. The specific format by which the information is identified depends on the protocol used to access the information. In general terms, an URL is presented this way:

```
<protocol>:<information-identifier>
```

Because most of the information you will access via the Web uses HTTP as its scheme or method of access, most of the URLs you will see will be for HTTP. The general format for an URL for HTTP is:

```
<http://[host.]domain[:port number][/filepath/filename]>
```

The information in brackets is optional. The host computer is the server from which your browser is requesting information. At minimum you must specify the host. When you do so and nothing else, you will be taken to the host site's default home page. The port number is the communications port the computer is using and is generally included only if the computer is using a nonstandard port. As you recall, every computer on the Internet has a unique identification or IP number. Those are long strings of numbers very difficult to remember. Fortunately, there is a way to assign a name—called an alias—for the those numbers. So, instead of remembering the numbers for a computer, you can remember a name. For example, the magazine division of the Association for Education in Journalism and Mass Communication (AEJMC) has a Web site running on a computer at Loyola College in Maryland. The computer's IP number is 144.126.254.129. That computer has been assigned the name (or alias) of www.aejmcmagazine.org The URL for the magazine division of AEJMC is http://www.aejmcmagazine.org. The computer running the home page of the television network CBS has been assigned the name www.cbs.com. The URL for CBS is http://www.cbs.com/. Cable News Network is http://cnn.com/.

Once you reach the computer on which the information you want is stored, you then have to access the specific information in which you are interested. Information is stored on Web servers in the standard path/file format used by personal computers. The different directories, subdirectories and file names are separated in the URL by the / mark.

To fully understand the anatomy of an URL, consider this example. Every year, the Investigative Reporters and Editors organization sponsors a contest honoring the best investigative journalism. The 1998 winners are posted on the IRE Web page at http://www.ire.org/history/pr/1998awards.html. That means the information uses the HTTP protocol and is on a computer called www.ire.com in a directory or folder called "history" that has a subdirectory called "pr." The file that will be accessed is called "1998winners.html." The files contain text and links to graphics files, plus links to information stored on computers elsewhere on the Internet.

What You Can Learn from the URL

As noted earlier, the Web supports access to a wide range of Internet protocols in addition to HTTP—including FTP, Gopher, Telnet, news and nntp (which are Usenet news groups protocols), mailto (electronic mail addressing), WAIS and other less-used protocols. The first element in the URL indicates the protocol being used. Consequently, when you see an URL that begins ftp:// you recognize that you will be accessing information from an FTP server. Once you have jumped to that location, you may have to be able to use FTP commands to access the information.

In most cases, however, while you are using the Web, you will be using the HTTP protocol. You will move from link to link in hypermedia documents, in the process jumping to new URLs. It is the hyperlinks that make the Web such a dynamic service. The hyperlinks are based on HTML, the Hypertext Markup Language.

The second element in the URL is the host name. If the host has an alias or name, the name will have two or three parts divided by a period. A typical host name will have the following form:

www.name.topleveldomainsignifier

In the first wave of Web sites, many sites started their domain name with "www." It was meant to signal that the site was, in fact, a Web site. But "www" generally has no meaning. Many Web domains are now registered both with and without the "www" in the front. The second element is meant to be a distinctive name, so people can easily remember the Web site. For example, it is easy to remember that the Web site name for the *New York Times* is www.nytimes.com.

The third element signifies the top level domain. As you know, when the Internet was first launched, it was sponsored by the United States government and used primarily by academic, government and military researchers. Each community had its own set of rules and requirements for Internet access and usage. The three-letter suffix was developed to identify the different communities.

Currently there are seven top level domains. Countries other than the United States also have a suffix to identify them. The current top level domains are listed in Figure 3-2.

Fig 3-2: The Internet addressing scheme tells what type of organization is associated with an Internet address. In nations outside the United States, a two-character suffix is added. For example .uk = United Kingdom; .au = Australia; .be = belgium; .ca = Canada; .de = Germany; .se = Sweden; .mx = Mexico; .es = Spain; .fr = France.

Top Level U.S. Internet Domains

.edu = Educational
.gov = Government
.com = Commercial
.org = Nonprofit organizations
.mil = U.S. military
.net = Network providers
.int = International organizations.

As the number of domain names increases, schemes for adding top level domains have been proposed but not yet implemented.

The Essentials of HTML

HTML is based on something called the Standard Generalized Markup Language or SGML. SGML is basically an international language to describe documents. It is an outgrowth of the methods proofreaders use to mark documents before they are sent to be typeset and printed.

In essence, HTML codes are like word processing codes. When you are working with a word processor, tags are embedded in a document determining the way a document looks when it is printed. For example, working with a standard word processor, when you change a typeface in a document, a tag is placed in the document. Those codes are generally concealed from the user. In the same way, if you want to center, boldface or underline text, the word processor surrounds the words with hidden tags.

HTML has a series of tags which determine the way a document looks when it is viewed by a Web browser. It also has tags which link text or images in one document or file to text or images in another document or file. When you click your mouse on a link while using your Web browser, you will automatically access the linked information. That information could be text, images, video, audio, or computer programs that perform designated tasks such as searching a database.

Your Browser

Understanding the basic elements of the Web will help you maximize your benefits. But to use the Web, all you need is a Web browser, which is the term used for the client software for the Web. Unlike e-mail, for which you may need your own mailbox, with the Web, you can basically use any computer running Web client software. The browser is the client software that makes the requests to Web servers for information, then displays on your computer the information that is accessed.

Any computer linked to the Internet and running the TCP/IP protocol can run a Web browser. Generally, whoever provides your Internet access will provide Web browser software as well. Like other software applications, browsers allow you to perform many tasks. The most important, of course, is that the browser allows you to request information from Web servers, then displays the information. In addition, Netscape and Internet Explorer allow you to copy, cut, and paste information from the screen into word processing documents. There are also tools (bookmarks or hot lists) for saving the URLs of sites that you visit often and the sites passed through during a single session. Properly set up, current browsers allow you to send e-mail directly from them without exiting to a separate e-mail client program.

If you find yourself in the position of having to evaluate browsers, the most important consideration may be the speed at which the browser displays information. While the speed depends to a large degree on the Internet connection itself, the amount of Web traffic at the site you are visiting, and other factors, the way a browser handles data is a factor as well. Faster browsers will first display text then fill in the graphics. Some allow you to jump from Web site to Web site while the graphics are still filling in. Many functions of browser operation may be configured by the user.

Another important feature is called cache memory. With cache memory, information from one file can be temporarily stored in your computer's memory after you move to another page of information on the Web. Then, if you want to see the information from the first file again, it can be recalled from the computer memory, rather than from the original source of the information on the Web. Loading information from memory is a lot faster than loading information from a Web server.

Browsers and File Types

The Web is changing rapidly. HTML is continually developing. Moreover, one of the strengths of the Web is that different types of information can be transported over it. Different types of data are stored in different files using different formats. As in other areas of computing, the basic structure for a file name on the Web is filename.extension. The extension identifies the specific kind of file. For example, files created in Microsoft Word end in .doc. On the Web, audio files, graphic files, video files and other kinds of files have different file extensions. Table 3-1 contains common file types and extensions.

But as new and more sophisticated information is developed for the Web, not all browsers, particularly the older browsers, can display all the information available. To compensate, companies have developed what are called "plug-ins" for browsers. Plug-ins are ancillary programs that are automatically launched when a browser encounters a file type that it cannot view by itself.

Both Netscape *Navigator* and *Internet Explorer* display both .gif and .jpeg graphic files and come with viewers for some video and audio file types. For other kinds of information, however, you will have to download plug-ins, which are also sometimes called readers or viewers. Plug-ins are generally distributed for free because companies that develop new media types want the viewers for that file type distributed as widely as possible *Shockwave*, which creates multimedia material for the Web, was developed by

Macromedia (http://www.macromedia.com) which supplies a viewer. A Real Media plug-in plays back streaming audio and video content created using software from Real Media (http://www.real.com). Adobe Systems Inc. (http://www.adobe.com) offers a reader for .pdf (or Acrobat) files (which keep their formatting even when they are displayed on the Web).

Table 3-1: Common file types encountered on the Web, their origins, and how they can be recognized by their filename extension.

File Format	File Type	Extension
HTML	Text	.html .htm
ASCII Text	Text	.prn .txt
PostScript	Formatted Text	.ps
Portable Document Format	Text & Graphics	.pdf
Graphics Interchange Format	Graphic	.gif
Joint Photographers Expert Group	Graphic	.jpeg .jpg
AU Audio	Audio	.au
Wav Audio	Audio	.wav
AIFF	Audio	.aiff .aif
Real Audio	Audio	.ra
Motion Picture Expert Group	Video	.mpeg .mpg
Quicktime Video	Video	.mov
AVI Video	Video	.avi
Real Player	Audio and Video	.rm
Director	Multimedia	.dir

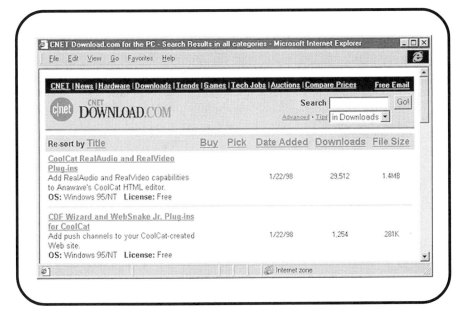

Fig. 3-3: Download.com has a section that specializes in providing plug-ins for World Wide Web browsers. Plug-ins help browsers to display (or play) Web content like audio and video files.

The Netscape Web site (http://home.netscape.com/) has a large repository of free plug-ins with easy instructions on how to download them as does Download.com (http://www.download.com). Both Netscape and Microsoft introduce new versions of their browsers at a heated pace. The competition is so heated, in fact, that browsers are free.

Working the Web

When you start a Web browser, the first thing that happens is that it calls out to a Web server. By default, Netscape opens the home page of Netscape Communications, its publisher. Because it is a very busy home page, people often change the initial home page—also called the default home page—to a chosen favorite. In some browsers, the default home page can be changed by pulling down on the options menu across the top of the browser and choosing "preferences." Many universities and employers use their own home page as the default. Others use the home pages of specific sources of information, such as academic departments. Journalists may want to use one of the "Journalists' Hotlists" described in Appendix A as their default home page. For example, the *FACSNET* service for journalists at http://www.facsnet.org/ provides a wealth of links, topic tutorials, and background information for working journalists (see Figure 3-4).

Fig. 3-4: *FACSNET* is a service for journalists that provides topic tutorials, background information, vetted Internet site links, and a database of experts on a wide range of topics.

Once the browser is operating, you can then jump to virtually any location on the Web. If you know the URL of the information you want, you can enter the URL of the location from which you are requesting information in the address line.

When your browser requests information from a Web server, a three-part process occurs. First, if the Web server has an alias, your browser sends a request to what is termed a Domain Name Server (DNS), to determine the IP number for the computer. Once the IP number has been determined, the appropriate server is contacted, and the information is requested. Finally, the data is transmitted to the browser on your computer for viewing.

For example, assume you are an environmental reporter and you want to access information from the Environmental Molecular Sciences Laboratory at the Pacific Northwest Laboratory, where of some of the most cutting-edge, basic environmental research is currently underway. You heard the Web site there has descriptions of the research being conducted. In the address line, you enter the URL, which, in this case, is http://www.esml.pnl.gov.

The request from your browser is sent to the DNS to determine the IP number of the computer called www.esml.pnl.gov. The request is then sent to that computer and the information—in this case the Web site's opening page—will be transported to your browser for display.

But suppose you are not interested in all the environmental work being done at the lab. All you want is to periodically survey the research reports and selected projects that they have published online. In that case, you can go directly to http://www.esml.pnl.gov./proj/homepage.html. In reply, you will receive the file which contains a sample of the research with links to information found elsewhere on the Internet.

There are two important lessons to be learned from this example. First, every file available via the Web has its own unique URL. You do not have to first access the home page of the Web site, then travel down layers to find what you want. Every file of information on the Web is ultimately accessible from every other place on the Web.

Second, you don't actually log on to the remote computer. You simply make a request for information, which is then accessed and sent to your computer for display.

Opening a specific URL is only one way to travel the Web. Many people begin at specific starting places, then just follow the links. For example, assume you are tracking the latest presidential campaign. You could start at CNN's All Politics site (http://allpolitics.com/) which offers insider coverage of different campaigns. From there you could jump to the home page of the Gallup Organization at http://www.gallup.com/, one of the premier polling groups, and review the back issues of their newsletters at http://www.gallup.com/newsletter/index.html. By moving from site to site, you could get a comprehensive picture of the developments during the race.

Here and Back Again

As you move from site to site on the Web by clicking on linked information, it is useful to know the URL of the Web servers you access. If you find useful information, you may want to return to the same site later.

As you move through the Web, you may find that you want to move back and forth among several pages. The most efficient way is to select the "go" command from the pull-down menu bar of the browser. You will see a history of the sites you have visited during that session. Highlight the site to which you want to return, and you automatically return there. Keep in mind, though, that if you visit a lot of sites during a single session, the history list may get truncated at some point.

If, while moving through the Web, you find a site that you are sure that you will want to return to regularly, you can "bookmark" the site. When you are at the page of information to which you wish to return— perhaps the opening page of the site of a competitor such as Time Inc. (http://pathfinder.com/)—select the "Bookmark" command ("Favorites" in *Internet Explorer*) from the pull-down menu and select "add." The URL will automatically be added to a list of URLs bookmarked earlier. To access an URL on your bookmark list, simply select it and off you go.

Remember, however, that if you are working at a computer to which other users have access, such as a computer in a computer lab or a single computer in a newsroom, the other users could delete your bookmarked URLs if they choose. To be safe, you may wish to compile a list of the URLs of your favorite sites on paper or on a floppy disk. If your list is on a disk, you can cut from the list and paste the URLs into the Open Location or address line when you wish to revisit sites. Chapter 11 offers an in-depth look into using the browser effectively.

Enhanced Reporting

The Web can be used in many different ways to enhance reporting. You can use the Web to scan favorite news sites to stay abreast of breaking news, search for in-depth material, find sources, find story leads and attend online events. Finding sources and story leads, and attending online events will be discussed in future chapters.

Using the Web to scan favorite news sites is perhaps the easiest and most straightforward application of the Web in journalism. Most accomplished journalists are news junkies, and read or view several newspapers and news broadcasts a day. Using the "bookmark" feature of the browser, journalists can create a list of six or eight news sites to monitor regularly.

Journalists must also always stay aware of what the competition is doing. Once again, the Web can provide faster insight into the way the competition is reporting the stories on which you are working

Finding What You Need

New Web users frequently enjoy simply browsing Web sites, happily discovering interesting information. But few reporters have time for that. The Web is also a dynamic source for finding information that you need for an article or project, or to simply give you a better insight into the subjects you cover.

There are many different methods of locating information on the Web— some systematic and some based on understanding the way the Web works. For example, journalism student Tanya Zicko was once assigned to write about proposed budget cuts in public broadcasting. She knew that many companies and organizations use a standard format for their URLs. The URL is www.company-name-or-initials.domain. As you learned, the domain indicates the type of organization operating the computer network on the Internet.

So Zicko sat down with her Web browser and entered http://www.pbs.org in the address line. She reasoned that the Public Broadcasting System would go by the initials PBS and that, because it is a nonprofit organization, it would be in the .org domain. She was right. She accessed the opening page of the Public Broadcasting System's Web server. There she found many press releases and transcripts of congressional testimony relating to her topic. She also visited www.cpb.org, the home page of the Corporation for Public Broadcasting, PBS' parent organization, where she found additional information. Zicko's analysis was filled with the most timely facts, figures and perspectives.

While many Web URLs follow the general format www.company-or-organization-name.domain, many more do not. Moreover, many times you will not know where the information in which you are interested is located. In those cases, there are two primary vehicles for finding information about the topics you want on the Web: Web search sites and Web subject directories or catalogs.

As the Web began to grow in popularity, several teams of researchers began to explore ways to automatically index all the information available online. These researchers created software "robots" that travel through the Web to identify new Web pages. They then index the pages according to key words and other mechanisms. The researchers then created methods to access the index according to key words. Taken together, the indexing and accessing of Web information serves as what is called a search engine.

Fig. 3-5: Browsing software tracks the history of your online sessions, making it easy to return quickly to any place you have recently visited.

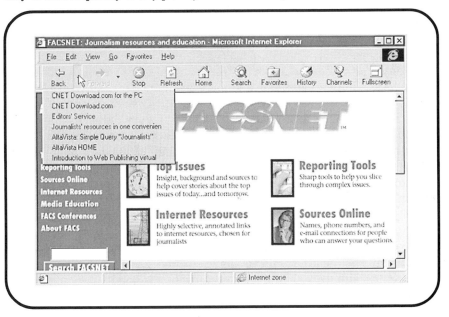

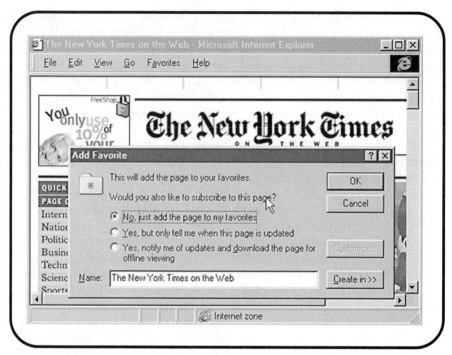

Fig. 3-6: When you find a Web page to which you expect to return frequently, you may add that page to your Bookmarks (*Navigator*) or Favorites (*Internet Explorer*) list.

Currently, hundreds of active search sites occupy the Web. Among the more popular are *AltaVista* (http://www.altavista.com/, Figure 3-x), *Infoseek* (http://infoseek.go.com/), *Google* (http://www.google.com), and *Yahoo!* (http://www.yahoo.com).

Many "meta-sites" search sites have emerged that combine the results from different individual search engines. Among the best known are *Dogpile* (http://www.dogpile.com/) and *Ask Jeeves* at http://www.ask.com. The *Yahoo!* subject guide on search engines at http://www.yahoo.com (under the Internet category) lists more than 40 multiple-site search engines.

In general, the search procedures work like this. Once you access the search site, you may enter key words describing the information you want. For example, assume you are writing a retrospective piece about Spiro Agnew, former vice president of the United States who died in 1996. You enter the words "Spiro Agnew" as key words into a search engine. The results will be a list of documents from the Web, Gopher, news groups, and other sources, in which the title of the document or some of the key information matches the keywords you have entered. Every entry on the list is linked to the site, so you can then jump from site to site, looking for the precise information you want.

While search sites are very powerful tools, they have very notable limitations. First, a search site will return only a small percentage of the Internet sites that actually match your search. It may take several months for new sites to be indexed. Second, because searches are driven by keywords, the results may not always match your intentions. For example, the search for Spiro Agnew on AltaVista turned up everything from an issue of the ezine Dirty Phrack to a discography of the folk singer Tom Paxson.

To conduct a thorough search, you should vary your keywords from search to search. Furthermore, you should use several different search engines when you are actively seeking information.

Initially, searching for information via search engines is a lot like searching for needles in haystacks. You may find yourself looking at many irrelevant pages before you find something appropriate. Once you find a good source, you will probably want to follow links on that page to other appropriate pages. To return to the results of your search, you can use the history list in the "go" menu as described earlier.

Using Subject Directories

Subject directories represent an alternative to keyword search dialogs for finding information on the Web. In this approach, sites organize information into subject categories. You can click on the subject Art History in the Arts and Humanities section at Yahoo (http://www.yahoo.com), for example, and get links to 500 sites on the Web that have information about Art History. The Poynter Institute's Nora Paul gives a good explanation of the different search sites and catalogs in her online book, *Computer Assisted Research: A Guide to Tapping Online Information*. The explanation is accessible at http://www.facsnet.org/report_tools/CAR/carfind.htm.

Most major search sites have both keyword search dialogs and subject directories. If you know exactly the type of information you want, subject guides are often a productive way to start a search on the Web. Using subject guides is comparable to using the subject guides in libraries. You can easily scroll through many listings looking for the most promising.

On the other hand, search dialogs often turn up resources you would never find via subject guides. For example, many college students are creating their own home pages with links to a lot of other interesting Web sites. Search engines treat the home pages of college students the same as all other home pages and often will link you to an obscure but useful page of information you would not have otherwise found.

Searching the Web for information can be time consuming. Consequently, if you know that you are going to be working on a project over time, it is worthwhile to subscribe to one of the appropriate online discussion groups

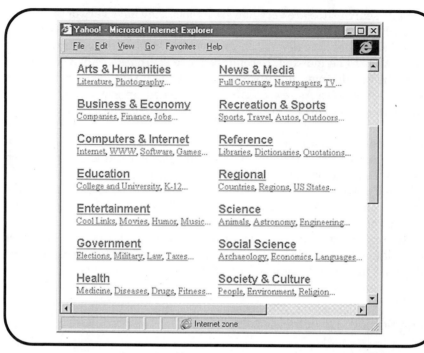

Fig. 3-7: Subject Guides, such as *Yahoo!*, permit you to browse through directories of Internet material arranged by topic. Most portals and keyword search sites now also provide subject directories

described in Chapter 5. The URLs of Web sites of interest are usually posted in discussion groups. After you are familiar with the flow of information among group members, you can post a message asking for good sites with information about your project.

Nevertheless, the payoff of sustained searching can be dramatic. Tom Johnson, a professor at San Francisco State University, reported this result from a computer-assisted reporting conference he conducted in Lima, Peru. One person at the conference, who worked for a major Lima newspaper, wanted to know about the military expenditures of Chile. Using *AltaVista*, he entered the Spanish terms for Chile and arms and nothing much came up. Then he entered the words "Chile weapons" in English. Near the top of the list of sources was a site which maintained a database of arms imports and exports by country. The database was maintained by a peace group in Sweden.

There are many different ways to search the Web. And there is so much information available that a reporter could easily spend too much time and find too little information. Reporters must develop a solid strategy for searching the Web. Search strategies will be discussed in depth in Chapter 6.

When You Find What You Want

Usually, the primary purpose of surfing the Web is to locate information you can use for assignments. In most cases, that means you will want to save the information you find.

In many cases, the best approach is to print the information you wish to save for future use. Most browsers allow you several options to save and print information When you select the print command, the file at which you are looking is printed at the printer associated with the computer you are using. Remember, that printer may not be the one closest to you. So, if you are going to simply print the file directly from the browser, be sure to know where that file will be printed.

Printing from the browser has some drawbacks. The file at which you are looking may be quite long. Don't be fooled because a file appears to be presented in fairly small chunks and there are hyperlinks from section to section in the text. For example, it is easy to find online *A Beginners Guide to HTML*. The first screen you see is a table of contents. Click on any entry and you move down to that section of the document. But the whole guide is only one file, fourteen pages long. If you simply press the print command, the whole file will be printed—even if you only wanted to save one section on troubleshooting.

Most often, you will be interested only in a small part of the information you view. For example, you may not need the graphics on the page. If you only want to save parts of a document, you should open your word processor and copy from your browser window and paste into your word processor the desired portions of the file on the Web into a document on your word processor. The cut and paste commands are under the Edit menu item on the browser. After you have copied and pasted all the information you need, you can treat the file as a regular word processing document.

The copy-and-paste approach is very effective if you wish to save bits of information from different pages. It is also a good approach if you wish to use the information on a personal computer off the network. If you use the cut-and-paste approach, be sure to carefully document where you found the information. The easiest way to accurately document the site from which you accessed information is to cut and paste the URL from the "Show Location" line.

If you do want to save a long file, you may want to store it electronically on your personal computer. You can do this using the Save As command under the file menu on the browser. Alternatively, you can mail the file to your e-mail address. To use the e-mail feature of the Netscape browser, however, you must know how to configure the mailer. You will need to know the IP number or alias of your mail server and other information. Moreover, if you are using a public access computer, anybody can change the configuration.

Sourcing Cyberspace Material

A cardinal principle of journalism is to report to the reader or viewer the source of your information. Traditionally, that process has meant quoting people whom you have interviewed or referring to a report or document. On the other hand, if the information has come from a press release or is generally known, often journalists cite the sponsoring organization or spokesperson but don't mention that the information came from a press release.

Sourcing material you find on the Web presents three problems. First, no universally accepted standard citation format for Internet material has evolved. Second, the Internet is always changing. There is no assurance that the information you found today at one address will still be at the same location, should somebody what to check the sources later. For example, most of the basic background information about the Web itself was transferred from the server at CERN in Switzerland (info.cern.ch), to one at MIT (www.w3.org). Users are no longer forwarded to the new location. Third, URLs are often long and cumbersome to include in the body of an article. It is also easy to make mistakes in transcribing an exact URL, and URLs can be time-consuming to verify.

The precise method of indicating the source of material you have obtained via the Web should be determined by your publication. If you have found a report or a document on the Web, you can refer to it as you would any report or document; that you found it via the Web makes no difference. But, if the material you are using was created specifically for the Web, you may want to indicate when and where you found it. The precise URL is probably not needed. After all, when reporters quote people, they rarely indicate whether the interview took place over the telephone, in person, or at lunch. On the one hand, Internet information does not have to be held to a higher standard than other information. On the other hand, the Web and the Internet do not free reporters from the obligation to indicate the sources of their information.

It is important, however, to develop a consistent method of citing material obtained via the Web. The minimum information should probably include, if it can be determined, the name of the person who created the material, the affiliation of that person, and the base URL showing where you found the material. In that case, if readers want to follow up, they can communicate directly with the creator of the material you used.

A New Medium

Here is a headline that ran in 1999 that you may have missed: "Corruption in Bosnian Government Reveals Existence of Bosnian Government." The headline was satirical and was published by the online version of *The Onion*, a humor magazine at http://www.theonion.com.

Thousands of companies and individuals have created their own Web-based publications. Although some of the more ambitious efforts using the Web as a new publishing media will be examined in Chapter 9, many individual reporters and students may find it advantageous to create their own Web sites as well.

One of the reasons so many Web sites have been created is that simple Web pages are very easy to make. The only requirement for creating a Web page is to be able to post HTML documents on a Web server. Many schools and third-party Internet providers routinely offer Web server space to students and subscribers.

There are many excellent books about HTML and Web publishing. Briefly, HTML is a plain ASCII text format and can be created using any word processor or text editor, though many find it easier using specialized programs such as Microsoft's *Front Page* (http://www.microsoft.com/), Macromedia's *Dreamweaver* (http://www.macromedia.com) and Adobe's *PageMill* (http://www.adobe.com/). Some of the latest generation of word processors, desktop publishing software, and office suites include an automatic conversion to HTML option. After the document is completed, it is saved as an HTML file in ASCII format.

As you will recall, HTML allows you to format a document and link sections and documents by embedding tags within text. Together, the tags and text are called the source code. Tags are embedded using angle brackets < >. Some common tags are <TITLE> for the title of the document, <H1> for a headline and <P> to separate paragraphs. A title is generally displayed separately from the text and is used to identify the contents. There are six levels of headlines (H1 to H6), with H1 being the most prominent. Unlike word processors, HTML text needs the <P> to separate paragraphs. Browsers ignore indentations and blank lines in the source code.

The main feature of HTML is linking documents and sections of documents—either text or images. Browsers highlight hypermedia links so users will know to click on them to be connected to another file. All links use the anchor tag <A>. The link includes the name of the document to which the link connects plus the text or image which is to be highlighted. The name of the document begins with the letters HREF and is enclosed by quotation marks. The full form for an anchor tag is <A HREF="name-of-document">highlighted text</A>. This form can be used to link documents running locally on the same Web server and documents that are running on different servers.

Most Web browsers can also display what are called in-line images; that is, images next to text. In most cases, the images should be in a GIF or JPEG format. To include an in-line image on your Web page, use the tag <IMG SRC=image_URL> The URL is the file name of the image and must end in either .GIF for GIF files or either .JPEG or .JPG for JPEG files.

The tags just outlined are enough to create very simple Web pages. For an example of a simple page using just the tags you can visit http://nmc.loyola.edu/ols/oljexample.html.

More sophisticated pages use short computer routines termed CGIs (an acronym for Common Gateway Interface) to enable database searching, creating links to sections of an image and other advanced features. Moreover, HTML is still being developed and there are many other tags that can be embedded.

A good method of learning HTML programming is to study other pages on the Web. To see the source code for pages you are viewing, simply select "source" under the View menu item on your Web browser.

Individual students and reporters may wish to create their own Web pages for several reasons. It can be an excellent method to showcase your work. And, it can be a way to express yourself in an unfettered fashion. An example of journalism students' Web sites from the Graduate School of Journalism at Columbia University can be found at http://www.jrn.columbia.edu. A basic understanding of HTML and Web publishing is an excellent skill for journalists to acquire. In many ways, the Web is like the early days of television. It represents a nearly unlimited opportunity for journalists. In fact, many young journalists now begin their careers in online news.

When the Web Goes Wrong

Despite the popularity of the Web, it does not work flawlessly. Indeed, few people realized how popular it would become in such a short period of time. So, much like the streets in a rapidly developing city, there is a lot of traffic and an occasional traffic jam.

For a user, a traffic jam makes itself felt in several ways. First, if you are requesting large amounts of information, it may take a long time for the information to arrive and to be viewed by your browser. In general, text is the fastest to load. Images represent a lot more data than simple text and take a longer time to be displayed. Audio and video are extremely data intensive. Depending on the exact link to the Internet, it is not uncommon for it to take a while to retrieve 20 seconds of audio.

The speed at which information is transferred and viewed depends on the traffic on the Internet itself, the speed at which information is transferred from the Internet to the network on which the computer you are using is located—the computer which manages that transfer is called your gateway computer—and the traffic on your local network. The busier the Web and your local network, the slower the information will be transferred.

Sometimes the traffic jam is not on the Web or your gateway or local network, but at the server from which you request information. Servers can only manage requests for information from a set number of browsers at any one time. If that limit has been exceeded, you may receive a message indicating that your connection has been refused and you should try again later. This is a fairly common occurrence with very busy Web sites.

Another common problem is that the connection between your browser and the Web server may be unexpectedly disconnected. You may not realize that you are off line for some time, particularly if you are mainly viewing pages that your browser has cached. One indication that you have been disconnected comes when you request information from an URL you know is correct and you receive a message saying that the Domain Name Server cannot find the computer. Or, it may respond "host not found." If you receive that message consistently as you try different servers, you can be almost certain your connection has gone down and you should restart your browser or redial your provider.

As you know, URLs are generally composed of long strings of characters. It is very easy to make mistakes when you enter an URL into the open location line. If you have incorrectly entered the name of the Web server on which the information you want resides, you will receive a message "host not found." When that happens, you should check the first part of the URL.

If you incorrectly entered the directory path and file name for the information you want, you will probably receive a message which says "404 File Not Found." That means you have sent your request to a legitimate Web server but the specific file you asked for could not be located. Table 3-2 lists several of the most common error messages.

If you spend long periods of time on the Web, you will have to manage your own computer memory as well. Remember, Web information is often stored in the computer's cache memory for easy recall. If the cache is full, you may not be able to open additional programs, such as a word processor should you need to. Therefore, it is prudent to have all the application programs you need open before you begin your searches.

Finally, as you move through the Web, from time to time you will come to sites that will ask you to register. Some will allow you to buy things online. While it is up to you to decide if you wish to register at a site, unless you are alerted otherwise you should assume that transactions on the Internet are not secure. That means people can intercept and monitor information as it travels through the networks. The security risk may be about the same as giving your credit card number over the telephone. You should consider the Web a public place and act accordingly.

Some sites ask you to register and select a password even though they are not secure sites. In those cases, don't use the same password you use for your ATM card, computer access or any other meaningful, secure account. One technique is to use your name as your password for sites

Error Message	Meaning
Unable to Connect to Server	The URL is valid but the server is not responding. It may be turned off.
Connection refused	Too many users are attempting to access information.
Broken pipe	An error occurred when the information was being sent through the Internet.
404 Document Not Found	A part of the URL after the first / is incorrect and the specific file cannot be found on the Web site.
403 Forbidden	Access to the Web site is blocked.
Document Contains No Data	You have found a file but there is no content in it. These are often files that draw information from a database.
Server has no DNS number	You have made a mistake in entering the name of the Web site, that is, the part of the URL between the // and the first /.
Location is not recognized	You have entered an incorrect URL.
Enter name and password	Web site is password protected.

Table 3-2: Common error messages encountered while you are navigating the World Wide Web and things do not go as planned.

that are not secure. One advantage is that your name is easy to remember when you return. And, be sure to record the name and password you have entered for each site at which you have registered.

Conclusion

With the World Wide Web, you can search the world for the information you need. Literally millions of people are making information available on Web servers to be accessed by people with Web browsers.

On the other hand, with the World Wide Web, it is as if the Library of Congress just opened, but people are still relatively unfamiliar with books. It is thrilling to be able to access all sorts of information. But inevitably, at some point you will want to locate information for specific purposes.

Finding specific, high quality information is still a challenge. To integrate the Web into your work, you will have to invest time to gain experience. You will want to develop your own hotlist and bookmarks. You should leave enough time in each project to follow links to see where they lead. You should explore.

As you obtain access to more information, you will face new demands.

For example, Kara Kiefer decided to write an article about assisted euthanasia. As she pursued the story, she read an article in the *New York Times* that referred to a New York state legislative report on law and dying. She knew she needed that report so she went to the Web. Working through subject guides, within an hour, she found a copy of the original report on the Web site of the Indiana University Law School.

Kiefer's success meant that she then had to read a long, complicated report. Finding the report on the Web meant she had to do more work. But her finished product was also much better.

4

Contacting People by E-mail

The Johns Hopkins University is the intellectual crown jewel of Baltimore. Birthplace of the modern research university, Johns Hopkins is the home of one of the most prestigious medical schools in the country. It is the leading academic recipient of federal funding for scientific research. Its students have earned well-deserved reputations as academic grinds.

The Johns Hopkins University is not a customary venue for shootings. But on April 10, 1996, a student pulled a .357 Magnum from a bag and shot sophomore Rex Chao in the back of the head and then again in the chest. Chao, an honor student and member of the Johns Hopkins Symphony Orchestra died shortly thereafter. Tobert Harwood, Jr., who had been chairman of the College Republicans club, was charged in the crime.

The campus and the city were shocked. How could this happen among the cream of the crop? To answer that question, a team of reporters from the *Baltimore Sun* interviewed the people who knew the men. They also examined the e-mail correspondence the two men had, printing excerpts of their electronic exchanges on April 21.

The material was moving, revealing between the two men an intensely personal relationship that had gone horribly wrong. It provided insight into the incident that probably could have been gained in no other way.

Since the early 1990s, the use of electronic mail, or e-mail as it is generally known, has exploded. As far back as 1992, a survey of corporate management information and telecommunications managers indicated that electronic mail was among the most important technologies in meeting their companies' messaging needs. As more and more companies have connected to the Internet, e-mail has become even more important. When the United States government sued the Microsoft Corporation for violating antitrust laws in 1998, a large part of the evidence Justice Department lawyers presented was e-mail exchanged among Microsoft executives. The e-mail often contradicted the executives' recollection and testimony at the trial.

The use of e-mail by journalists has steadily increased. In fact, Neil Reisner, a journalist for the *Miami Herald* who has pioneered the use of computers in journalism, argues that journalists who cannot effectively use e-mail cannot effectively do their jobs.

Journalists can use e-mail to communicate with their colleagues and with sources. They can use e-mail to check facts and quotes. They can use e-mail to gather ideas and insights not available in other ways. Finally, they can also use e-mail to subscribe to discussion lists in which like-minded people communicate about specific topics. E-mail is becoming as important as the telephone as a means of communicating for journalists.

This chapter will

- explore the basics of e-mail, including how to get started, how to understand the anatomy of an e-mail address, and the structure of the e-mail network,
- describe how to construct an e-mail message and manage your e-mail account,
- review some of the rules of etiquette which have emerged in relation to the use of e-mail,
- point out some of the legal ramifications of using e-mail, and
- suggest ways to effectively use e-mail in reporting.

Subscribing to and using e-mail discussion lists in journalism will be discussed in Chapter 5.

The Basics of E-mail

Conceptually, e-mail is not much different from regular mail (affectionately known to the initiated as "snail mail"). You create a message. You address the message to the intended recipient. You deposit the letter into the transmission system, which carries it to its intended destination.

There are differences, however. First, e-mail arrives at its destination much more quickly than regular mail. This aids communications considerably. For example, a reporter for a science journal needed leads to scientists and engineers, who were using Microsoft Windows technology, for a story she was doing. She sent e-mail to three contacts she had at software companies publishing technical packages that run under the Windows operating system for scientists and engineers. Within a half hour, she received the names of six scientists working at such organizations as Sandia National Laboratory and the National Weather Service.

E-mail is also more convenient than regular mail. Generally speaking, when you reply to an e-mail "letter," you don't have to find a piece of paper, locate an envelope, remember the person's address, buy a stamp, and put the letter in the mailbox. Instead, you can reply to the message with just a few keystrokes. E-mail programs automatically address the reply to the sender of the initial message. Moreover, most e-mail programs allow you to copy all or part of the original message with just a few keystrokes; therefore, you can respond point by point. For example, when one of the public relations people sent the names of people working with the Macintosh instead of Windows, the reporter copied that part of the message and sent it back, reiterating the request for Windows users.

Finally, e-mail is still more informal than regular mail. In many circumstances, a formal salutation is unnecessary. And you can create a signature that will be attached automatically to all your e-mail correspondence.

Used correctly, e-mail is a powerful and convenient tool for journalists. Used incorrectly, e-mail can create serious problems for journalists.

Getting Started

The first step in using e-mail is establishing an account on a computer connected to the Internet and setting up a mailbox. There are three basic approaches to establishing an e-mail account. The first is to establish an account through your school or employer. Almost all colleges and universities now offer their students electronic mail. Most large- and medium-sized news organizations do so as well. The second method is to set up an e-mail account through a commercial Internet Service Provider. Let's say you use Earthlink Communications to access the Internet and the World Wide Web. As part of the service, Earthlink also provides an electronic mailbox. The final approach to setting up an e-mail account is to use a free service via the World Wide Web. Netscape *WebMail*, Microsoft *HotMail*, *Yahoo!*, and other Web companies allow you to set up an account that can be accessed using your Web browser.

At least two variations on these themes should be mentioned here. More than 10 million people gain e-mail and Internet access through such commercial hybrid services as CompuServe, America Online or Prodigy. Some providers such as Juno.com offer free Internet access to anyone willing to tolerate a certain amount of e-mail advertising.

Each approach has its advantages and disadvantages. If you set up an account through your school or company, it will not cost you any money. If you set up an account via your Internet Service Provider, you can use a range of different e-mail clients to access your mail. If you use Web-based e-mail, you can access your account easily as long as you have Web access. Commercial hybrids offer a lot of hand-holding support, but generally require you to use their branded software, which may be noticeably slower than other software.

In all cases, when you set up an electronic mailbox, you will be assigned a user name and a password, which only you will know. That means that other people without authorization will not be able to access your e-mail without your permission. A certain amount of computer storage space will also be reserved for your use. Finally, you will be given a procedure describing how to log on to the computer on which your account resides.

Nevertheless, your e-mail account is not private. It resides on your college's or company's computer, the Internet Service Provider's computer or the Web site's computer and can be accessed by the system administrator and others who are authorized to manage the system. Legal issues associated with e-mail will be discussed later in this chapter and in Chapter 10.

Anatomy of an E-mail Address

When you set up an electronic mail account, you receive an e-mail address. The address has two parts: the user name (in this case the name you use to sign on to the computer on which you have the mailbox) and the Internet name of the computer. As you learned in Chapter 2, every computer attached to the Internet has a unique identification number. Most system administrators then associate a name with that number to make it easier for people to use and remember. By convention, the two parts of electronic addresses are separated by the @ symbol.

For example, early in 1999, before Sarah Cohen took a position with the *Washington Post*, she was the training director for the National Institute for Computer Assisted Reporting (NICAR). Her e-mail address was sarah@nicar.org. Her user name, assigned by the system administrator when Cohen had her mailbox set up, is sarah. Nicar.org is the domain name for NICAR. The .org top level domain reflects that NICAR is officially chartered as a nonprofit organization.

For computers located in the United States, the last three letters of the address indicate the type of setting, or top level domain as it is termed, in which the computer is located. In addition to the .org domain for not-for-profit organizations, there are six other primary top level domains: .gov for governmental computers; .edu for computers in educational institutions; .mil for computers associated with military organizations; .com for computers in commercial organizations; .int for international organizations; and .net for computer networks, many of which provide direct access to the Internet.

The e-mail addresses for computers located outside the United States end in a two-letter country code. For example, the address for computers in Canada end in .ca; in France, with .fr, Germany .de, Singapore .sg, Japan .jp, Australia .au, and the United Kingdom, .uk.

For the purposes of e-mail and the part of the address which follows the @ sign, different organizations organize their computer networks differently. Some include the exact name of the computer on which the account is located. For example, the International Technology Research Institute is a research center at Loyola College that studies developments in technology around the world. The addresses for the researchers there are username@loyola.edu. ITRI represents the specific computer on which the editors' accounts reside. Loyola is the name for the computer that serves as the gateway out of the college to the rest of the Internet. The .edu indicates that the college is an educational institution.

Other companies, organizations, and many college campuses totally omit the name of the computer that serves as the host for e-mail. For example, an e-mail address at the University of California, San Diego is *username@ucsd.edu*. Once a message arrives at the domain ucsd.edu, it is internally routed to the specific computer on which the user has an account. Actually, the computer that serves the needs of most of the people in the social sciences at UCSD has been named "Weber." But UCSD routes e-mail from the gateway to the appropriate computer, so the name "Weber" does not have to appear in the e-mail address. Thus in the generic formula for an e-mail address the name of the host computer is shown as optional because many systems simply use the system domain name.

Knowing how to decipher an electronic mail address will give you some insight into the people with whom you may be corresponding. For example, a person with an e-mail address that includes upenn.edu has an account at the University of Pennsylvania. People with accounts at America Online have e-mail addresses which end with aol.com. The e-mail addresses of reporters at the *Seattle Times* are username@seattletimes.com. The e-mail account of the President of the United States ends with whitehouse.gov.

E-mail Software Comes in Different Flavors

Establishing an account is only the first step in the process of getting started. Next, you will have to familiarize yourself with the software you

---

Fig. 4-1: E-mail addresses use the syntax of a user's name (or ID) followed by an @ sign, an optional host name, and the host computer's Internet domain. Below the generic address above are two addresses that have been used by one of the authors.

username @ [host.]domain

wurlr @ ttacs.ttu.edu

reddick @ ttu.edu

need to read, create, send, delete, and manage your mail. As with other Internet applications, e-mail is a client-server application as described in Chapter 2. The client software issues requests to the server, which actually performs the task. In addition, with e-mail, the client software may also help you manage and manipulate files on the computer on which your account is located.

As the use of the Internet has grown, three varieties of client software have emerged. Each variety is associated with a specific e-mail setup. If you have set up an e-mail account through your company or college, you will probably be using Microsoft *Outlook,* Lotus *Notes,* or Novell *Groupwise,* e-mail software that has been designed with the needs of corporate messaging in mind. If you have established your e-mail via an Internet Service Provider you will probably be using the e-mail client the service has provided or a commercial program such as Netscape *Messenger, Outlook Express,* or *Eudora Light.* If you have opted for Web-based e-mail, the e-mail client will be lodged in the Web page of the service you have selected.

At some colleges and universities you may be required to make a connection to a central computer and use the software on that computer. If that is the case, it may be more convenient to establish a Web-based e-mail account. They are free, easy to use, and accessible as long as you have access to the Web.

Despite these differences, most e-mail clients work in basically the same way. They use a point-and-click approach to the major functions—sending, receiving, reading, composing and deleting mail.

Creating and Sending an E-mail Message

Creating and sending short e-mail messages is very easy regardless of the computer system you are using. The steps generally will be the same regardless of the system you use; however, the specific commands needed to complete each step will vary from system to system.

To create and send a short mail message, first open the e-mail client program. This is either a typical application program or, if you are using Web-based e-mail, a Web site. Once you are into your mail program, work through the pull-down menus until you find the "New Message" command.

The computer responds with a form that includes at least the following fields for the e-mail header: **To:, From:, Subject:.** You may also see such fields as **CC:, BCC:, Reply To:,** and **Attachment:.** A line and then a blank space usually follow that. The fields on the top of the form can be considered the top page of a memo or, in some ways, the envelope for the message. In the **To:** field you enter the e-mail address of the recipient. In the **From:** field, you enter your e-mail address. (You usually can modify your e-mail client to automatically include your e-mail through a pull-down

```
            To:
          From: reddick@facsnet.org (Randy Reddick)
       Subject:
            Cc:
           Bcc:
   Attachments:
```

Fig. 4-2: When you compose e-mail, typically your mail program fills in the "From:" field for you, and you must fill in the "To:" line. Although the "Subject:" line is optional, it is good practice to describe the content of your mail message here.

command called options or preferences, which is often under a section called tools. In the **Subject:** field you should enter a brief description of your message. The **CC:** field allows you to send the same message to other people. Some e-mail clients will only accept one additional e-mail address in the **CC:** field. Others will accept multiple addresses, separated by a semicolon, or a comma. The **BCC:** allows you to send a copy of the message to another person without the original recipient knowing to whom you have sent the copy.

Except for your own e-mail address (if you have configured your client correctly), you have to enter the information in all the fields listed above. The attachment field allows you to attach another file such as a word processing file, an image file or a spreadsheet to your e-mail. In this case, you must return to the menu bar and find the attachment command. When you click on this command, the software will allow you to browse through your hard disk to locate the file you wish to attach. When you have found the file, you highlight it and click "attach." Then, when you send the e-mail, the attached file also will be sent.

Only the To: and From: fields are necessary for you to send e-mail. The other fields, including the Subject field, are optional. However, because people often get a lot of e-mail, it is wise to include a short description of the topic of your message in the subject field.

Editing Messages

E-mail was among the first and remains the most popular Internet application. Before the widespread availability of e-mail clients with graphic user interfaces, editing text for e-mail was awkward. In many programs, it was hard to move between lines to correct mistakes. Once you had moved to another line, it was difficult to move back. Moreover, you could not cut and paste information from your word processor, let's say, into an e-mail message.

The difficulty in composing messages led to a certain e-mail culture. Messages were generally short and informal. Moreover, many recipients tolerated spelling mistakes. They understood that it was difficult to edit the message. E-mail was seen as the equivalent of dashing off a short, handwritten note.

With contemporary e-mail clients, however, it is as easy to compose a message as it is with a standard word processing program. In fact, if you use Microsoft *Outlook* as your e-mail client, you can compose your message in Microsoft *Word*. Also, with many e-mail clients, it is easy to cut and paste information from other application programs into the text of the message.

Nonetheless, to a large degree, the more relaxed culture that developed in the earlier days has continued. Few people structure e-mail the same as a formal letter. The salutation is generally more relaxed than the typical "Dear So and So" of a letter, and the sign-off is less stiff as well.

But fewer people are tolerant of mechanical mistakes such as misspellings. You should compose your e-mail messages with the recognition that your e-mail projects an image. Be sure that it projects an image you want.

Sending E-mail

Once your message is written and addressed, sending the message is simple. All e-mail clients have a send button or menu command. Simply hit the "send" and your message is on the way.

Many e-mail clients allow you to compose mail off-line and then automatically send the messages when you log on. Others allow you to delay sending the message until a specific time. You should scan the tool bars at the top of your e-mail client to survey the exact features your program contains.

When e-mail arrives at its destination, the message will have a header in the following format:

```
TO : Recipient's e-mail address

FROM : Sender's e-mail address

DATE: Date (and time) message was sent

SUBJECT : Subject of the message
```

There are ways to include your personal name in the "From:" line, if you choose. Nevertheless, you should always include your e-mail address as well, either in the "From:" line or in the body of the message, to ensure that the recipient knows how to respond to you via e-mail. Usually, the header also indicates the date the message was sent.

Including a Signature File

Many people like to create what is called a signature file. A signature file, which usually includes your name, contact information (such as address, telephone and fax numbers, and e-mail address), as well as personalizing information such as a saying or graphic, is automatically appended to the end of every message you send. In most e-mail client programs, signature files are extremely easy to create and edit. Some clients permit you to designate virtual "stationery" upon which your e-mail messages will appear.

Chapter 11 describes specific steps for creating signature files in the three freely available e-mail clients, *Eudora Light*, *Outlook Express*, and Netscape *Messenger*. Once again, the signature file need not be as rigid as the signature on a formal business letter. It is a good place to personalize what can be a relatively impersonal form of communication.

Addressing Your Mail

As you know, the first step in sending e-mail is filling in the recipient's address. As described earlier, e-mail addresses generally adhere to the following structure: username@computername.domain. Username is the name of the recipient's e-mailbox. Computername is the name of the computer on which the mailbox is located. Domain describes the type of network the computer is on.

The exact form of the address you need to use, however, depends on where the recipient's electronic mailbox is located in relationship to your own. If the recipient's electronic mailbox is on the same network as yours, you usually only have to fill in the username part of the address. If the recipient's electronic mailbox is not at your school or business, you will need to use the full Internet address: username@computername.domain.

For example, assume you are a reporter at the *Los Angeles Times*. If you wish to send a message to another *Times* staffer, you would only use their user name. But, to send mail to people outside the *Times*, you will have to use the full Internet address.

Once you begin to communicate with people electronically, you will want to save their e-mail addresses. The easiest method is to add e-mail addresses to your standard address/telephone directory entries. Many mail programs support their own electronic directories as well. Often, those directories allow you to associate the e-mail address with the person's name. Once you have made the appropriate entry into the directory, to send mail, enter the person's name at the "To:" prompt.

Another approach to saving people's addresses is to save at least one e-mail you have received in your in-box. To write to them, you can hit the "reply" button, change the subject line, compose, and then send, your message. By using the "reply" function, you do not have to worry about incorrectly entering an e-mail message. The address of the person to whom you are responding is automatically entered into the "To:" field.

Once you have sent your message, a copy of the message will usually be saved in the "out-box" or "out-folder" of the e-mail client. You can also retrieve e-mail addresses from the messages in your out box.

If you communicate regularly with a small group of people, many programs allow you to set up nicknames for recipients. Then, instead of entering an entire e-mail address, you could just enter the name "Mom," for example, and your mother's e-mail address will appear in the angle brackets in the "To:" field.

In addition to sending e-mail to individuals, many clients allow you to create distribution lists. In general, creating a distribution list involves a two-part process. You must name the list and enter the e-mail addresses of the people to whom you wish to receive the mail. Many people create lists of small workgroups or friends and relatives.

Getting to the Destination

Although widely used, the e-mail network is not as well developed as the telephone network. As you know, the Internet is actually a network of many different networks. Sometimes the individual networks do not communicate with each other as smoothly as we would like.

Consequently, when you send electronic mail, you can never be sure exactly how long it will take to arrive. While many messages will be delivered to their destinations within a matter of seconds, others can take hours or more. Furthermore, if the network has problems delivering the message, it may try for some time before returning the message to the sender.

From time to time you will have messages returned to you. When mail is returned, you will also receive a message from what is called the postmaster, which is the software handling your message at different points in the network. If you read the message closely, you should be able to determine the source of your problem—frequently a mistake you have made in the address. If you have made a mistake in the part of the address which follows the @ sign, the message from the postmaster will read "host unknown." If you made a mistake in the part of the address preceding the @ sign, the message will read "user unknown." In that case, you know the part of the address which follows the @ symbol is, in fact, connected to the Internet.

Receiving and Responding to E-mail

Of course, correspondence is a two-way street. When you start writing to people, they will write back. All of the e-mail clients named in this chapter except host-resident *Pine* will signal you when you receive new mail, if you wish. You can generally configure the program to check for new mail at regular intervals (like every 10 minutes) and to signal when it finds some.

If you do not keep your computer on all day, you must log on to a central computer to access your account. In any case, once you start using e-mail, you must make a commitment to check your mailbox regularly. If you do not, not only are you sure to miss messages, but you give up two of the main advantages of e-mail—the timeliness of the delivery of information and the ability to immediately respond.

A sound strategy is to incorporate checking your e-mailbox into your daily routine. For example, you may want to check your e-mail after you open your mail in the morning, at mid-day, and before you leave for the evening. Or you may want to check your e-mail each time you check for voice messages. If you check your mailbox regularly, reading, responding to, and managing your e-mail is easy.

Once you log on to the computer that handles your e-mail, you will receive a notice if you have any mail. If you do have messages, start your mail client program using the procedure described in the previous section. Once the mail software is running, you will receive a list of messages. The directory listing will indicate the e-mail address (or name, if the sender has personalized this line) of the person who sent you the message and also the subject line of the message.

At that point, you can read the full text of a specific message by clicking on it. Once you have read the message, you can delete it, file it electronically, respond to it, or forward it to another person at another address. The commands for performing each of those tasks vary from mail program to mail program, but all these functions are point-and-click operations from the tool bar.

Receiving Attachments

In the same way that you may attach files created in other programs such as spreadsheets or images to your e-mail, you may also receive attachments. If you are using a standard e-mail client, attachments may be automatically saved in a subdirectory of the directory of the e-mail software itself.

To view the attachment, you will need to have the same application software in which the file was created. For example, if somebody sends you a presentation created in Microsoft *PowerPoint*, you will need to have a copy of *PowerPoint* to view the file. In fact, when you click on the file name, which will appear labeled as an attachment in the e-mail message, the appropriate application program to view the file may be automatically launched. If the appropriate program is not available, you will be asked with which program you wish to view the file. Once you have read an attachment, you can save it in any subdirectory you choose. For some programs, such as Microsoft's *Word* and *PowerPoint*, free viewers are available at the software manufacturer's Web site. The viewer software will permit you to read the file but not to edit it.

Managing Incoming Mail

As e-mail becomes more and more integrated into your daily communications, you will find that the volume of mail you receive will grow. Moreover, as with the telephone and regular mail, you will use e-mail for both business and personal reasons. You may find yourself conducting several different conversations simultaneously via e-mail. Moreover, you will probably subscribe to at least a couple of mailing lists and periodically receive unsolicited e-mail, unaffectionately known as spam.

With that in mind, many e-mail programs have advanced features that help you manage your mail. Some let you set up rules to filter mail—blocking mail from certain addresses that regularly send you spam, for example. Some e-mail clients will sort messages into different discussion threads based on the subject line, or color-code incoming mail to assist you in identifying the contents of each message you receive.

Responding to E-mail

In general, responding to messages sent to you by another individual is simple, requiring only one-command operations—"reply." The address to which the response will be sent and the subject line will be filled in automatically. The subject line will generally read "RE:" and the subject of the original message.

However, as e-mail has grown in popularity, you may find yourself on mass mailing lists. You may subscribe to some mailing lists yourself, a process that will be described in Chapter 5. In some cases, your name and e-mail address will have found their way onto a commercial list that companies use for marketing. In these cases, the person's address may not be listed in the "From:" field. Instead, the address to which the e-mail will be sent if you hit the "reply" command is listed in a field called "Reply-to." The "Reply-to:" field is also contained in the "header" section that contains the To:, From:, and Subject: fields.

If you have received mail from a list to which you want to respond but you want to respond to the sender and not to the person or address listed in the "Reply-to:" field, you can still first click on the "reply" command. Then you must cut and paste the correct address into the "To:" field of the header.

From time to time, you may receive e-mail that you wish to pass along to another person. In this situation, you can use the "forward" or "redirect" commands. After you have clicked on the command, you will have to enter the e-mail address of the person to whom you wish to forward the message. After you have done so and clicked on the "send" command, a complete copy of the e-mail, including the original information in the header, will be sent. If you redirect mail, it generally arrives at the new destination appearing as though it were originally addressed to and intended for the person you sent the message to. The only difference is that the "From:" field will say something like "From: *Original Sender* (by way of *your name*)." If you forward mail, on the other hand, the message header shows the message coming from you, usually with a forward designation. Depending on how your client is configured, the original message content of a forwarded message will be indented and may be set off by some kind of marker such as greater-than symbols (>).

After you read and/or reply to a message you will probably want to delete it. By default, most non-Web-based e-mail clients automatically download messages from the central computer to a directory on a local hard drive and erase them from the central mail server. Some corporate and college systems and Web-based services e-mail do not. Those messages will reside on the central server for a specified period of time (or, in some cases an unlimited period of time) until you delete them. If you will have only a limited amount of space reserved for your mail on a central server, you will want to be sure that you delete your messages from the server regularly. Remember that it is easy to keep copies of the messages on your local hard drive.

By default, all three of the free programs (*Eudora, Outlook Express,* and *Messenger*) download mail from your host mail server, bring messages to your hard drive, and then delete the messages on the server. Deleting mail from your in box is a two-step process. After you have read a message, you click on the delete button. The message, however, will not actually be deleted at that time. Depending on how you have your e-mail client configured, your trash may be emptied when you exit from the mail program. In all cases, when you first delete a message, the deleted message is taken out of your in box and sent to a special folder called "Trash" (*Eudora* and *Messenger*) or "Deleted Items" (*Outlook* and *Outlook Express*). You can "empty the trash" at any time. You can also retrieve messages from the trash until they are deleted from the trash folder..

If you read a message without deleting it, it will be saved either in your in-box or in a special folder for old mail. Most programs also tag messages to which you have replied. Remember that all the messages you do not delete continue to fill up the storage space on the computer reserved for you. In most cases, you should delete messages after you have read them and responded.

Saving Your Information

In many cases, after you have received e-mail, you will want to save it. Many people simply let their messages accumulate in their in-boxes. As long as you are sure that you are automatically downloading your messages to your personal computer and deleting them from the mail server, there is nothing wrong with this approach. Over time, the in-box will have hundreds or even thousands of messages in them. But most e-mail clients allow you to sort through your messages by subject, date, sender and other criteria, which helps you find old messages.

Alternatively, you can use the "save as" command, which works the same in most e-mail software as it does in word processors. The "save as" command lets you rename the file and save it virtually anywhere on your hard drive. Let's say that you are working on a story about gun control and you have sent questions via e-mail to Charlton Heston, who has long played a leading role in the National Rifle Association. You could save his reply as "Heston_reply_date" in the same subdirectory as the other material you have gathered for the story. This approach is more systematic than having to sort through hundreds of messages when it comes time to write the story.

Another approach is to print the message and save the hard copy. Many journalists still prefer to work from notes on paper. Most clients have a "print" command. If for some reason yours doesn't, you can copy and paste the contents of the message into a word processor and print the information from there. If you go this route, be sure to include all the identifying header information with the message.

Viruses

E-mail has proven to be a very powerful new method of communication and millions of e-mail messages are sent safely every day. However, using e-mail also means you are receiving messages from people across the

Internet, which increases the chances of you recieving a computer virus. A virus is computer code that in some way interferes with the normal operation of your computer. Malicious viruses can destroy your hard disk and all the information on it. Worse, the code can copy itself and spread from computer to computer, once it has been embedded in a file, much like a virus in the natural world spreads from person to person.

One of the most common ways to spread viruses is via e-mail. People will attach a file with a virus to an e-mail message. When recipients open the attached file containing a virus, the virus goes to work. Consequently, it is extremely unsafe to open attachments sent by people you don't know. And sometimes it is unsafe to open attachments from people you do know. A *Word* macro virus named "Melissa" caught a lot of press in 1999. Melissa would read people's personal e-mail address books and send itself to all the people listed, fooling people into thinking they had received the attachment from a person they knew. Instead, their computers were being infected with a virus.

A virus must be what is called an executable program. That means that the text of a simple e-mail message cannot be infected. But many viruses are created using macros in Microsoft *Word*. When you receive a *Word* document as an attachment, frequently you will be asked if you wish to disable the macros. Unless you are sure that the document is from a trusted source and is free from viruses, you should disable the macros. In fact, it is better not to open any unsolicited programs or documents that might contain a virus. Microsoft *Excel*, the spreadsheet program used by many journalists for analyzing agency budgets and smaller data sets, is also vulnerable to macro viruses. The same care should be taken with *Excel* files.

Finding People

For several reasons, the best way to determine someone's e-mail address is to ask that person directly. Just because people have e-mail addresses does not mean they actually use e-mail regularly. Moreover, many people may have more than one e-mail account but only use one. If you access an address from a directory and send an e-mail message, you have no idea whether the intended recipient actually checks the mailbox or, if so, how often.

For example, a reporter once sent a note to a professor whom she knew was an active e-mail user asking for advice about a complicated story she was preparing. What she didn't know was that the professor had two electronic addresses and that he only occasionally looked at the one to which she sent her message. Indeed, her message was only one of 300 waiting for him at that address. By the time she called on the telephone, he had left town for a conference. She had to look elsewhere for guidance.

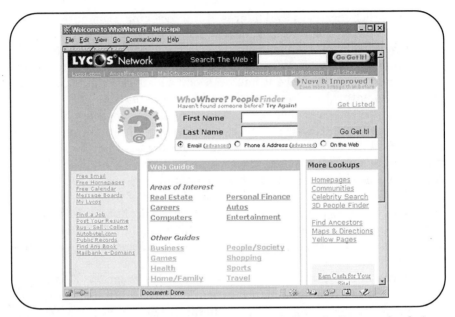

Fig. 4-3: WhoWhere is one of several services that help in finding people, their e-mail addresses, and physical locations.

Despite the dangers of just sending e-mail cold to somebody and sitting back for a reply, several directories have been established that make it easy to try to find a person's e-mail address. Still, actually finding a specific person's address is a hit-and-miss adventure.

Most of the large Web portals such as Yahoo at http://www.yahoo.com and Lycos at http://www.lycos.com have sections to help you find people online. WhoWhere at http://www.whowhere.lycos.com returns not only the address for the name you requested, if it can find it, but other similar names, which can be useful if you are unsure of the exact spelling of the name for which you are looking. Switchboard at http://www.switchboard.com also has a large directory of e-mail addresses.

Many of these directories provide telephone numbers and addresses as well as e-mail accounts. Switchboard, for example, has more than 100 million telephone numbers in its database and is much more convenient to use than the telephone company's directory assistance. One advantage—you don't have to know the area code to find a person.

The directories are growing rapidly, however, and they are trying aggressively to get people to register with them. They offer some interesting options for people who do register. People who register with Switchboard, for example, can use its "Knock-Knock" feature. Only people you want to reach can get your e-mail address. When Knock-Knock is on, you will be sent e-mail telling you who wants your address before it is given away.

In addition to directories, many people now have personal home pages on the World Wide Web. Sources or potential sources with home pages generally provide their e-mail addresses as well. If a search of phone book kinds of directories fails to produce the address you seek, a search of Web pages from a general search site such as *AltaVista* or *Northern Light* or *Inference Find* may turn up Web pages that give you the information you seek.

The Law and E-mail

In 1995, a person lodged a complaint after seeing obscene words on the Web site of Master Sergeant Jeffrey Delzer of the United States Air Force. Air Force investigators then examined Delzer's e-mail and found that he had been exchanging sexually explicit stories and jokes with other consenting adults using his Air Force computer.

Delzer, a 19-year veteran of the service, was convicted of misuse of a government computer, distribution of obscene writing, and other violations of the law. He was sentenced to three years in jail and demoted to Staff Sergeant, a reduction of two ranks, which cost him $300 per month in retirement pay.

In that same year, Pillsbury fired sales manager Michael Smyth after it was learned that he had e-mailed his boss that the boss' superior was a "backstabbing bastard." Smyth filed a wrongful discharge suit. He lost.

In both cases, the judges ruled that individuals gave up any reasonable expectation of privacy when they use a company network, even if the message was only intended for one person. Through these cases and others, it has been well established that the enterprise that owns the computers on which an electronic mail account is lodged can, under the right circumstances, read the messages in so-called private mailboxes. Companies can read the e-mail of their employees, and presumably universities can read the e-mail of their faculty and students.

It is also important to keep in mind that the same rules of speech that govern regular communication also apply to electronic communication. It is illegal to libel someone online by spreading false information that will damage his or her reputation. It is unlawful to threaten them. It is illegal to send or store obscene material.

If you act in a way that violates the law, you can be prosecuted. Indeed, the way you behave online can put your organization at risk as well. For example, in 1995, Prodigy, a commercial information service, was the subject of a lawsuit because of information one of its subscribers had distributed electronically. In another case, a person was arrested for having illegal telephone credit card numbers stored on his computer. He said that he had received the numbers via e-mail and didn't even know they were there. Nevertheless, he was prosecuted.

Also, just because you have downloaded and deleted your e-mail from the mail server does not mean that it cannot be reconstructed. First, when you delete files from the hard drive, you only remove the identifying information. The rest of the file remains there until it is actually overwritten. Many tools exist to retrieve "deleted" files.

Moreover, most large companies routinely back up all their e-mail. That means copies of your mail will remain on back-up tapes for some period of time.

Netiquette and E-mail

In addition to the legal constraints concerning online communication, a code of etiquette, termed "netiquette," has evolved for e-mail as well. First, messages you send may be forwarded to others, and security in some systems is not what it should be. Consequently, you would not want to say anything via e-mail that you would not say face-to-face or that would make you feel uncomfortable if others heard secondhand. Moreover, because your files are accessible to people who have system privileges, you will not want to store private information.

You want to make your e-mail messages as easy as possible for others to read and for them to respond to. Consequently, try to keep e-mail relatively short and to the point.

Attachments are another area of concern with e-mail. Images generally represent a lot of information and can take a long time to download if the person to whom you have sent the image is using a dial-up modem. You should also be sure your recipient knows when you are sending a large attachment and is able to manage the attachment efficiently.

The objective of e-mail is to communicate. So, don't forget to include your name, affiliation, e-mail address, and other ways to get in touch with you at the bottom of the message.

Because in many ways e-mail is similar to other public behavior, many media organizations are now establishing codes to govern its use. Among the tenets of the Associated Press guidelines for the use of electronic service is the admonition that accounts are for business use only; people should conduct business online as if they were appearing at a public meeting representing the AP; people should abide by the mores of the electronic community; and, AP wants people to empty their mailboxes and clean out their home directory regularly.

E-mail Is a Tool for Reporters

There was a time when much of journalism was conducted via the mail. Indeed, the word "correspondent" was not a misnomer. Reporters corresponded with their sources, their readers, and their newspapers.

For the last 100 years, however, the interview has been the mainstay of reporting. Face-to-face and telephone interviews are the primary vehicles most journalists use to obtain the quotes they need to produce articles, as opposed to research reports or some other form of writing. E-mail has added another technique for journalists to use.

For example, Sally Squires joined the *Washington Post* in 1984. As a staff writer for the health section, she has used e-mail to contact sources, interview experts, query people about studies of interest, and to clarify information. Christine Gorman, an associate editor for the science section of *Time* magazine used e-mail when sources were not easily available or in a different time zone. In 1996, she told a reporter writing for *Merck Media Minutes* that "We can't live without e-mail anymore."

Person-to-person e-mail can be a valuable tool for reporters in several ways. First, it can enhance the interaction they have with their sources. Second, it can be a channel via which readers can funnel their ideas to reporters. Finally, in some cases, e-mail correspondence is considered part of the public record. Therefore, journalists can access the e-mail of government officials to learn what is going on behind the scenes.

The most common way for reporters to use e-mail is as an enhancement for personal interaction. For example, e-mail is an effective way for reporters to lay the groundwork for face-to-face interviews. A message can be sent to a potential source who is a stranger, introducing the reporter and letting the source know the reporter plans to call and why. It is a good icebreaker.

From time to time, it may be appropriate to send a source a list of potential questions in advance. It may relax the person and give him or her time to prepare. Many public affairs officers for the military request that reporters submit questions in advance before interviewing a senior officer. They do this for two reasons: to be sure that the officer has the necessary information to answer the questions and to see how well informed the reporter is.

E-mail can be used to follow up interviews as well. After a long telephone conversation, you may find that your notes are unclear at certain points. You can then e-mail your source for clarification and amplification. Sources can respond to the questions in a timely fashion without disrupting the rest of their schedules. Checking quotes is a controversial practice among reporters. Those covering government, politics and business are loath to allow their sources to see their quotes before they appear in print. They fear that official may try to "edit" a quote to make it appear better in print.

E-mail also allows reporters to approach sources in a new way and sometimes get information which they could not otherwise obtain. For example, a reporter for a communications newsletter in Washington, D.C., got wind of shoddy bookkeeping at the National Science Foundation concerning a very high profile project. He repeatedly called the administrator in charge of the project, but the administrator never responded. Then the reporter sent e-mail, laying out the facts as he knew them and asking some pointed questions. To his surprise, he soon received a detailed response. Over the next several days, he was able to clarify several issues and write a detailed, informed and balanced story.

E-mail Produces Story Leads

In the same way that e-mail enhances the interaction among reporters and sources, e-mail can enable readers and others interested to more conveniently reach reporters. For at least the past 50 years, news media have basically provided one-way channels of communication. Journalists produce stories; viewers and readers see and read them.

It has been very difficult for viewers and readers to interact with reporters. Newspaper reporters and television news broadcasters don't make their physical addresses readily available for their audiences. Calling a busy reporter on the telephone can be an even more unpleasant experience.

Some journalists have begun to make their e-mail addresses more readily available. The results can be dramatic. For example, the e-mail address for Scott Adams, the creator of the comic strip *Dilbert* (a chronicle of the lives of the employees in the cubicles of a typical high-tech company, which runs in 1,000 companies in 30 countries) is readily available. Adams has reported that he receives nearly 1,000 messages a day and those messages are the source of many of his ideas.

E-mail and the Public Record

As more public officials use e-mail to communicate, reporters and others have argued that their electronic correspondence is part of the record and should be available for review. The National Security Archives in Washington, D.C., which gathers and makes available official documents concerning national security issues, successfully sued to obtain 5000 e-mail messages generated during the Bush administration.

A journalism student at Metropolitan State University in Denver, Colorado, used the Open Records Act to request the e-mail messages of Governor Roy Romer and top state lawmakers for a two-week period. The correspondence included such important morsels as the leftover food available to the governor and his staff.

On the other hand, some local officials may try to use e-mail to avoid state sunshine laws requiring official government meetings to be held in public. For example, after reviewing 70 messages in one month, the executive director of the Arizona Center for Law in the Public Interest has argued that members of the Phoenix city council were violating the state's open meetings laws.

Documentary material has long been an important element in journalism. E-mail creates a new type of document for reporters to survey.

Conclusion

Not long ago, two schoolgirls in Massachusetts decided to do an experiment for their school's science fair. If they sent two e-mail messages on the Internet, how many responses would they get in two weeks? The girls guessed 53; one of their moms thought the figure would reach 1,000. After 50,000 replies, the girls had to pull the plug on the experiment, which clearly had mushroomed beyond their wildest expectations. After a year, people were still receiving mail asking them to help the girls with their experiment.

The point is that e-mail is an important, new, dynamic way to communicate with people. Used correctly, it represents an important new technique for reporters. Used incorrectly, e-mail can produce unforeseen and unfortunate results.

Chapter

5

Online Communities

A powerful explosion ripped through the Albert Murrah Federal Building in Oklahoma City on the morning of April 19, 1995. Armed with scant details, rumors, and a few solid leads, dozens of journalists "gathered" online in the hours immediately following the blast. They continued sharing notes and asking each other for help on aspects of the story that stretched out for weeks.

Lines of inquiry on e-mail discussion lists included leads on Muslim terrorists, the Michigan Militia, other attacks on federal buildings, and the making of the bomb itself. The Internet abounded with answers, if only you knew what questions to ask and where to look. Journalists "gathering" in CARR-L (Computer Assisted Research and Reporting List), IRE-L (Investigative Reporters and Editors List), and SPJ-L (Society of Professional Journalists List) and other online discussion lists exchanged hundreds of messages on the topic in the weeks following the blast. More than five dozen such lists provide homes for journalists to discuss their craft.

When Karla Homulka pleaded guilty to the mutilation murders of two girls, a Canadian court banned publication of any details of her trial until the trial of her husband Paul Bernardo was completed. The court reasoned that defendant Bernardo's right to a fair trial outweighed freedom of the press in this case. The judge was particularly worried that the American press just across the border would violate the ban, so he excluded foreign media from the courtroom and forbade anyone to publish any circumstances of the deaths mentioned in Homulka's trial until the conclusion of the Bernardo case.

The judge's ban could not stop the flow of information about the trial to mass audiences in the United States and around the world. Soon after Bernardo was arrested, several electronic bulletin boards containing facts and rumors about the affair were launched. For example, Justin Wells and Ken Chasse set up a Usenet newsgroup about the trial on Chasse's Sonic Interzone BBS, a public access bulletin board in Toronto. The Usenet newsgroup, which was named alt.fan.karla-homulka, distributed information around the world about the trial, in defiance of the publication ban. Net-connected Canadians and other interested folks found information on the case in newsgroups and in e-mail discussion lists.

Every quarter, business journalists report the earnings of major companies in the United States. And every quarter, companies explain their earnings and describe their perspective for the months to come in a conference call to Wall Street analysts. Journalists used to be excluded from those sessions. But in the summer of 1999, journalists and other individuals, could go to the NASDAQ-AMEX Web site and listen live to Intel Corporation's conference call with analysts.

Finally, millions were shocked when the news that John F. Kennedy, Jr.'s small airplane was missing in the waters off Martha's Vineyard in Massachusetts. In covering the story, many reporters wanted to know if people in their 20s had a different relationship to JFK, Jr., than people in their 40s and 60s, who were alive when John Kennedy was president. To find the answer, many reporters went to chat rooms in which teens and 20-somethings were interacting with each other about the tragedy.

In this chapter, we will discuss

- e-mail discussion lists of interest to journalists,
- common listserv commands used to subscribe to and manage traffic in discussion lists,
- commands to search listserv archives,
- Usenet newsgroups, including what Usenet is, how newsgroups are organized, and how to access network news,
- the spread of public and private chat rooms,
- the development and use of Webcasts, and
- the promises and pitfalls these services hold for reporters.

Discussion Lists and Listservs

E-mail discussion lists have emerged as significant tools for journalists. Let's say you are a young reporter assigned to cover the Iowa caucuses at the beginning of the next presidential primary season because a candidate from your state is running. The only problem is that you have never been to Iowa and have few sources there. You could subscribe to the e-mail discussion list at ia-caucus-subscribe@groups.com. Once you subscribe (subscriptions to e-mail discussion lists are free), you would be able to interact with citizens in Iowa and elected officials in Iowa to gauge the political climate. It would give you a dramatic head start in establishing a network of sources for later use.

If you have e-mail access to the Internet, you can participate in these groups. Discussion lists can be thought of as electronic mass mailings in which people holding similar interests exchange their views and information about issues of concern. It works in this way: Individuals send e-mail to a specific address for the particular discussion list; that mail is automatically distributed to everyone who subscribes to that list; and everyone who subscribes to the discussion or distribution list receives every message sent to the list.

Two addresses are associated with e-mail discussion lists. The first is the address of the list distribution software; a specialized mailing program designed to manage the list functionality and located on a host server. This is generally called the "Listserv," named after the software created to manage e-mail distribution lists. We will use the term "Listserv" to refer to all such programs even though there is other software, notably *Listproc* and *Majordomo*, designed to perform the same operations.

The second address for the list is that of the discussion list itself. You send messages you want to share with the group to the discussion list address. Once your subscription is set up, this is the address you use most frequently as you participate in the discussions of the list. You send all commands governing your subscription including "SET" parameters (discussed later), to the Listserv.

For example, if you wanted to subscribe to the CARR-L list mentioned earlier you would send a message to the Listserv:

Listserv@ulkyvm.louisville.edu

After you are subscribed to CARR-L list, you send messages you want to share with everyone to the discussion list:

CARR-L@ulkyvm.louisville.edu

The only difference in the two addresses is what is on the left side of the @ sign. In one case you are giving commands to the machine that handles your mail, the Listserv. In the other case, you are sharing correspondence with people, the list. Understanding the distinction between the list and the Listserv—and how you use each—will save you a lot of grief as you begin to use e-mail discussion lists in your work.

Subscribing and Unsubscribing to a List

The list service software at a particular location often manages many different discussion lists. The primary function of the list service software is to allow a person to subscribe or terminate a subscription to a particular list. To subscribe, you would send a message to the Listserv. In the body of the message, you would enter

```
sub listname your name
```

where you insert the name of the list followed by a space, your first name, space, and your last name.

To terminate a subscription, address a message to the Listserv and in the body of the message type

```
unsub listname
```

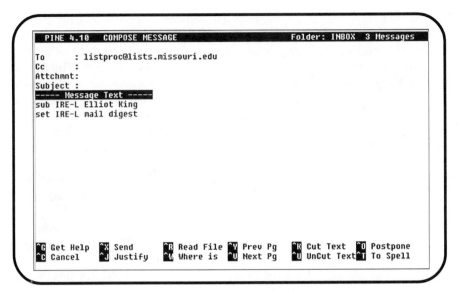

Fig. 5-1: Subscribing to a discussion list and setting parameters for the list may be done with the same message.

Instead of the command "unsub" you can also use the command "signoff."

For example, to subscribe to IRE-L you would address an e-mail message to listproc@lists.missouri.edu. In the body of your e-mail message you should type "sub IRE-L jane doe," substituting your name for jane doe. Figure 5-1 shows a sample message for subscribing to IRE-L and for setting the manner in which you get the list to digest (see the following section on setting parameters).

This exact procedure works for lists managed by *Listserv* or *Listproc* software, a large portion of the discussion list universe. Some mailing list software uses variations on this theme. Instead of sending the subscribe message to "listserv@(Location)" you would send it to "(name of list)-request@(location)." For example, to subscribe to the "Digital News" discussion list maintained by the Radio and Television News Directors Foundation (RTNDF) you would send an e-mail message to Digital_News-request@rtndf.org and on the subject line of your message put the word "subscribe."

Another popular list managing program is *Majordomo*, which uses a command structure of its own, but performs the same functions as *Listserv* and *Listproc* software.

Setting Your List Parameters

After sending a subscription request to a Listserv, you will receive a message welcoming you to the list, describing the list's purpose, and sometimes giving basic commands for controlling your receipt of mail from the list. Save these messages in a place where you can easily find them. Mail lists have frequent postings from people who are asking for help getting off a list or giving other commands described in the welcome message because they have failed to record the instructions.

After you receive the welcome message you will receive all e-mail messages that are being sent to the list. With some active lists, you may receive 50 or more messages a day. Consequently, you should check your mailbox regularly. If you subscribe to just a few active lists, you could receive more than 100 e-mail messages a day. These messages will arrive one at a time and they will be interspersed with your personal mail. If you subscribe to more than one list, the messages will arrive in a random mix, and you may have a hard time separating one set of messages from another, or from your personal mail.

To better manage the possible deluge of messages you receive from lists, you can set your mail to "digest" or to "index." When your list mail is set to "digest," you receive only one message a day from the Listserv. The message generally starts with a table of contents telling you how many messages there are for the day, then listing the topics of the messages followed by the number of messages touching each topic. Following the table of contents, you get the complete text of each message sent that day.

When mail is set to "index," you also receive only one message a day. The index message, as the name implies, is only an index of the day's messages. Each message has a two-line entry that includes the message number, the name of the sender, and the subject. Usually, the index is followed by instructions about receiving the messages you want, and a sample script for sending to the Listserv to get the messages you seek.

In order to set your mail to digest, address an e-mail message to the Listserv. In the body of the message, type

```
set listname digest
```

where you provide the listname, such as IRE-L or SPJ-L. If you prefer the index format, just substitute the word "index" for the word "digest."

Other set commands that might prove useful include "nomail" and "ack." If you are going on vacation and you don't want your mailbox to fill up, you can send to the Listserv the message

```
set listname nomail
```

That will turn off your mail without unsubscribing you. When you return, just send to the Listserv the message

```
set listname mail
```

REpro and NOREpro are also opposites. If, when you post messages to the list you want to see your own posting, you need to set your mail to "Repro." Some lists are set that way by default, others are set to "NOREpro," meaning your own postings will not be sent to you.

For instructions on these and other commands, send a message to the Listserv. In the body of the message, type "info refcard" and you will get a short e-mail message identifying commands available to you. Also, many listservs automatically send you a list of the most common commands when you subscribe.

Caution: Any time you send a message to the Listserv (the machine or the software, as opposed to the list of people), you need to take precautions against some unwanted responses. The Listserv software expects that every line in the body of your e-mail message is a command that you are asking it to execute. If you have set up a signature file to be automatically added to your e-mail messages, you should delete the signature. The Listserv will try to interpret your signature as commands. You may wind up with a flood of error messages in your mailbox. For the same reason, you should send only plain text messages to a Listserv. Most e-mail software today permits you to use virtual stationery, and/or to send text in either HTML or Rich Text Format. This makes for much prettier-looking e-mail messages. However, such messages include a number of tags and other hidden codes that are not friendly toward list management software.

Two-Way versus One-Way Lists

As you can see from the set of commands described earlier, e-mail discussion groups were originally developed as an interactive, one-to-many form of communication. In recent years, however, many companies, particularly specialized online publications and information sources, have used the same technology to send what could be thought of as e-mail newsletters. Newsletters are basically a one-way channel of communication. Once you subscribe, you receive a single e-mail message. You can request more information about a given topic using Listserv commands. Or, frequently, the e-mail newsletter will have links to information posted on the World Wide Web.

For example, Newsdesk at http://www.newsdesk.com is a service of PR Newswire (http://www.prnews.com) that sends news releases to journalists. At selected intervals, subscribers receive a list of headlines in an e-mail message. You can then click on the headline and be taken to a Web site with the full news release, or you can retrieve the news release by creating an e-mail addressed to headline-request@newsdesk.com. You then enter your Newsdesk Username into the Subject: field of the message and type get <filename> into the body of the message. When you have requested all the files you want, you type the word "end" on the next line and send the message. The files will be returned to you via e-mail.

Finding Relevant Lists

Tens of thousands of e-mail discussion lists, treating all manner of topics, are scattered about the Internet. Two general kinds of lists are of particular interest to journalists: those catering to particular interests of journalists, and those specializing in topics relevant to the beats journalists cover. The challenge seems to be to identify relevant lists. Several tools exist to help find these.

First, there are more than six dozen lists catering to the various crafts and interests of journalists. Some of these are listed in Table 5-1. We have used CARR-L, IRE-L, and SPJ-L as examples in this chapter. Messages on these lists routinely provide tips on how and where to find valuable information on the network. CARR-L is very strong here. Barbara Croll Fought at Syracuse University maintains two extensive lists of e-mail discussion lists focusing on public communications topics. Her lists are available on the World Wide Web at http://web.syr.edu/~bcfought/nnl.html.

In order to find discussion lists relevant to your beat, you may use one of several Web-based finding tools. The following sites are good starting points:

- http://tile.net/ – The Tile.net site will help locate e-mail lists, newsgroups, and ftp servers.
- http://www.liszt.com// – Started in the 1970s, this server claims to have a database of more than 90,000 discussion lists.
- http://www.neosoft.com/internet/paml/index-index.html – Stephanie da Silva's Publicly Accessible Mailing List index
- http://alabanza.com/kabacoff/inter-links/ – This site is an Internet navigator and resource locator.

Sending the message "list global *keyword*" to listserv@listserve.uga.edu will produce a similar list. The keyword is a string of letters that could be included in the list name. Let's say you are looking for lists discussing chemistry. The message would read "List global chem." You would receive a description of all the lists whose name or topic matched your term.

Posting Messages and Using Lists

Reading and participating in discussion lists can be extremely useful. It puts reporters in contact with people who generally know a lot about a specific topic. The reporter can then follow up with those people, ask where more information can be found, or ask who else would be a good source to interview. In other words, discussion lists can provide reporters with a wealth of leads to more information. We recommend

Listserv	Listname	Topic of List
listserv@ulkyvm.louisville.edu	CARR-L	Computer assisted research and reporting
listserv@cornell.edu	COPYEDITING-L	Interests of copy editors, including grammar, punctuation, style concerns
Digital_News-request@rtndf.org	Digital_News	Implications of new news technology. "Subscribe" in Subject field.
listserv@listserv.syr.edu	FOI-L	Freedom of information issues
listserv@american.edu	INTCAR-L	Internationally oriented computer-assisted reporting
listproc@lists.missouri.edu	IRE-L	Interests of investigative reporters
listserv@acfcluster.nyu.edu	JHISTORY	Issues related to the history of journalism, job placements, and research
listserv@qucdn.queensu.ca	JOURNET	Journalism education and research
listproc@ripken.oit.unc.edu	NEWSLIB	Researching news stories
listproc@lists.missouri.edu	NICAR-L	Computer-assisted reporting
listserv@cmuvm.csv.cmich.edu	NPPA-L	Visual communicators, news photographers, and graphics editors
listserv@vml.spcs.umn.edu	RADIO-L	Digital audio broadcasting issues
listproc@listserv.umt.edu	RTVJ-L	Radio–TV journalism trade, ethics, classes, and equipment
listserv@psuvm.psu.edu	SPJ-L	Broad area, including SPJ chapter information

Table 5-1: Partial listing of e-mail discussion lists focusing on the interests of journalists and journalism educators.

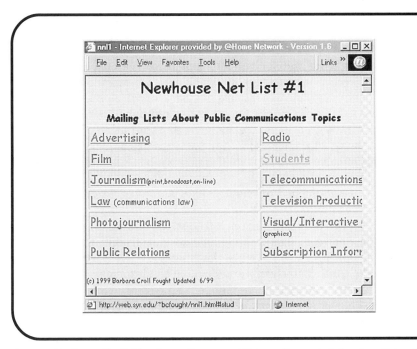

Fig. 5-2: Barbara Croll Fought at Syracuse University maintains two lists of e-mail lists with topics of interest to communications professionals. Her lists at http://web.syr.edu/~bcfought/nnl.html describe more than 75 e-mail lists.

that you "lurk" in a list for a while before posting any messages to it. "Lurking" means that you "listen" or read without talking.

After you understand the tenor of the list and what kinds of discussion it encourages, you are ready to post. To post a message to a discussion group, you send e-mail to the list (not the Listserv) by following the normal procedures for sending e-mail. To respond to a posted message, with most lists you can simply use the reply function of your mail program while you are reading the message. Hundreds of different listserv-based discussion lists operate with people communicating about topics ranging from the use of computers in Eastern Europe to bird watching to jazz.

To Quote or Not to Quote

As you monitor discussion lists, from time to time participants will engage in an exchange that may relate directly to a story on which you are working. Should reporters directly quote from messages that have been posted on discussion lists?

This question has been hotly debated. At one level, when people send messages to discussion lists, they know scores, perhaps thousands, of people will read the message. Those people clearly have chosen to communicate publicly. On the other hand, they may not have realized that they are talking on the record to reporters, with the added factors that entails.

Moreover, should e-mail messages posted to discussion lists be considered the same as talk in a public forum or like published, written works in which authors have greater control over the dissemination of their words? Most people agree that discussion list postings are copyrighted written works. But what constitutes "fair use" of the material? Legal issues will be further discussed in Chapter 10.

Ideally, you should use discussion lists as places to obtain leads to information. You should then follow up those leads through more interpersonal methods. The best journalism is frequently the result of one-on-one interaction between a source and a reporter. Learn from the material that is distributed; but, if you want to use that material in a story, try to establish one-on-one contact to clarify and develop the information.

In short, using material garnered from an e-mail, while probably not illegal in most cases, should not be considered as a sound practice either. In essence, you are taking material out of context and using it in ways in which it was not intended to be used.

Discussion List Archives

In general, when you subscribe to a discussion list, you will monitor or participate in an ongoing discussion. Often it is like walking into the middle of a conversation.

Commonly, the interaction taking place at any particular moment will not be of immediate interest or use. Months later, however, you may receive an assignment on a topic that was discussed earlier by a discussion group. Alternatively, after you receive a specific assignment, you may identify what you think is an appropriate discussion list and wish to know if the topic has already been discussed.

Fortunately, many discussion lists keep archives of past postings. To receive an index of archived files you send a message to the listserv. The body of the message should state "index (list name)." You can retrieve messages that look like they may be of interest by sending the message "get (list name) (name or number of file)." This process was first described in the section above discussing list parameter settings.

For some lists you may have to subscribe to review the archives of its messages. You can see which groups have archives at a specific location by sending the message "database list" to listserv@location. In other words, to see what archives are available at the location at which the CARR-L discussion list is managed, you would send the message "database list" to listserv@ulkyvm.louisville.edu.

Once you have the list of archives, it can be searched using keywords by sending the message "search (keyword) in (listname)." You can then retrieve the message using the procedure outlined above.

Listserv software supports several other database features as well. For instructions about accessing advanced commands, send the message "info" to listserv@(location).

Listserv software permits some very powerful searching through a scripting language. If you wanted to get a listing of all messages sent to CARR-L during 1995 that discuss the bombing of the federal building in Oklahoma City, you would send a message to the Listserv containing the following script in the body of the message:

```
//

Database search DD=rules

//Rules DD *

Search Oklahoma and (bomb or bombing) in CARR-L since
95 to 95

Index

/*
```

What is returned to you is a listing in index form of all the messages that meet your search criteria. Each message is assigned a number. Let's say your index came back with three documents you wanted to read, and they were numbered 3106, 3110, and 3112. You would then send the following script to the Listserv:

```
// JOB

Database search DD=Orders

//Orders DD *

Select * in CARR-L.3106-3112

Print 3106 3110 3112

/*

// EOJ
```

Using these scripts as models, you can search any Listserv archives for topics of your choosing simply by adjusting the name of the list, the topics, and the dates. You need to be sure your message is addressed to the appropriate Listserv.

To search Listproc archives you would follow the same process, except that the syntax for the search line follows this pattern:

```
Search IRE-L Oklahoma and (bomb or bombing) since 95 to 95
```

One cautionary note is due here. List owners do not maintain endless archives. Typically, messages are saved for a year or two, and then they are deleted (or at least taken offline). So actually doing the search today that we have specified here, will produce no hits if the archive only goes back to 1997.

Usenet Newsgroups

In addition to e-mail discussion lists, newsgroups also serve as a place for people to gather around predefined topics. Usenet newsgroups, which are sometimes referred to collectively as "network news," make up a large distributed conference system in which people with shared interests interact with each other. In many ways, Usenet is like the forums on America Online, CompuServe, and other commercial information services, and smaller electronic bulletin boards. People post and read messages on boards or in newsgroups organized around topics of common interest.

While Usenet newsgroups appear to be like e-mail discussion lists, they operate differently. Once you subscribe to a discussion list, every message posted to the list is sent to your account as electronic mail. When you read the messages posted to a newsgroup, you are reading messages that are located on a server, not in your own account. In the same way, when you post a message, the message stays on a server. It is not automatically distributed to thousands of people.

The development of Usenet preceded the development of the World Wide Web. It was created by computer system administrators who agreed to feed the newsgroup postings to each other, adhering to a specific communication protocol. The protocol is known as the Network News Transfer Protocol (NNTP), which is now considered an Internet protocol.

Given its origins, it is a very informal network with no governing body and few specific usage rules. Each system administrator controls the traffic at his or her particular site. If you know of a newsgroup (such as "alt.journalism") that your news site does not carry, you can ask to have it included. Many colleges and universities and most commercial Internet Service Providers offer Usenet access.

The structure of network news has some advantages over listserv-oriented, mailing list-based discussion groups. Because the messages are not actually sent to an account but reside on a central server, people who are reading newsgroup postings do not find their mailboxes filled with mail if a discussion gets lively. Nor do they have to suspend mail if they plan to go on vacation or cannot monitor their computer account for a couple of weeks.

On the other hand, not everyone with Internet access can conveniently access Usenet newsgroups. You must have access to a news server. And even if you do have access to a news service, your system administrator will probably offer a subset of the tens of thousands of newsgroups available. For example, subscribers to America Online can only access newsgroups carried on AOL news servers. As noted later, people whose system administrators opt not to receive a news feed will have to access alternative systems if they want to read postings on an excluded newsgroup. There are some open news servers, but that can be a cumbersome way to access Usenet. Information about public access Usenet servers can be found at http://home1.gte.net/docthomp/servers.htm. Also, some services offer access to 25,000 to 65,000 or more newsgroups for as little as $25 a month.

Another concern for journalists is that the quality of the information communicated in these groups is very uneven. Some information is excellent. Some is just wrong. And, often, it is hard to tell which is which. Nonetheless, the amount of information circulated through network news is enormous. While it is hard to find accurate statistics about the current size of Usenet, hundreds of thousands of messages are posted daily.

Network News Hierarchies

Network newsgroups are organized according to hierarchies ranging from the general to the specific. The name of each newsgroup is divided from its parent and various subgroupings by a "dot" (period). For example, the newsgroup alt.fan.karla-homolka was initially placed in the hierarchy of newsgroups reserved for discussion of alternative and controversial material. All newsgroups in this hierarchy begin with "alt."

The second element in the newsgroup name "fan" designates fan clubs. Other fan clubs listed that begin with alt.fan. range from Alyssa Milano to Woody Allen. In fact, the Homulka murder case is not the only crime to have its own fan club. The highly publicized Amy Fisher-Joey Buttafucco attempted manslaughter case in which a teenage girl shot the wife of her purported lover was also the subject of a newsgroup under the alt.fan hierarchy. So was the O.J. Simpson case.

Traditionally, Usenet newsgroups fell into seven categories, listed in Figure 5-3. But newsgroups can also be created locally. And, because system administrators can arrange news feeds for any group that is of interest, many locally created groups gain as wide a distribution as standard network newsgroups and are generally considered part of the Usenet newsgroup family. Locally created newsgroups often use the "alt" prefix or create prefixes of their own. Some other common designations include "bionet" for topics of interest to biologists and "biz" for business-related subjects. Currently there is a huge number of domain prefixes reflecting the huge number of topics under discussion.

Seven Major News Categories

comp ....Computer science and related topics
news..........Network news itself
rec ....Hobbies, recreational activities
sci ....Scientific research and applications
soc ....Social issues, either political or simply social
talk ....Forum for debate on controversial subjects
misc...........Anything that doesn't fit into the categories above.

Fig. 5-3: Traditional top-level domains for naming of news groups. Others include "alt," "biz," and "bionet."

There are newsgroups about major political events and leaders in both the alt and social hierarchies. The soc.politics designation includes politically oriented newsgroups. Soc.rights.human is a newsgroup that discusses human rights issues. Finally, most major professional sports teams as well as many entertainment activities and industries are the topics for newsgroups in both the alt and rec hierarchies. For example, in the rec hierarchy there is rec.sport.baseball, rec.music.bluenote for discussions about jazz and the blues, and rec.mag for discussions about magazines.

Configuring Your News Reader

Most Web browsers include a newsreader. Consequently, all you need to find out is the name of the news server to which you have access. Once you know the name of your news server, you configure your Web browser to access the browser. In *Internet Explorer*, select News from the Go Menu. The first time that you access your newsreader using *Internet Explorer*, a software Wizard will help you through the setup process. Subsequently, to modify your configuration, under the News command, you click on the options command.

In Netscape *Navigator*, the installation wizard for the Usenet News readers is activated by clicking on the *Collabra* Discussion Group command under the Communicator button in the main tool bar. To make adjustments to the newsreader or to add a news server, you click on Mail and News Groups in the Preferences section found under the Edit Menu.

Organizing Your Newsgroups

There are two ways for you to access Usenet newsgroups. The most common way is for you to download the list of newsgroups available on your

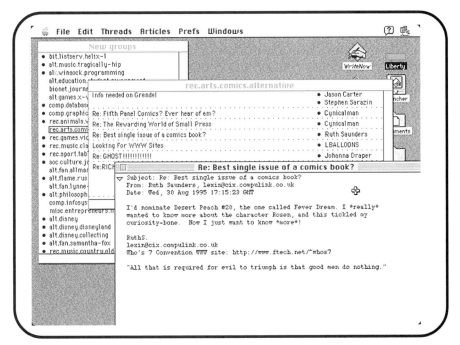

Fig. 5-4: Levels of Usenet news operations are graphically illustrated by these three windows from a *Nuntius* news-reading session. You select a newsgroup from a list (left window), then an article from within the group, and finally you read the article (foreground, right).

news server. To do this using *Internet Explorer*, you simply click on the "Newsgroup" button. In Netscape *Communicator*, you click on the *Collabra* Discussion Group button.

However, local servers may offer access to 7,000 newsgroups or more. When you first begin to read network news, the system assumes that you may want to read all the news from all the newsgroups. Consequently, the process of eliminating newsgroups can be time consuming.

Most newsreaders, however, have features that allow you to eliminate newsgroups according to major designations and categories. For example, you may not be interested in anything that has to do with computer science, so you will want to exclude all newsgroups that begin with the comp. prefix.

The newsreaders in both *Internet Explorer* and Netscape *Communicator* walk you through a step-by-step process to subscribe and unsubscribe to different newsgroups.

Newsreaders keep a log of the newsgroups to which you subscribe and which articles within that group you have already read. Therefore, when you select that group again, you are brought directly to messages that have been posted since you last read the postings.

A second method to access newsgroups is to go to a site such as http:// tile.net.

Navigating Usenet Levels

When you read Usenet news, you enter a program that functions on three tiers: (1) a group listing/directory level, (2) an article listing/directory level, and (3) an article reading level. Additionally, you may be in screen mode or command mode at either directory level. This three-tiered structure and what it means to you as a user is the same no matter which news reading software you are using.

In the graphical environment, the three-tier structure is expressed this way. The news reader screen is divided into two windows. Above the top window there is a line that looks similar to the line in which URLs are displayed in Web browsers. The name of the newsgroup is displayed in that line. The list of messages (lists of related messages called threads) to be read appears in the top window. The message itself is displayed in the bottom line. Basic navigation selections are made by clicking on icons.

Reading and Responding

When you select newsgroup messages to read, what you see on-screen has all the appearance of an e-mail message or a message posting to a bulletin board. If you wish to respond, you have the option of writing a "follow-up" message, which then will be displayed to the network. Or, you can "reply," which will send a mail message privately to the originator of the message. Newsreaders offer point-and-click commands to do both.

Most newsreaders track what you have read through a system of marking files. When you are in the article directory level, you are reading articles that are described by one-line subject tags. You may know that you don't want to read certain articles. By issuing the "mark" (or "skip" in some systems) command, you instruct the newsreader to treat the article as if it had been read. You can mark all messages as read or all the messages in a related thread (or clusters of responses on a single topic) as read as well.

Finding the Right Newsgroups

For journalists, network news can serve many functions. Reporters may want to monitor beat-related newsgroups to stay current on specific topics

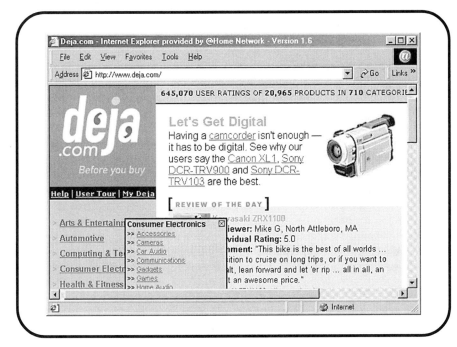

Fig. 5-5: Deja.com is a service that both helps to find relevant newsgroups and permits searching of newsgroup archives.

and to find potential story ideas. In that case, the reporter may have the time to select several newsgroups and monitor the messages on them for several days to see if the information is relevant.

In other cases, however, you will be on deadline and looking for precise information about well-defined topics. You won't be able to leisurely survey 20 newsgroups to find what you need.

In those cases, you can start by reading the FAQ or "Frequently Asked Questions" posting, which generally describes the newsgroup and its charter. The FAQ also often contains other valuable information and leads about the topic in question. Most newsgroups routinely repost their FAQs.

There are several directories available for Usenet newsgroups. Many will allow you to search through the newsgroups to identify where postings in which you may be interested are listed. Some Usenet directory listings and search mechanisms are those located at:

http://tile.net/
http://www.deja.com/
http://www.liszt.com/news/

Some Web sites also offer listings of appropriate Usenet sites. For example, *Science Daily* at http://www.sciencedaily.com offers access to over 600 science-related newsgroups. It also provides a newsreader embedded in its Web page.

Archived Usenet Information

Most newsreaders retain Usenet newsgroup messages for a limited period of time. The quantity of messages being posted daily makes it impossible to save everything. Consequently, when you read newsgroup posts, you will only be able to read the messages that have been posted within that specified period.

These days, old newsgroup messages are often not saved. There are often good reasons for this. First, to save all Usenet newsgroup messages would be similar to saving a record of all telephone conversations. It represents a huge amount of data. Second, as the Usenet FAQ puts it, the signal-to-noise ratio, that is, the amount of good, useful information compared to the amount of useless information on many newsgroups is very low. In other words, the information is not worth saving in many cases.

Nonetheless, *AltaVista* (http://altavista.digital.com/) and other search services permit you to search Usenet newsgroup postings for the past several weeks. In *AltaVista*, you click on the Useful Tools command on the opening page and select Usenet. You can then search for newsgroups using the form "newsgroups:groupname," specific people using the form "from:username@address" and by subject using the form "subject:text" in the search window.

Proper Usenet Behavior

Like other groups of people interacting, people communicating with each other via newsgroups have developed their own rules of etiquette. If you begin to assert yourself in a group without understanding how to behave, at least some people in the group are bound to get mad at you. While you might think that might not make a difference, boorish behavior may mean that you will miss a good lead or contact.

People just starting to read network news should probably read several of the FAQs about Usenet itself prepared for new users. The news.answers newsgroup carries most of the relevant FAQs for new users, including what to do if you have questions about network news. A primer by Chuq Von Rospach for new Usenet users is available in the news.answers newsgroup. It summarizes the rules for working with the Usenet community.

As a journalist, you may not find yourself fully participating in the discussions in a particular newsgroups. More often, you will monitor the traffic—which is called "lurking" in online jargon—to identify people with whom you may either want to be in touch outside the context of the newsgroup or contact to develop leads to other sources of information.

You can think of a newsgroup as any other kind of public forum. As a reporter, if you attended a community meeting, you probably would not grab the microphone and begin interviewing a person you thought made an interesting comment. Instead, you would try to take the person aside, identify yourself as a journalist, and talk privately. You should follow the same process with a newsgroup.

On the other hand, it certainly is not impolite to inform the group of the reason for your participation and invite people to get in touch with you via e-mail if they have information they wish to share.

Using Chat

In the summer of 1999, the financial planner Alan Weiss was scheduled to appear on CNBC, the financial news channel. Unfortunately, traffic on the George Washington Bridge from New York to New Jersey was tied up and Weiss missed the scheduled time slot. Instead, CNBC producers arranged a live chat on its Web site for Weiss to respond to viewers' questions.

Chat has emerged as an important mechanism for people to communicate via the Internet. Consequently, it has also emerged as a viable vehicle for journalists to identify people who may be useful sources for specific stories.

Although the word "chat" conjures up the image of casual conversation, in essence, chat rooms are more like electronic bulletin boards in which messages are posted in real time. Because of the speed at which messages are posted, people can interact with each other immediately.

Most chat rooms are organized in a similar fashion. When you enter a chat room—they are now found on many Web sites including all the major Internet portals—your screen will be divided into at least two windows. In one section you will see text scrolling up the screen. These are the messages that people are posting at the time.

In the second window, you will see the screen names of the people who are chatting at the moment—that is, the people who are posting the messages. You choose a screen name when you register to chat at a specific site.

In a chat room, you can post messages to the general conversation and you can post messages to specific individuals who are participating in the conversation. Finally, many chat rooms are subdivided into different rooms. You can move from room to room to participate in different conversations.

Both *Internet Explorer* and *Netscape* Web browsers allow you to participate in chat rooms. Some chat rooms also encourage you to download special plug-ins or Java-based applets that will speed up the chat interactions.

Some of the common command used in chat rooms include:

/go roomname	This command moves you into different rooms.
/goto name	This commands moves you into the same room as the person you have named.
/help	Generally, this command calls up a user's guide.
/tell name	This command sends a private message to the person named.

To use any of these commands, simply type them into the box you normally type your conversation into.

Another way to send a private message to somebody in a chat room is to double click on that person's name and fill in the box with your message. When you hit "enter" your message will be seen only by the person on whose name you clicked.

Chat and News

Over the years, the conversations in chat rooms have sometimes become newsworthy in their own right. For example, chat at the Silicon Investor Web site has been the origin of many rumors that have moved the stock market.

In many ways, chat rooms are the ultimate online version of talking with strangers. When you enter a chat room, you usually know virtually nothing about the person behind the screen name you see. There have been many stories of people meeting in chat rooms and agreeing to meet in person with dire consequences.

Moreover, information in chat rooms can be false and malicious. Negative information about companies, for example, can be spread by disgruntled employees. In fact, some companies have hired detectives to track down people who spread damaging information about them in chat rooms. Obviously, as a journalist, you must judiciously evaluate the information you encounter in a chat room.

Nevertheless, people do congregate and communicate in chat rooms. Consequently, particularly in times of breaking news, such as when students attack their schools and other major events, chat rooms can widen the range of sources to include in a story.

Moreover, hosted chats have emerged as an interesting way to interact with newsmakers. AOL, *Yahoo!*, Ivillage—a Web community catering to women—and other Web sites regularly invite newsmakers to host chat sessions. In a single week in July 1999, for example, people could chat with pop singer Brittany Spears, actor John Turturro, and family therapist Deb Sheehan on *Yahoo!*

Instant Messaging

Instant messaging programs such as America Online's *Instant Messenger* and *ICQ* and services from Microsoft, *Yahoo!*, and others, is a modified form of chat. Instead of public venues, instant messaging software allows you to chat with a closed circle of friends and acquaintances maintained in what AOL calls buddy lists.

To participate in instant messaging, you have to download a separate software client. *AOL Instant Messenger* is available from http://

www.netscape.com/. The Microsoft and *Yahoo!* software is available from their Web sites as well. Once you have downloaded the software, you can use instant messaging without having your browser open. (You must be connected to the Internet, however.)

As with chat, you will see at least two open windows. In one window, you will see everybody from your buddy list who is online at that moment. In the second window, you will see a scrolling display of the messages being posted.

Instant messaging is, in essence, a private version of chat. Consequently, it is not likely that you will be able to use it to identify new sources. However, you add your most commonly used sources in your buddy list. If they use instant messaging, you could easily contact them for quick quotes or to clarify information. Moreover, it is an intriguing way for teams of reporters or students to collaborate on different projects.

Instant messaging has emerged as one of the most dynamic new methods of interaction on the Internet. By 1999, by some estimates, more than 70 million people had downloaded AOL's *Instant Messenger* software and were sending more than 700 million messages daily.

Webcasts

DCI Corporation is a leader in high-tech education, trade shows and management consulting. One of its mandates is to keep the press and others informed about key trends in information technology. To fulfill that mandate, in 1999 the company sponsored a series of Webcasts. A distinguished speaker would brief the press. The speaker's remarks would be transmitted live via the World Wide Web to whoever had registered for the event. Moreover, the speaker's slides would also be transmitted simultaneously. Those who participated in the event could post questions via a chat box.

The series proved to be a cost-effective way to brief large numbers of people about significant topics. Indeed, many more people could participate than could attend a live event at a specific site. To participate, all people had to do was to make sure that they had downloaded the Real Player plug-in (http://www.real.com) or Microsoft *NetShow* plug-ins for streaming audio and video over the Web.

The use of streaming audio and video over the Web is in its infancy but it is growing rapidly. In the summer of 1999, the technology magazine *PC Week* reported that more than 100,000 people had participated in its Webcasts with computer industry illuminaries such as Microsoft chairman Bill Gates. In the long run, however, it should provide an extremely effective alternative to live press conferences. When it does, it will become a common activity for journalists.

Conclusion

E-mail discussion lists, Usenet newsgroups, chat, instant messaging and Webcasts represent methods of communicating with people around the world about predefined topics of interest. By talking to people, journalists can get interesting ideas for stories as well as interesting leads to information.

However, just because someone is computer savvy enough to partici-pate in a newsgroup or discussion list, does not mean he or she has any special expertise or knows anything factual about the issue. Many newsgroups and chat rooms are filled with rumors and mistakes, particu-larly about current affairs. Information gathered there has to be carefully checked out and verified.

And, while an argument can be made that people who are participat-ing in a newsgroup or discussion list are engaging in a public forum, they often do not know that a reporter is present and that their comments are "on the record." Consequently, online journalists repeatedly debate whether you can or should use information posted to a newsgroup. You should care-fully consider all the ramifications of your actions, including how much confidence you have in the accuracy of the information, how necessary the information is to your story, who will, or could be, hurt by the quote, and other issues before you make a decision.

On the other hand, Usenet newsgroups, e-mail discussion lists and chat rooms offer an intriguing possibility for journalists: the opportunity to include the views of informed nonexperts in stories. Media critics have observed that, in many cases, the information reporters use comes from a narrow slice of elite and expert opinion.

Though there are many reasons for that, one is that it was hard for journalists to identify and interview nonexperts whose opinions may be significant. With the emergence of Usenet newsgroups concerned with professional sports teams, sports reporters could include information from fans as well as the usual quotes from the players and management in their stories. The alt.fan discussion groups on Usenet give reporters easy access to loyal fans for all teams.

Usenet newsgroups and e-mail discussion lists can provide journalists with access to people who may not be experts on a subject or part of the elite but yet are interested and have informed opinions. How that access is and should be managed and made to work for reporters has not yet been determined. Over time, however, it could change the flavor and sourcing of many different types of reporting. And even today, Usenet and discus-sion lists are viable for reporters gathering information and leads when more traditional means are cut off.

Chapter **6**

Search Strategies

Long before the Internet captured headlines in newspapers or hearts of people around the world, reporters assigned new beats resorted to a number of established journalistic traditions to learn who's who and what's important in the new "territory."

A newspaper reporter newly assigned to City Hall might start by reading appropriate clippings in the morgue followed by a visit to the library. Armed with a preliminary sense of who the players are and what the issues might be, the reporter then noses around City Hall, meeting people, and making firsthand observations.

A longer period of developing and nurturing sources that help the reporter in developing stories follows. Over time, a good reporter nurtures relationships with news sources, learns where relevant documents are stored, and develops a keen sense of precisely where to go and whom to see in the process of tracking down news leads. Under deadline pressures, the seasoned reporter can rely on a number of documents, reference materials, and sources he or she has previously fostered during months on the beat.

The same journalistic traditions apply to online journalism. The Internet abounds with useful documents, reference materials, and other resources. Online analogs of newspaper clip files can be found. And a little nurturing of online sources can pay big dividends down the road. This chapter describes several strategies for getting to know online resources off deadline so you know where to find the information you need quickly. Readers of this chapter will

- understand the basics of how search sites work,
- learn a comprehensive strategy for efficiently gathering source materials online,
- understand the uses of online tutorials and directories to get familiar with the Internet,
- explore pre-screened resources through journalists' hotlists,

- comprehend how to structure successful search queries,
- benefit from the work of Internet "scout sites," and
- learn how to manage bookmarks wisely.

The primary goal of the practices outlined in this chapter is to help you become so familiar with the Internet and its tools off deadline that you can locate what you need under deadline pressures. This is largely a process of successful searching, so we open this chapter with a few words about how search sites work, we lay out a comprehensive strategy for learning to use the Net, and we dissect that strategy.

How Search Sites Work

Not all search sites are created equal. Any journalist who has performed the same search at several different search sites quickly reaches this conclusion. Different sites report different results—give different answers—to the same questions. The experience frequently leads to one of two questions: "Which search site is best?" or "Which site should I use?" The answer to both questions is "It depends on your question."

The truth is that no one search site—or any group of search sites—will at any moment contain a list of everything on the Net at that time. By some estimates, most general search engines track only 15 percent of all the information on the Web or less. Some sites focus on just one topic. Some specialize in finding people or businesses, not documents. The World Wide Web itself is expanding so rapidly, that no search utility can keep up with everything on the Web. But this is not all bad.

The first principle to understand about search sites is that none of them actually searches the Web (or any other zone of the Internet) at the time you construct your search. Instead, search sites rely on indices that are created *before* you do your search. A search device then searches its index, not the actual Web sites themselves. The different ways that those indices are created and the manner in which those indices are queried account for most of the result differences obtained on any given search.

A telling distinction in the way search sites work has to do with the relative roles that humans play versus the roles of software robots. Danny Sullivan, who runs a service called *Search Engine Watch*, divides search sites into three groups: **Search Engines**, **Directories**, and **Hybrid Search Engines**. A true *Search Engine* creates its index automatically. A search engine's software robot or "bot" crawls the Web (hence these engines are often called "spiders"), reading pages and page links, and looking for new or changed material. *Directories* build their indices through human activity. The owner of a Web site nominates his or her site to the directory owner, and human editors decide whether to review the site and ultimately whether and how to list it. *Hybrid Search Engines* are directories maintained in association with a search engine. A site may get listed by being nominated or by being discovered by a spider. Sullivan's site at http://searchenginewatch.com/ offers detailed descriptions of the working of search engines.

Another important distinction among search sites is the scope of the site's index. Some sites focus on one clearly defined topic or confine listings to resources in one geographical region. Others attempt to catalog everything from aardvark to zymurgy.

A Comprehensive Strategy

Your objective is to develop a set of strategies for getting to know—ahead of deadline—where useful resources are buried, and for being able to find new ones you have not already located on deadline. Used together, the ideas described below can form a comprehensive approach for searching the Web.

1. Consult online tutorials to learn what the Internet is and how it works.
2. Learn from other journalists.
3. Visit subject catalogs and directories to get an organized sense of what the Internet contains and how some "librarians" have organized the Net.
4. Use "scout sites" that are relevant to your reporting beat.
5. Employ specialized search sites where appropriate.
6. Learn well how to use two or three all-topic search sites.
7. Use agent software and meta-search sites to cast big nets.
8. Manage your bookmarks wisely.
9. Employ appropriate update and alert services.
10. Use common sense and naming conventions to locate common sites.

Each of these strategies will be explained in detail.

Using Online Tutorials

Early in 1997 Reuters News Service in New York provided Internet access to all reporters in the newsroom. In March, Reuters management told reporters to spend 30 minutes a day browsing the Internet. One way to become familiar with resources available to you is simply to browse the Net. If you focus your browsing, you stand a better chance of connecting to useful and credible information than if you wander aimlessly about the Internet. If you are new to the Internet or if you need help understanding

Internet resources beyond the World Wide Web, then online tutorials should be useful.

Online tutorials teach concepts and principles important to understanding the Internet. Some teach how to navigate the World Wide Web, how to construct searches, how to use the different protocols beyond the Web to access information. News organizations have created some good general tutorials for the Internet. One of the best is the *Internet Academy* created by the *Los Angeles Times*. The *Internet Academy* is organized into three graduated courses of study: Internet 101, 201, and 301. Each course has several segments. The Internet Academy is available at http://www.latimes.com/HOME/BUSINESS/ACADEMY/.

Other Net tutorials prepared by journalists or journalism organizations include:

- Public Broadcasting System's "Beginner's Guide" in its *Understanding and Using the Internet* at http://www.pbs.org/uti/begin.html
- The *Newbees* guide at http://www.ok.bc.ca/netguide/nubee.html, a product of the Okanagan Valley Group of Newspapers in British Columbia
- The "Net Tour" of the National Institute for Computer Assisted Reporting at http://www.ire.org/training/nettour
- "A Journalist's Guide to the Internet" provided by the St. Louis Chapter of the Society of Professional Journalists at http://www.stlouisspj.org/surf/surf.html

But news operations do not hold any patent on Internet tutorials. Patrick Crispen's "Internet Roadmap" garnered so much attention when he created it that it is available many places on the Internet and has inspired several imitations. One site, http://www.mobiusweb.com/~mobius/Roadmap/ also includes links to Crispen's "Internet Tourbus." *Dr. K's Best of the Internet Tutorials* is the work of Bruce Klopfenstein and may be found at http://www.bgsu.edu/Departments/tcom/tutor.html. Michael Lerner Productions serves up its "Learn the Net" tutorial in several different languages. Each language site sports a drop-down menu of other language options. The English language version is available at http://www.learnthenet.com/english/index.html.

Each tutorial site has its own take on the Internet, what is important, and how things work. Not all sites agree on all subjects. Most will reinforce each other and what is taught in this book about how the Internet and its tools work. You should return frequently to these tutorial sites until you can safely say that you have mastered all that is in them and you understand where and why they may disagree on some topics.

Learn from Other Journalists

John Makulowich, a senior writer for *Washington Technology* (a business newspaper for U.S. government computer systems integrators), has been "on the Net" about as long as any journalist. Before the World Wide Web was created, Makulowich began developing lists of Internet resources valuable to journalists. One of those lists evolved into the journalism entry of the *World Wide Web Virtual Library* (*VLJ*), freely available at http://www.cais.net/makulow//vlj.html.

The *VLJ* is the most extensive of a class of Internet resources we call "Journalists' Hotlists." These hotlists are in their simplest forms sets of bookmarks developed by the journalist in question. They represent the best Internet resources the creating journalist has found. Reporters benefit from the lists because somebody who shares the concerns of journalists has vetted these Internet sites for us and found them worthy of use. Some of these lists contain annotation that provides helpful descriptions of the sites in question. Some journalist hotlists include forms for passing search queries on to favorite search sites.

A journalist off deadline could invest a few minutes a day visiting these sites in a systematic manner, making bookmarks on sites that appear useful. The return on investment is much higher than randomly surfing and often is higher than browsing general topic catalog sites. A few worthwhile hotlists include:

- http://www.stlouisspj.org/resources.html, an offering of the St. Louis chapter of the Society of Professional Journalists
- http://npc.press.org/library/reporter.htm, "Reporter's Internet Resources" maintained by the library staff at the National Press Club
- http://reporter.umd.edu/, *A Journalist's Guide to the Internet* maintained by Chris Callahan at the University of Maryland
- http://saturn.vcu.edu/~jcsouth/hotlists/hotlists.html, a list of hotlists kept by Jeff South at Virginia Commonwealth University
- http://www.reporter.org/beat/, the "Beat Page" of the IRE Web site
- http://www.seanet.com/~duff/, the *Reporter's Desktop* maintained by Duff Wilson of the *Seattle Times*
- http://www.journalismnet.com/, *Journalism Net* from Canadian TV producer Julian Sher
- http://scoop.evansville.net/, *Scoop Cybersleuth's Internet Guide* maintained by the *Evansville* (Indiana) *Courier*
- http://www.facsnet.org/internet_resources/main.html, the "Internet Resources" section of *FACSNET*
- The Journalism Web Ring, some 35 or more interconnected sites of interest to reporters and generally maintained as hotlists by

journalists and journalism professors around the world—http://
www.webring.org/cgi-bin/webring?ring=hacks;list

E-mail discussion lists provide yet another way one journalist may
learn from another online. Discussion lists are described in Chapter 5. As
noted in that chapter, Barbara Fought of the S.I. Newhouse School of Public Communications at Syracuse University maintains two separate lists
of "Net Lists" directed at journalists. Fought distinguishes between one-
way "newsletter" types of lists (at http://web.syr.edu/~bcfought/nnl2.html)
and two-way discussion groups listed at http://web.syr.edu/~bcfought/
nnl1.html. Combined, these are called the "Newhouse Net Lists." Her
Newhouse Net List pages describe each list and give instructions on how
to join each list.

Using Subject Catalogs and Directories

If you embrace the Reuters directive to browse the net 30 minutes a day
with no other objective than to discover resources useful to your beat, you
may want a little direction to get started. Using subject catalog sites and
directories is one way to give direction to your "off deadline" browsing
time. In simple terms, these sites have set out to catalog Internet resources,
developing focused or all-topic lists organized by subject, much as a library organizes books on shelves by broad topic areas.

Pure directory sites are browse-only catalogs without keyword search
capabilities. The subject catalog will list a screen full of broad topics into
which many other subtopics fall. Finding useful documents is a process of
selecting (browsing through) increasingly more specific topics until you
finally land at the document or site you find useful. This process may not
be productive on deadline, but it can lead you to finding excellent primary
sources or indices of sources you want to employ. In practice, few directory
sites are browse-only, but they also offer keyword search options.

Not All Indices Are Created Equal

Remember, directories and general search sites "find" Internet resources
by inspecting indices created by the specific catalog or search site.

One significant distinction among sites is whether the index is created by human beings or by software robots, sometimes called "bots," "crawlers," or "spiders." Software spiders spend their lives exploring the World
Wide Web (or other Internet resources), looking for new material. When
they find new pages, they read the pages—or predetermined parts of them—
and use what they find to add to their existing index of the Net. This

method has the advantage of being able to catalog vast quantities of documents. The disadvantage is that much less relevant or even spurious information finds its way into machine-generated indices.

When trained human beings do the indexing of resource material, on the other hand, intelligent decisions can be made in selecting only the best material on a given topic. The advantage, from the reporter's point of view is that there is a higher proportion of quality, relevant material turned up by human-edited indices. The down side of building human-generated indices is that it is labor intensive, and a lot of material gets missed.

Some Representative Directory and Catalog Sites

Several all-topic catalogs or directories on the World Wide Web recommend themselves for various reasons. Nearly all have search utilities to augment the browsing-oriented catalog. Some search resources beyond the Web. Some have rich indices developed by trained information specialists. Others use bots or a combination of software robots and human beings.

One of the oldest of the subject catalogs is *Yahoo!* at http://www.yahoo.com/. The *Yahoo!* index is maintained by human beings. As such, it does not list as many resources as some machine-generated sites. The broad subject categories generally correspond to academic subject divisions one might find in a university catalog. *Yahoo!* is a commercial venture that also maintains keyword search forms, customizable "My *Yahoo!*" home pages, and a series of country-specific, state, region, and even city-specific catalog sites. For example, *Yahoo!* France is accessed at http://www.yahoo.fr/. The U.K.-Ireland *Yahoo!* is http://www.uk.yahoo.com, the Germany-specific site is http://www.de.yahoo.com/, and so forth. Each of these serves information in the language of the country it represents. The state, region, and city Yahoos may be accessed from the "Get Local" links on the main *Yahoo!* top page.

Other similar commercial catalogs include *Excite* at http://www.excite.com/. *Excite* also maintains country-specific versions, keyword searching, and personalized home pages. *Infoseek*, a part of Disney's Go Network (http://www.go.com/), features several index tabs that let the user reorganize the browsing topics organization scheme. Both *Excite* and *Infoseek* tend to organize information more along consumer interest lines than academic topics. All three of these sites offer news: *Yahoo!* through Reuters, *Infoseek* through association with ABC, and *Excite* through the wires of Reuters and United Press International.

One human-indexed directory stands out from others in some of the options it allows for its advanced search. The *Tradewave Galaxy* advanced search (http://galaxy.einet.net/cgi-bin/wais-text-multi) offers the option of searching not only its Web index, but also databases of Gopher and Telnet resources. Telnet resources have been indexed for years in the Hytelnet database created by Peter Scott at the University of Saskatchewan. A similar ability to search Hytelnet is offered at http://www.lights.com/hytelnet/.

Three noncommercial sites especially rich in their own rights are the *World Wide Web Virtual Library* (http://vlib.org/), the *Internet Public Library* (http://www.ipl.org/), and the Louisiana State University Library's *Webliography* at http://www.lib.lsu.edu/weblio.html.

The *World Wide Web Virtual Library* is the oldest of all the subject catalogs on the Web. It was started by Tim Berners-Lee, creator of the World Wide Web. In their own words, the *Virtual Library* "is run by a loose confederation of volunteers, who compile pages of key links for particular areas in which they are expert." In its origins, the *Virtual Library* sought to list the very best resources on the Web, in part to show that the Web contained worthwhile resources. While that battle is won, the standards of listing the best resources and of retaining volunteer experts worldwide to maintain the catalog lend its resources a high level of credibility.

The *Internet Public Library* began its life at the University of Michigan and then migrated to the nonprofit sector. The *IPL* includes many original library type resources beyond just being a catalog of Internet resources. The *IPL's* Reference Center (http://www.ipl.org/ref/) is an especially good place for journalists seeking reference materials and guides on various topics.

The *Webliography* at Louisiana State University is maintained by librarians and staff of LSU Libraries. The *Webliography* is a collection of annotated listings for Web sites and resources. It is organized into eight large categories (business, engineering, government, humanities, science, social science, electronic publications, and reference materials) each of which has a number of more specific topic lists. The *Webliography* also has a section on patents and trademarks.

Scout Sites Focus on a Single Topic

Since 1994, subscribers to the *Scout Report* have received weekly reviews of the best new Internet sites. Today, the University of Wisconsin Department of Computer Sciences distributes by e-mail each Friday a new issue of the *Scout Report*. Like its older sibling, *Net Happenings* (also still being distributed), and many more recent imitators, the *Scout Report* is a labor of love. You may find back issues of the *Scout Report* on the Web at http://scout.wisconsin.edu/.

The idea of "scouting" the Internet for the pure satisfaction of cataloging the best resources on a given topic has led to creation of what Nora Paul of the Poynter Institute for Media Studies calls "scout sites." Paul and Margot Williams of the *Washington Post* have written a book called *Great Scouts* (CyberAge Books, 1999) focusing on these sites that can be of great help to a journalist needing a crash course on a clearly defined topic. Typically, a scout site is one created by a person who has a deep interest in one topic, say, dolphins. Because of an intense interest in "everything dolphin" and perhaps with a little missionary zeal, a person might set out to create a Web site that gathers into one place all the best information on dolphins. The person might include everything from the natural history of dolphins to their depiction in art and literature; from campaigns to save them from fishermen's nets to research into their "speech;" from roles they've played as entertainers to wartime military missions.

In creating such a site, the person would have to do a lot of "scouting" for good information to include in the author's Web site. Scout site authors may make no special claim to expertise, other than a passion for the topic and knowledge borne out of much reading. Often, that is good enough. A few scout sites are created as a public service by businesses or nonprofit groups. During the Third Conference of the Parties to the U.N. Convention on Climate Change summit in Kyoto, Japan, in December of 1997, *CNN Interactive* (http://www.cnn.com/) created a special scout site focusing on Web resources on Global Climate Change. A good scout site will tell who created the site, why, and something about the expertise of the person who created the site.

Earlier, we listed several examples of journalists' hotlists. Each of those is an example of a scout site. The first of those sites listed was that of John Makulowich's contribution to the *World Wide Web Virtual Library*. Much of the *World Wide Web Virtual Library* is comprised of scout sites. So the library itself, at http://vlib.org/, serves as both a catalog and a directory to a great number of scout sites. One site incorporated in the *Virtual Library* offers a keyword search capability for the library. It is located at http://vl.bwh.harvard.edu/htdig/search.html.

Some organizations have taken the scout site claim so seriously that they aspire to be *the* portal through which all people seeking certain kinds of information must come. One of these is *Hieros Gamos*, which lists itself as "The Law and Government Portal." *Hieros Gamos* is located at http://www.hg.org/. Others may be less ambitious, but still create powerful scout sites. The Cardinal Fund Management investment firm has developed a "Killer Links Page" for resources helpful to investors. It is accessible at http://www.cardinalfund.com/Linkspage.htm. Totally independent scout sites can also be powerful resources. More focused (U.S. only) law and government resources are maintained by Ira Sterbakov, a retired software engineer, at http://www.erols.com/irasterb/gov.htm.

Specialized Search Tools

Closely related to scout sites are sites with specialized search indices. These sites, mentioned under catalog sites, build indices of Internet resources

Fig. 6-1: Gary Price's *direct search* site indexes specialized search sites that get at data often missed by general search services sush as *AltaVista, Hotbot,* and *Google.* The site is located at http://gwis2.circ.gwu.edu/~gprice/direct.htm.

relating to a specialized topic, such as law, medicine, cancer research. *Findlaw* (http://www.findlaw.com) is one of these sites. A number of the more sophisticated scout sites also develop specialized search indices. For example, the *Hieros Gamos* site just described has search capabilities focused upon law and government resources.

The *Medline Fool* (http://www.medportal.com/) provides search mechanisms for the National Library of Medicine's Medline and Pre-Medline databases. It also provides for searching other health-related resources on the Net. For some of the same resources, a journalist could go directly to the *Internet Grateful Med* site (http://igm.nlm.nih.gov/) run by the National Library of Medicine. The site offers access to 15 databases including the Medline database.

The Edgar database (http://www.sec.gov/edgarhp.htm) of information on publicly traded companies in the United States gives several options for searching its highly focused database. Other search sites focused on publicly traded companies include the Vancouver Stock Exchange (http://www.vse.ca/). A site specializing in information on British companies, Companies House (http://www.companies-house.gov.uk/) offers some information for free and some for fee.

Gary Price at George Washington University maintains something of a scout site for specialized search devices, which he calls *direct search.*

Price's site also provides direct links to the advanced search features of some of the larger search sites such as *AltaVista, Inference Find, HotBot,* and *Yahoo!* The site is located at http://gwis2.circ.gwu.edu/~gprice/ direct.htm. As subsets of *direct search,* Price has also built an index of U.S. state and city online directories located at http://gwis2.circ.gwu.edu/~gprice/ state.htm and an index of online archives, library catalogs, and bibliographies at http://gwis2.circ.gwu.edu/~gprice/bibs.htm.

Match the Tool to the Job

The good news for reporters is that for any given beat or any particular task there are likely to be several specialized finding tools. This leads to a very important principle about searching the Internet: *Use the right tool for the job you want to complete.* Why use a pair of scissors to drive a screw into a cabinet when you have a perfectly fine set of screwdrivers? If you need simple facts, you can go straight to almanac style resources and not bother with some massive search site query. Ask yourself, "What am I trying to find?" and then use the appropriate tool.

For example, if you are trying to locate a specific person or business, you might use one of the all-purpose phone books on the Web. Some of these are:

- *WhoWhere People Finder* at http://www.whowhere.lycos.com/
- The *Yahoo! People Search,* http://people.yahoo.com/
- *Switchboard,* http://www.switchboard.com/
- *Internet Address Finder,* http://www.iaf.net/
- ThinkDirectMarketing.com offers several reverse directories for businesses and individuals at http://web.thinkdirectmarketing.com/freesearch/
- *WorldPages,* http://www.worldpages.com/global/

Phone book resources assume you know whom you seek. If you are seeking an expert on some topic, you could try the following resources:

- The *Sources and Experts* page at http://metalab.unc.edu/slanews/ internet/experts.html is the work of Kitty Bennett at the *St. Petersburg Times*
- The CVCP *ExpertNet,* http://www.cvcp.ac.uk/What_We_Do/ ExpertNet/expertnet.html for finding academics in the United Kingdom
- *ProfNet,* a service of PR Newswire, at http://www.profnet.com/
- The CCSO *Phonebook-Server Lookup* at the University of Illinois, is good for locating academics, http://www.uiuc.edu/cgi-bin/ph/ lookup?Query=

- *Amazon.com* http://www.amazon.com searches will produce lists of books or recordings that match a topic, giving you the names of authors who have written on your topic

Another kind of informal expert, is the person in the street. Deja.com (http://www.deja.com/) facilitates searches of postings to Usenet news groups. Journalists looking for people having experience with a certain kind of product or company have searched news group postings to identify people carrying on discussions about the matters.

If you are seeking facts or statistics, try some of the sites that specialize in providing such information:

- The U.S. Central Intelligence Agency's *World Fact Book*, *Factbook on Intelligence,* list of foreign government chiefs of state and cabinet members, and other publications are all available from http://www.odci.gov/cia/publications/pubs.html
- Bob Drudge's *My Virtual Reference Desk* http://www.refdesk.com/ outline.html sports links to online almanacs, dictionaries, encyclopedias, maps, statistics and other reference tools
- *Statistical Abstract of the United States* is accessible at the U.S. Census Bureau at http://www.census.gov:80/stat_abstract/
- For statistical data on nations other than the United States, the U.S. Census Bureau has links to other statistical agencies at http://www.census.gov/main/www/stat_int.html

The listings provided here suggest just a few samples of specialized search sites. Most scout sites will provide you with background material on the topic for which the site was constructed. As you nurture your sources online, you will find others that are relevant to your research and reporting interests. You will want to place bookmarks on the sites you find and continue to be alert for new ones. The important lesson here is to use the right tool for the job. Don't wrestle with one of the big search sites when a smaller, more focused one will get you what you need with less grief.

Constructing Productive Searches

A natural tendency for reporters—and anybody else doing research online—is to go straight to one of the big name search sites the moment you want to find some information. Many journalists new to Internet searching have entered a select term into a search box only to face tens of thousands of hits. A quick inspection of some of those hits discovers a lot of irrelevant material.

Two courses of action will help ensure that you get what you are looking for. First, if a specialty search site is called for, use it. Second, take time to learn search commands specific to the search site you are using, and then construct careful searches. All major search

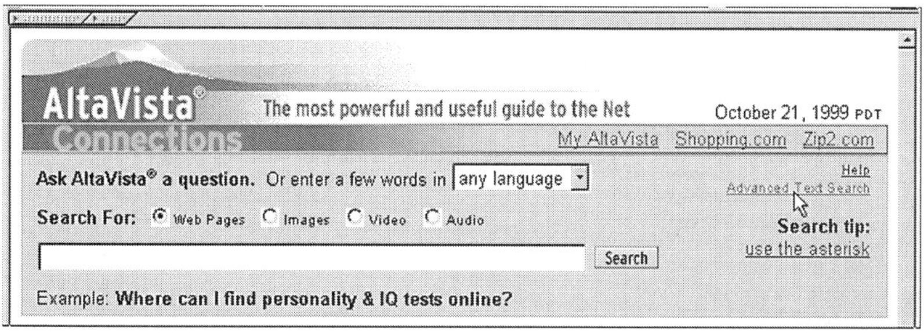

Fig. 6-2: Like many other search sites, *AltaVista* has a link to "Advanced Search" options (see mouse arrow). You can go straight to the advanced Web search section by opening http://www.altavista.com/cgi-bin/query?pg=aq&what=web.

sites support Boolean logic, and all provide help files that show how to do searches in the site. Take time to print out the help files and study them off deadline, performing test searches so that when you face deadline pressures, you already know how the search site works. If you choose to keep the help file for reference, you should check the site periodically looking for changes in the search syntax or in the help instructions.

Be alert for links to "Advanced Search" or "Power Search" capabilities or to search "Options"—or some similar terms—that give more powerful search tools. *AltaVista* offers an "Advanced Search" selection, and *Yahoo!* offers an "Options" choice from the top page of the site. These advanced options will give you ways to limit your search that will increase the likelihood you find the very document you seek. The first "advanced" option you should learn is the use of Boolean logic.

Using Boolean Logic and Literals

Boolean logic uses the terms AND, OR, NOT, and NEAR to define sets of objects. Those objects may be Web pages, Web sites, stamps in a collection, photographs in an archive or any other grouping. If you wished to research immigration policies for the United States, Canada, and the United Kingdom, you might construct a simple search on the term "immigration." If you did so, you would produce a large listing of hits, including many documents and sites that were absolutely useless to you.

By using Boolean terms when you construct your search, you can eliminate many unwanted hits. Thus you might construct a search such as "immigration AND policies" because you are interested specifically in policy matters. You still are producing hits on documents that deal with nations

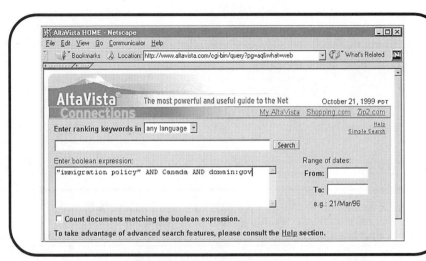

Fig. 6-3: Boolean expressions that help to narrow searches may be placed in the large dialog box of the *AltaVista* advanced search section. Other advanced search parameters permit you to restrict date ranges and select document language.

other than those you seek. You might further limit your search by searching on "immigration AND policies AND Canada." This search narrows the field further but it also excludes the United States and the United Kingdom. And it still produces documents we don't want.

Major search engines support the use of literals to get even more precise results. In the searches we have described so far, the search engine will report all documents that contain both words, "immigration" and "policy." These documents are not necessarily about "immigration policy." They could be about insurance policies and mention immigration in passing. To overcome this, we employ literals in our search. By placing "immigration policies" in quotes, we are telling the search engine that we want documents that use exactly that phrase. Now our search looks like this: " 'immigration policies' AND Canada."

We still have excluded the United States and the United Kingdom. We could now include them by using the Boolean OR. Our new search could be phrased " 'immigration policies' AND Canada OR 'United States' OR 'United Kingdom' " and will include all documents that include the phrase "immigration policies" with either Canada, United States, or United Kingdom. We will explore other strategies to help us refine our search, but first let's explore those other Boolean terms, NOT and NEAR.

If we constructed the search " 'immigration policies' AND Canada AND NOT 'United States' " we would get a listing of all documents containing both our literal "immigration policies" and "Canada" as long as the document does not contain the phrase "United States." Thus "NOT" becomes a way of excluding hits on related topics that sometimes cloud and confuse our results.

The search " 'immigration policies' AND Canada NEAR 'United States' " would produce only documents that contain all three of our terms ("immigration policies" and "Canada" and "United States") and furthermore the term "Canada" must be found in the document near the term "United States." NEAR generally means within five to eight characters. Some search engines allow you to define what NEAR means.

Throughout this discussion we have capitalized our Boolean operators, AND, OR, NOT, and NEAR. Some search sites require you to capitalize Boolean operators. Most sites allow you to use shorthand like "–" for NOT and "+" for AND. Some sites do not support the use of NEAR. Boolean operators are not the only tools for helping us to refine our searches, but they are basic tools and may be combined with other tools to construct even more narrowly defined searches. Most sites allow other search limiters beyond Boolean operators. In our current example (at *AltaVista*), we added the qualifier, "domain:gov" following the last Boolean AND.

Other Search Refinements

Suppose that in the research on immigration policies we want only "official" pronouncements coming from government resources. The advanced features of some search engines allow us to specify site domains and/or URL contents. We know that all U.S. government sites will have the top level domain of ".gov." Incorporating that into our search at *AltaVista*, we might come up with this query: " 'immigration policies' AND 'United States' AND 'domain:gov'. "

Table 6-1 shows differences in the numbers of hits obtained using these various constructs with the *AltaVista* advanced search (http://www.altavista.com/cgi-bin/query?pg=aq&what=web) utility. We have used Boolean search terms, literal phrasing, and finally limited our search to government sites. Still other ways exist to limit or to expand your search results.

Search Construct	Pages Found
immigration	646,850
immigration AND policies	42,297
immigration AND policies AND Canada	13,009
"immigration policy"	9,126
"immigration policy" AND Canada	2,235
"immigration policy" AND Canada AND NOT "United States"	897
"immigration policy" AND Canada NEAR "United States"	578
"immigration policy" AND Canada AND "United States" AND domain:gov	33

Table 6-1: Number of Web pages found by *AltaVista* using different Boolean operators.

Word form variations: We have been using the plural form, "policies" in all our searches to this point. There might be a perfectly made-to-order document that spells out the *policy* (singular) of the United States (or Canada or the United Kingdom). In constructing your searches, be alert to variations in the form of the words you are using in your search. In our current example, two strategies suggest themselves. We could do two separate searches, one using "policy" and the other "policies." We could use a highest common denominator variation in our keywords as we construct our search. If we searched on "immigration polic" as a literal, it would return all documents whether they used the singular or the plural form of the word. This course reduces the number of searches you have to do, but it also has a danger. If the search engine encounters the phrase "immigration police" we will get those documents also.

Wild cards: Another way to approach the previous search is with wild cards. We could have constructed a search for "immigration polic*." The asterisk tells the search mechanism to accept any word strings that begin with "polic." Many search sites support wild cards. In our example, there would be no difference in the result because we are looking for a literal. Where wild cards become more useful is in a Boolean expression outside of the literal. Thus a search on "Canada AND immigration NEAR polic*" will give us a listing of all forms of our target word—policy, policies, police—where the word is near "immigration" and the word "Canada" also occurs.

Date limitations: Any time a computer file is created or edited, the software involved "stamps" a date on the document. Some search engines permit you to specify a range of dates within which you want your "hit documents" to fall. This can be useful if you are trying to track down a report on a specific, dated event.

Limiting boxes: Some search sites will give you the chance to click options for your search that will help narrow the range of results you get. These boxes are usually found on the "advanced" search area or "options" area. Learn what these are; they often simplify the process of constructing a search.

Defaults: Every search site has defaults in the ways that it responds to a multi-word search. Some assume the Boolean AND. Some assume OR. Some assume a literal. In the process of learning to use a search site, you need to find out what those defaults are. They are usually reported beneath a "Search Tips" or "Help" button.

The message is simple: Study help files at your chosen search site, and practice using different search qualifiers and combinations. In other words, pick two or three search sites and invest the time and energy to learn them well. The dividends will include increased proficiency at finding what you want when you want it.

Danny Sullivan lists less than two dozen "major players" among the hundreds of general search sites. Among those listed, there is an even smaller number of search engines. For example, *AltaVista* is powered by *Ask Jeeves* and *LookSmart*. NetFind, Netscape, and WebCrawler are powered by *Excite*, and Inktomi powers such sites as GoTo, HotBot, MSN, and Snap. These are the sites Sullivan lists as major players:

- Alta Vista   http://www.altavista.com/
- Ask Jeeves   http://www.askjeeves.com/
- AOL NetFind   http://www.aol.com/netfind/
- Direct Hit   http://www.directhit.com/
- Excite   http://www.excite.com/
- Go / Infoseek   http://infoseek.go.com/ or http://www.go.com/
- Google   http://www.google.com/
- GoTo   http://www.goto.com/
- HotBot   http://www.hotbot.com/
- Inktomi   http://www.inktomi.com/
- LookSmart   http://www.looksmart.com/
- Lycos   http://www.lycos.com/
- MSN   http://www.msn.com/
- Netscape   http://www.netscape.com/
- Northern Light http://www.northernlight.com/ or http://www.nlsearch.com/
- Open Directory http://dmoz.org/
- RealNames   http://www.realnames.com/
- Search.com   http://www.search.com/
- Snap   http://www.snap.com/
- WebCrawler   http://www.webcrawler.com/
- Yahoo!   http://www.yahoo.com/

What the Search Engines Miss

At any given moment in time top search engines will have indexed a fraction of the information on the the World Wide Web. One of the reasons is easy to understand. The engines (bots, spiders) that crawl the web, inspecting sites for new content, simply cannot make it to every site on the Net every day. The end result is that new material has to wait to be discovered until the spider pays its regular visit. That typically is several weeks to several months.

One reason to perform a search at several different sites is that you increase your odds of finding more recent material if you are looking in several indices. But even that strategy won't find everything, because some good material simply doesn't get indexed. One class of material not indexed by the search engines is material kept in data tables and served up by cgi scripts.

What happens in these sites is that the page you see on your screen was created by the server when you asked for it. It does not reside as an HTML page on the remote host. Instead, it resides as a record (or group of records), often in plain text format and stored in data tables on the server. Links on such pages often are calls to record numbers or lines in a data table on the host site. A search engine visiting the site is confronted with what is essentially a private database. Unless the owners of the site take extraordinary measures to make their site visible to search engines, then pages in the site will not be indexed.

Still other material is hidden from search engines. Many public sites maintain private resources "for members only" or accessible only by paying a fee. Many newspaper archives are maintained this way. You may freely look at today's news—or maybe even the last week's news. At some point, however, articles get moved to an archive, and to get the text of the article you have to pay a fee. The *Wall Street Journal* requires subscription fees of anyone seeking access to its articles—even today's news. All of these controlled access documents are kept hidden from search engines.

A similar situation arises when a page that was indexed by a search engine gets moved or replaced by new content. You perform a search at a site like *InfoSeek*. The search site finds in its index an article that seems to be a perfect match for what you seek. You click on the link, only to get a "404" error—"Document not found." If the item was moved after the search indexed it, the only way you will get the page is if some other site stored it. The search site *Google* (http://www.google.com/) may give you the option of viewing a cached version of the page in question.

Meta-Searches and Agents

Sometimes you want to cast a really big net for information. You may be looking for information on a very obscure topic, or you may just want to be sure that you don't miss anything that might be helpful. One option you have is to perform your search at several search sites. Another option is to use either meta-search sites or agent software. In either case, the general idea is the same.

Meta-search sites and agent searching tools take your search dialog and submit it to several different search sites. They then compile the results from each site and report the hits back to you. The difference between the two methods is where the computing work is done, subtleties in both flexibility of searching and how results are reported back to you, and what you might do with the results.

Two general meta-search sites enjoy some popularity among journalists. They are *Metacrawler* (http://www.metacrawler.com) and *Dogpile* (http://www.dogpile.com). *AskJeeves* (http://www.ask.com) and *InferenceFind*

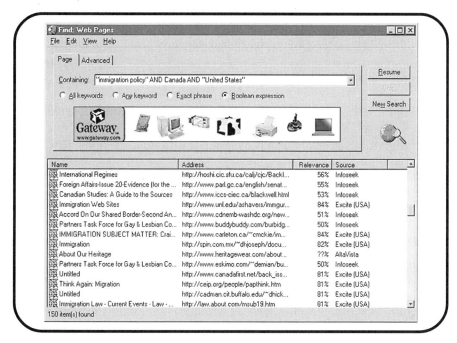

Fig. 6-4: *WebFerret* is a search agent that resides on your computer. You construct your search in *WebFerret*, selecting a number of options, including sites to search. The agent software hands your search off to several search sites, gathers results, eliminates duplicates, reports relevance, and captures the first few lines of the document.

(http://www.infind.com) also return results from several search engines from a single query. At each site, you construct your search, and the engine at the site takes your search to several other sites for you. All the computing work is done outside your computer on the servers of the search sites. The advantage is obvious. You have only to construct your search once, and you have the benefit of getting results from several separate Web indices.

The disadvantages are less obvious. First, your carefully constructed Boolean search may not be read the same way by every site, because different sites often use different syntax. In fact, you may wind up getting a more complicated, less relevant response than you should. A less obvious downside is that you may get a report that Site X has no hits on your topic when in fact it has great listings. One reason these sites miss hits rests in what happens when the meta-search engine files your request with Site X. If Site X is particularly busy at that moment or some other event slows things down, your search may time out. This means that the meta-search engine gets tired of waiting for a response and moves on, abandoning whatever hits otherwise might have been reported. One other disadvantage is that meta-search sites tend not to remove duplicates from the list of hits reported. Thus, you wind up digging through listings that may report the same sites frequently.

Agent software resides on your computer's hard drive. An agent is a small application whose sole purpose is to take your search around the Web, query various search sites, get the results, and compile a report—on your computer. The agent software may eliminate duplicates and generally may be custom configured in a number of ways. For example, you may tell it to search only the sites you choose. You may set up filters for the kinds of results you want. You may use Boolean logic. Because the report is delivered on your computer, it's easy to save the report in a format you can use later. One popular piece of agent software is *WebFerret* from Ferretsoft (http://www.ferretsoft.com/).

Managing Bookmarks Wisely

Duff Wilson at the *Seattle Times* creates a set of bookmarks for each project he is on. Alan Schlein of Deadline Online, a training service for journalists, offers classes in coping with information overload. Both efforts are aimed at a common problem for journalists, who by their natures tend to be information junkies with a wide range of interests. They get out onto the World Wide Web and they find all kinds of great sites. They start building lists of bookmarks that very soon blossom into expansive, unmanageable, disorganized catalogs replete with listings they forget about in just a few days.

Following a few principles can help to tame bookmark madness. These are:

- select only the very best sites to bookmark
- edit site titles and descriptions
- sort bookmarks into folders
- make use of multiple bookmark files where appropriate

When it comes to managing bookmarks, Netscape *Navigator* (v. 4.x)—at the time of this writing—has some clear advantages over MS *Internet Explorer* (v. 4.x). By default, *Navigator* bookmarks are stored in a single file called "bookmark.htm." *Explorer* bookmarks (Favorites) are stored in a series of folders within a master folder called "favorites." One advantage is that of space. In the fall of 1998 Chet Burgess of CNN taught some Internet classes at the annual meeting of the Radio Television News Directors Association in San Antonio. For each class, he gave his students a diskette that had his bookmarks on them. The bookmarks were in two formats: *Navigator* and *Explorer*. The *Navigator* file occupied 88 kilobytes of disk space. The same bookmarks, as *Explorer* favorites, occupied 315 kilobytes. More important for the present discussion, *Navigator* bookmarks are more easily customized, and the fact that all bookmarks are kept in a single HTML file that can be read (and edited) by any program that reads (and edits) text files gives them a greater flexibility.

Chapter 11 describes the process of setting bookmarks, organizing them into folders, and editing descriptions. Selecting which sites to add to your bookmark list and which not to can be very difficult. Two guidelines might help. First, place bookmarks on only those sites you expect to be using for regular work in the near future. If your beat has not changed recently, you may add to this list sites you wish you had known about when you did such-and-such a story last month. This means resisting the temptation to place a bookmark on any site that looks good for whatever topic.

Second, you might follow Duff Wilson's lead and create a bookmark file for each project or for each beat. If you are doing a project on Land Use, you create a LandUse.htm file that keeps your bookmarks on all related topics. Assuming you use Netscape *Navigator*, the easiest and safest way to do this is to copy your current "Bookmark.htm" file giving the new file the new name, LandUse.htm. Then, from within *Navigator*, launch the Bookmark editor (Ctrl-B). Open your new file (File | Open Bookmarks File) and select the new file you made by copying the old. The bookmark list at this point should look like the list you just replaced because it is a copy. However, the Edit Bookmarks window should have the name of your new file (LandUse.htm) in the title bar. If it does, then you need to select all your bookmarks (Ctrl-A) and then delete them. Now you have an empty bookmark file, and every bookmark you add becomes a part of the new file.

Set up folders to group bookmarks for similar sites. In our Land Use example, you might want to create a folder for bookmarks pointing at online "clippings" of other articles on the subject. Another folder might contain pointers to documents on environmental concerns, one folder could contain links to relevant government agency sites and/or documents, and still another to development agencies. As a general rule, you should limit the number of bookmarks you have in a folder to about 20-25 and limit the number of folders in one bookmark file to the same level. If you have significantly more, then when you open the folder under bookmarks, the display you get could be more confusing than helpful.

Keeping Current

The Web changes constantly. That great new sites appear daily is both boon and bane for a journalist. Having new material to work with may make doing a story easier next time. But it also places pressure on the journalist to invest time keeping up to date. Devoting 20-30 minutes a day looking for new sites is one useful strategy. Monitoring announcements in e-mail discussion lists can be helpful as other list members share their finds with the group. But there is one more tool at your fingertips. Both "update" and "alert" services will help keep you informed of changes in areas of interest to you.

Many sites offer **alert services**. You register with the site, reporting that you want to be notified of changes made in the site. Using mail list management software (such as *Listserv*, *Listproc*, or *Majordomo*), site owners then notify all people who registered when there are changes. One of these of interest to some business reporters is operated by PR-Newswire at http://www.prnmedia.com/prnemail/. Companies pay PR-Newswire to post their press releases. The PRN e-mail service sends press releases by e-mail to journalists who request the service. You create a profile online, listing the kinds of releases you want or the companies you are trying to monitor. Bill Dedman has compiled a list of some of these sites, organized by topic, available at http://home.att.net/~bdedman/alerts.html.

If a site you like does not offer an alert service, then you may be a candidate for an update service. Update services monitor pages or sites you specify for changes. At *NetMind*, http://www.netmind.com/, you specify a page you want monitored and what kinds of things you want to watch (links, text, images, keywords). When there is a change, *NetMind* notifies you in the manner you have chosen: by e-mail, pager, cell phone, or personal data assistant. A service at Dartmouth University, called *Informant*, tracks query results at search sites. Located at http://informant.dartmouth.edu/, *Informant* sends you e-mail notice whenever a specified search turns up new results. *Informant* searches *AltaVista*, *Excite*, *Lycos*, and *Go*. The *Deja* (http://www.deja.com/) Thread Tracker works in a similar way for news group postings. If you happen to be following a news group discussion on immigration policy, Thread Tracker will notify you by e-mail when new messages have been added to the thread.

Hybrid alert services, sometimes called gleaning services, profile services, or filtering services, blend characteristics of both alert services and update services. At these sites, you complete a profile of the kinds of things you are looking for, and the site then monitors a pre-defined universe of online resources looking for new material matching your profile. If it monitors only its own material, you have found a customizable alert service. If it monitors material created at other sites, you have a customizable update service. CompuServe has one of the oldest of these in its Executive News Service. You tell ENS that you are interested in "immigration policy," and that you want to collect all articles showing up in certain publications over a distinct period of time that mention that phrase. The CompuServe ENS sets up a folder for you, looks for such articles, and places them in a folder for you. You return periodically to check your folder and to read what ENS has harvested for you. The ENS service assumes that first you belong to CompuServe and then costs you a nominal fee per month on top of your membership.

Similar services are offered on the Web—for free. *NewsTracker* (http://www.newstracker.com/) says it "collects and filters thousands of late-breaking articles from online newspapers and magazines including the *Los Angeles Times*, *Chicago Tribune*, *Forbes Digital*, *Advertising Age*, and *Russia Today*." *NewsIndex* (http://newsindex.com/delivered.html) promises to monitor more than 250 news sources globally in response to the profile you establish. *Quickbrowse* (http://www.quickbrowse.com/) monitors the online sites of major U.S. daily newspapers.

All of these sites are monitoring what for journalists is secondary source material, all right for surveillance and tips on what the competition is doing, but still not primary news gathering material. There is a promise of primary source monitoring in some specialized areas. The FreeEDGAR Watch List (http://www.freeedgar.com/Search/WatchList.asp) accepts from reporters a list of publicly traded U.S. companies from the site user. When any company on the list submits an electronic filing to the Securities and Exchange Commission, the reporter receives an e-mail alert.

Common Sense and Naming Conventions

A lot of unnecessary energy is spent worrying about how to find this site or that, which search engine or scout site to use, when a clear understanding of domain naming conventions would give the answer. In other cases, a little common sense will go a long way toward leading one to a solution.

For example, there is widespread convention for companies to seek domain names that contain the company name, initials, or trademark. Thus global computer giant IBM will be found at http://www.ibm.com/, auto manufacturer Ford holds forth at http://www.ford.com/, and bookseller Barnes and Noble owns the domain barnesandnoble.com. The general pattern for company domain names is *companyname(or initials).com*. In the United Kingdom, the .com is often replaced with .co.uk.

Universities and colleges in the United States use the top level domain .edu. New York University resides at nyu.edu. California Institute of Technology, commonly known as Caltech, owns the domain caltech.edu. The pattern for institutes of higher learning in the United States is *name(or initials).edu*. One sometimes needs to be flexible when several schools are known by the same initials. The University of Southern California uses the domain usc.edu, while the University of South Carolina employs sc.edu. In the United Kingdom, the conventional pattern is *schoolname.ac.uk*. Thus City University of London resides at city.ac.uk and Aberdeen University is at aberdeen.ac.uk.

Government agencies in the United States likewise follow conventional patterns. For federal agencies, the pattern is *agencyname(or initials).gov*. Thus the U.S. Department of State Web server may be found at http://www.state.gov/, and the Department of Defense is at http://www.dod.gov/. In rare cases where two agencies claim the same initials, as in Department of Energy and Department of Education, then creativity is called for. Energy is at doe.gov while education is at ed.gov.

Official sites of state governments in the United States also follow a standard pattern. The convention is http://www.state.*statecode*.us/ where the two-character postal abbreviation for the state is substituted for the *statecode*. Thus Maryland's official state site is located at http://www.state.md.us/ and Texas is at http://www.state.tx.us/.

City government sites in the United States generally observe the pattern: http://www.ci.*cityname.statecode*.us/. You use the same, two-character state code as you use for state Web sites. The "cityname" portion of the address is a little more tricky. You'll find Atlanta at http://www.ci.atlanta.ga.us/ ; but Los Angeles is at http://www.ci.la.ca.us/; New York is at http://www.ci.nyc.ny.us/; and Chicago is at http:// www.ci.chi.il.us/. County government servers usually follow similar patterns to cities, using the following pattern: http://www.co.*countyname.statecode*.us. Some counties are almost as creative as cities when it comes to selecting the *countyname*. Where city and county government addresses may be less than intuitive, those official servers are often available through the state server.

In the United Kingdom, government site addresses tend to be straightforward. Thus the Parliament Web site is located at http://www.parliament.uk/, and the Ministry of Defense holds forth at http://www.mod.uk/. Branches of the military are contained within the MOD domain. Thus the Royal Air Force is at http://www.raf.mod.uk/, and the Royal Navy is at http://www.royal-navy.mod.uk/. Local government Web sites are not as easy to guess, but a fairly comprehensive list is found at the Local Government Association site. The LGA main site is at http://www.lga.gov.uk/. The LGA represents all 410 local authorities in England and Wales and lists those authorities who have Web sites at http://www.lga.gov.uk/lga/2searchlinkla.htm.

Conclusion

The art and skill of finding what you want on the Internet when you want it is a skill like many others in doing journalism—it is a skill developed over time through nurturing sources and careful digging. You have to study the tools of online research and practice with them off deadline if they are going to help you during a moment of deadline pressure.

Several small strategies can help you to develop those skills. Combined, over time, they will make you as proficient at using the Internet as you are at using any other group of communications and research tools. Knowing which tool to use for the research job at hand is important. Common sense and traditional journalistic values are just as important in the virtual world of online research as they are in the "real" world.

Chapter 7

The Internet beyond the Web

Swedish journalist Fredrik Laurin routinely gathers Swedish census data and mines the Swedish parliament's information system. Although the data are available via the World Wide Web, Laurin uses a less friendly Internet protocol called Telnet. Telnet allows people to log on to remote computers (as opposed to just requesting files), and then move through the remote computers' menus to gather information.

Why does Laurin use an older and more difficult method to get the information he needs? Laurin wants the data in raw form so he can analyze it himself. Gathering data via Telnet instead of the Web makes it easier to get the data in the form he wants.

When TCP/IP and the Internet were first developed, there were three basic services—e-mail (which was extensively discussed in Chapter 4), Telnet, which is the ability to log on to remote computers, and File Transfer Protocol, which is a method to transfer files from computer to computer on the Internet.

Telnet and FTP functions are incorporated within TCP/IP (which was discussed in Chapter 2), and, consequently are available to any Internet-connected computer. Before the development of the Web, many people realized that being able to store and access files on computers across the Internet would create a dynamic information resource. An early attempt at creating an organized, distributed information network with a uniform, browsing interface was called Gopher. Though now overshadowed by the Web, Gopher is still operating and diligent journalists can find useful information there.

This chapter explores non-Web and older resources still available through the Internet. Though perhaps not for everybody, intrepid reporters may find that using these resources can offer them an advantage. FTP is a particularly valuable application to be able to use. This chapter will describe:

- how to invoke Telnet and navigate Telnet resources,
- use of the FTP protocol,

- how to take advantage of Gopher resources,
- when you might want to use Gopher or Lynx clients in lieu of traditional Web browsers, and
- where to find listings of Telnet, Gopher, FTP, and other non-Web resources.

These Internet resources can be accessed in a number of ways. Standard Web browsers can be used to access Gopher resources and for some FTP applications. Separate client software is also available for FTP and in some cases is more efficient than using the browser. Telnet requires a separate client program. Telnet clients are standard on Windows computers running Windows 95 and above (it can be called via the browser like other plug-in programs). Macintosh users may need to download a separate Telnet client.

What Telnet Offers

Telnet is one of the basic Internet services. Created before the spread of point-and-click graphical user interfaces, Telnet is text-only. You must type in every command. Furthermore, it requires you to log on to most sites you visit. Despite the challenges in using Telnet, it may be useful in certain circumstances.

Telnet is still widely used for three applications. First, before many of the major and university libraries in America created Web sites, they made their card catalog systems accessible via Telnet. Many of these systems provide access to other information services, especially if you have an account with the library. The cards in some of these catalogs frequently contain brief abstracts of the documents they are indexing. Because card catalogs list books and other publications by topic, they can be great assets for journalists seeking to identify expert sources on a given topic.

Second, in some circumstances, Telnet can be used to log on directly to the computer that houses your e-mail server. For example, Dan Gillmor, Tech columnist for the *San Jose Mercury News* travels abroad frequently. He stays in touch with his office e-mail by using Telnet to get back to a mail server. When story assignments take you out of town, especially on extended trips, Telnet may offer one solution, if available to you. If you can get to any Net-connected computer that has Telnet, you connect to the host that contains your mailbox.

After you log on, you launch the e-mail client on your host, typically *Pine*. Many universities in the United States use *Pine* as their default e-mail editor. Then you manage your mail from the remote computer. All actions you take in this mode actually affect the original mail messages in your box. One advantage of managing mail in this manner is that you do not have to do any e-mail client configuring or any managing of user pro-files on the computer you are "borrowing."

Finally, Telnet may be a good alternative if you want to access raw data that will be imported into other programs such as spreadsheets for analysis. Fredrik Laurin notes that "copying data from the Web often gets very messy when you want to work with it further in *Excel*." Sometimes all Laurin wants from the Web pages he visits are the data, which he then sorts and manipulates in the process of developing his story. By capturing the data from a Telnet environment, he finds that he has less cleaning to do before he can use the data for story work.

To use Telnet, you must know where the Telnet resources are. A catalog of Telnet resources may be found on the Web at http://www.lights.com/hytelnet/. At least one search and catalog site on the Web permits you to search the Hytelnet database of Telnet resources. The Tradewave *Galaxy* site advanced search, available at http://galaxy.einet.net/cgi-bin/wais-text-multi, has search options that will point you to Gopher and Telnet resources.

How Telnet Works

In simple terms, Telnet lets you log on to a distant computer, run programs on that computer, and then log off. The Telnet client is used to log on and log off. When you are logged on, your local computer then acts as a dumb terminal. All the programs and action are run on the distant machine. The entire exchange between your computer and the distant machine is text-based.

If your browser is properly configured and you have a Telnet client, you enter the URL of the Telnet site to which you want to connect by typing "telnet://sitename.domain." This launches the Telnet client. Alternatively, you may launch the Telnet client separately. For example, in Windows, you would click the Start Button, select "Run" and type "Telnet [host.domain]" in the Open Program dialog. If you typed

    telnet fedworld.gov

that would launch your Telnet client and open the National Technical Information Service bulletin board system that provides a gateway to online services of many federal agencies.

On a Macintosh, you may launch your Telnet client in the same manner as any other program. On Windows, if at the Start | Run dialog you merely type "telnet" with no host and domain information you launch your Telnet client without opening a site. In either case, (Mac or Windows) you can connect to a Telnet server in one of two ways. If your Telnet client gives you a cursor in a command line, you need only type

    open fedworld.gov

If you don't have a command line, you would use your mouse to launch an open dialog from either a "Connection" or a "Session" menu.

After you connect to the site, you usually have to log on. Consequently, to use Telnet resources you have to know ahead of time the address and log-on procedure for the site you are visiting.

After you have logged on to the remote computer, Telnet is command line driven, meaning all commands to your Telnet client are typed directly at a prompt, rather than run by clicking with your mouse on some drop down menus. Indeed, you will not even seen your mouse anymore.

Closing Telnet Connections

Although opening a connection via Telnet is easy, closing a connection can be a little more challenging. If you are using NCSA/BYU Telnet or the Telnet client associated with Windows machines, select Close Connection, under the File button on the menu bar. If you are not using NCSA/BYU Telnet or another client with a graphical interface, the process can get a little tricky. When you first connect to a site, you don't know what type of computer is at the other end or what kind of software it is running, so you cannot be sure exactly what command will close the connection. After you have opened a connection, for the most part, you must use the commands of the computer you called.

Sometimes information detailing how to disconnect is provided when you first connect. For example, a site might display, "Escape character is '^]'." What that means is that by typing Ctrl-] (holding the Control key down and pressing the right brace key), you can escape the program and disconnect.

The combination (Ctrl-]) is common on the Internet. Other common commands for leaving programs include:

- Typing "Q" or "QUIT"
- Typing "E," "X," "EXIT," or "Ctrl-X"
- Typing "Ctrl-Z"
- Typing "Bye," "Goodbye," or "G"

A Sample Telnet Session

Opening and closing the connection marks the beginning and end of a Telnet session. What happens in between is important. Accessing information stored on the computer you called is the hard part. First, while thousands of computers are accessible via Telnet, many are not open to the public. You have to know specific log-on procedures. If you are logging on to a computer on your own campus or news operation, presumably you

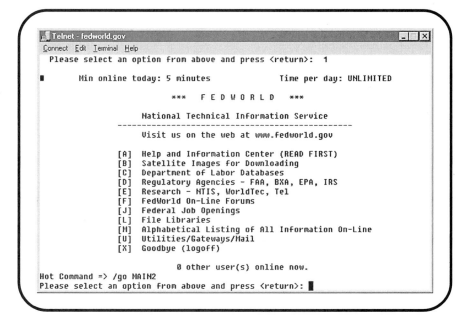

Fig. 7-1: The FedWorld BBS System maintained by the NTIS for the U.S. Commerce Department, requires you to select from menu options. You type the letter of the menu item to view that selection.

know the log-on procedures. Many Telnet sites require that you have a user name and a password (i.e., an account on that machine or knowledge of a public access account).

Other public Telnet sites may provide you with connect screens that offer advice for logging on to access special services. FedWorld is a BBS-type system available through Telnet. To access FedWorld by Telnet, type

telnet fedworld.gov

When you connect, you are prompted for your name. The first time you log on, enter "new," and FedWorld will ask you to fill out a form giving your organizational affiliation (your school or company), phone number, and address. You then choose a password, and you are encouraged to write it down so that future log-ons will proceed more quickly. FedWorld offerings include gateways to dozens of BBS systems run by various federal government agencies.

FedWorld currently automatically senses what kind of terminal your Telnet software is emulating. Some other Telnet sites require you to specify a terminal type during the log-on process. This is done so the host computer, the computer to which you have connected, knows how to read your keyboard and in turn how to speak back to your computer. Most communications software and Telnet client programs allow your

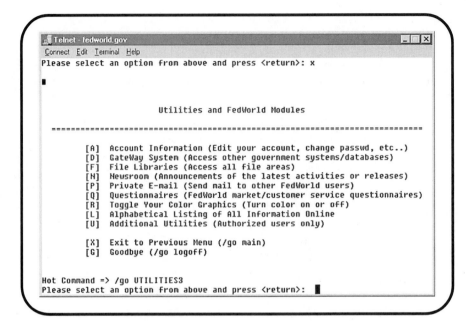

Fig. 7-2: A second level menu of the FedWorld BBS System gives you the option of selecting a "GateWay" to other government systems (choice [D]).

computer to "emulate" one of several different "dumb" terminals, often connected to larger computers.

Reflecting the legacy status of Telnet, commonly accepted terminals on the Internet are the DEC VT100 or VT102, which were used with minicomputers manufactured by Digital Equipment Corp. DEC is now owned by Compaq Computer Corp. If the site to which you are connecting asks for VT100 or some other emulation, be sure you configure your software to that specification. A few sites require an IBM 3270 terminal emulation. If you do not know what is required or accepted, try VT100 or TTY first.

At the FedWorld site, the registration process on your first visit establishes for you a user profile that FedWorld "remembers" for all subsequent visits. When you get past the registration and introductory screens, you are taken to a top menu in which you must choose whether you want to enter the FedWorld system or an Internal Revenue Service system. Choosing FedWorld brings up a new menu that offers several new choices (see Figure 7.1). Selecting item "[U] Utilities/Gateways/Mail" takes us to a menu from which we can choose "[D] GateWay System (Access other government systems/databases)" (Figure 7.2).

Through this system of menu hierarchies we finally work our way down to the Gateway Systems that provide access to dozens of U.S. government bulletin board systems. At the height of the system in 1994, more than 120 government agencies were represented, though now many have opted for the Web.

Capturing a Telnet Session with Log Utilities

When you bring files to your computer screen during a Telnet session, you can only read them unless you take advantage of a utility built in to nearly every communications program on the market—session logging. Session logging is like computerized photocopying. It copies all the text that passes your screen and writes it to a disk file that you name. You then have the full text on your computer so that you use it without having to re-enter it.

In the NCSA/BYU Telnet package, the session capture option is under the Session menu. In the Telnet client supplied with Windows, the logging utility is under the Terminal menu. Whatever your software, check your manual (or ask your systems administrator) for the procedure to start a log file or to log a session.

Most programs also allow you to suspend the log temporarily during a session. In Macintosh or Windows-based computers, you have a second option for saving information you find in a Telnet session. You can highlight text and copy it to the clipboard, then paste the text into a document in your word processor. You can actually have the word processor running in the background and switch between the word processor and your Telnet client.

Getting Help

As you explore your possibilities with Telnet, at times you may become confused about what to do. You can usually get online help in one of three ways:

- Type "?"
- Type "H" or "HELP."
- Enter the number, letter, or name of a menu choice.

Help screens generally summarize available commands. If you are accessing the network by telephone, be careful. Some Telnet commands may conflict with your communications software. For example, Ctrl-] is a common Telnet escape command we have noted. However, if you are using ProComm communications software, that key combination merely toggles on and off a status bar across the bottom of the screen; the command is not passed on to the Telnet host.

Moving Files with FTP (File Transfer Protocol)

Although reading and logging information found via Telnet serves many purposes, often you will find information on the Internet that you will want to grab and transfer to your own computer. It may be a large file located somewhere else or it may be a great piece of software available on the Net. The Internet protocol for moving large files around the Internet is called the File Transfer Protocol or FTP. FTP is also an excellent method for getting Frequently Asked Question (FAQ) files that abound on the Internet and address many topics.

When the Internet was first created, FTP was arguably the least friendly of all the Internet protocols. Over time, however, several excellent, friendly FTP clients have been developed. Moreover, World Wide Web browsers permit you to download files using the FTP protocol.

In general, FTP is used in two ways. The most common usage is in conjunction with the Web itself. A Web site will include a large file—often a video clip or an entire program—that will be transferred to the local computer in its entirety. In this scenario, when you click on an FTP link on a Web page, the first clue you have that anything is unusual is that you will get a screen labeled "file download" that will ask you how you want to save the file requested by your click. You designate where you want to save the file, and the transfer begins. FTP is used extensively to download software and software updates from the Web.

The second usage for FTP is when people set up FTP servers for the express purpose of letting others retrieve or send files that would be too big to send as e-mail attachments. For example, Aimee Kalnoskas, a science writer, was preparing a story on the work of the Cornell Theory Center (CTC), a major supercomputing center funded by the National Science Foundation and associated with Cornell University. Researchers at the CTC had created several striking visualizations of their research. Every visualization was more than a megabyte large.

Kalnoskas wanted to use the images to illustrate her story. Instead of having the researchers send more than a megabyte of information via e-mail or put the images on a disk and send them via regular mail, she had them put the images on an FTP server. She then fetched them within a matter of moments.

You can FTP large files much faster than you can e-mail them, and there are fewer limitations on what you can send. Often, authors who collaborate in writing books will transfer chapters via FTP.

FTP is also often used to post files to a Web site. In fact, HTML editors such as *Dreamweaver* from Macromedia, *FrontPage* from Microsoft, Adobe's *PageMill*, and Sausage Software's *Hot Dog* come with an FTP client to facilitate that process.

Anonymous FTP

FTP server sites operate similarly to Telnet sites. First you connect to the site. Then you must log on. After that you can navigate through the site to find the directory or files you want. At that point, you can then either retrieve a file or groups of files from that directory or place a file or group of files in that directory.

Many FTP server sites are private. That means you must have a user name and password to log on. But some are open to the public. Opening sites to the public is enabled through a convention known as "anonymous FTP."

In this case, when you connect with an FTP server, you enter "anonymous" as your user name and then give your e-mail address as your password. Because this is a standardized process, your browser can connect and log on for you.

When you log on under anonymous FTP, you have access to whatever files and folders on the FTP server are public. Commonly these are files and folders stored in a master folder called "pub" or "public."

Navigating FTP Server Directories

As noted earlier, several FTP clients with graphical interfaces are now available that translate your mouse clicks into commands typed to the FTP server. Those clients include

- For Windows: *WS_FTP*, *Cute FTP*, *Bullet Proof FTP*, *FTP Voyager*, and *1ˢᵗ Choice FTP*
- For Macintosh: *Fetch*, *Anarchie*, and *NetFinder*

These software programs put a pretty face on the FTP on your computer. You point and click on buttons, double-click on folder icons, and the software issues the corresponding commands connect to the FTP server, log on, navigate through directories and then send or retrieve files. Some of these clients, like *WS_FTP*, actually display a running log of the dialog between your client and the FTP server so that you can see the language of the "conversation" taking place. The files and directories on the remote computer are displayed in one window (on the right-hand side), and files and directories on your computer are displayed in another alongside the first (Figure 7.3).

Handling and Using Files

Once you have mastered the steps in grabbing a file and transferring it to your computer, you may not be able to directly put the file to use. Many files that are transferred using FTP are compressed. Not only do compressed files take up less storage space on a hard drive, they are more quickly transferred across the Internet. However, once you receive a compressed file, you must first decompress it before you can use it.

By convention, the file extension—the part of the file name after the "."—indicates whether a file has been compressed and, if it has, by what compression method. You might retrieve a file named "polyanna.zip." The extension ".zip" indicates that the file had been compressed and archived in zip format. In order to use the program, it would have to be "unzipped." Nico Mak Computing's *WinZip* for Windows and Aladdin Systems *Stuffit Expander* for the Macintosh can handle zip files and other compression and archiving schemes.

Other common compression schemes include .sit, native to the Macintosh, Compress/Uncompress (file extension .Z), and Pack/Unpack on UNIX (file extension .z). Fortunately, most decompression software – including *WinZip* and *Stuffit* are available via the Web. Some FTP sites will tell you in their welcoming screens about other compression schemes that the host site can uncompress "on the fly" if you follow instructions. See Table 7-1 for a list of common file compression/archive formats and the software needed to unpack the archive.

If FTP sounds complicated, it can be. But it is also one of the most efficient ways to transfer large files, software, and data. FTP is also a key to much of the collaborative work done by scientists on the Internet. For example, the Cooperative Human Linkage Center is a collaborative effort among researchers to map the human genome. In it, experimental data collected at the University of Iowa is automatically transferred via FTP for analysis at the Fox Chase Cancer Research Center in Philadelphia.

Fig. 7-3: An FTP session in WS-FTP presents the directory structure of the remote host (here Oakland University) in a right-hand window and your local directory on the left. You point and click while the client talks to the server.

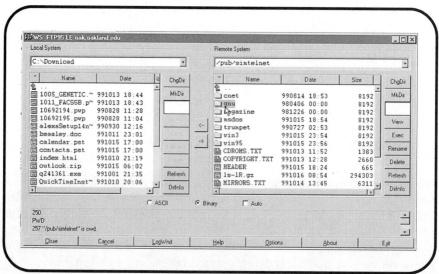

Although it requires effort to master, FTP can be very useful for journalists who need to access large files and graphics. Similarly, journalists and students who are publishing their work on World Wide Web sites will probably need to master FTP. The most efficient way to post material on a remote Web server is via FTP. Of course, Web servers are rarely "anonymous" FTP servers as well. Instead, you will need to have permission and a password to post material on a Web server. On the other hand, FTP means a journalist working for an online publication whose server is located in, let's say, Seattle, can post information via FTP from Washington D.C. as easily as a journalist sitting right next to the server itself.

Table 7-1: File name extensions provide clues to the nature of a file's contents and storage format. This table summarizes some of the more common file name extensions encountered on the Internet

File Ext.	Archive	PC	Mac	Extraction program to use
ARC	yes	X		PKUNPAK, ARCE, Aladdin Expander, WinZip
ARJ	yes	X		ARJ, Aladdin Expander, WinZip
COM	maybe	X		If archived, is self-extracting
CPT	yes		X	Compactor
DOC	no	X	X	Usually text-only file; may be MS Word (PC) file
EXE	maybe	X		If archived, is self-extracting
HQX	yes		X	BinHex
LZH	yes	X		LHARC, WinZip
MAC	no		X	Is a runnable application
PIT	yes		X	PackIt
PS	no	X	X	PostScript coded file; send directly to PS printer
SEA	yes		X	Self-extracting
SIT	yes		X	Aladdin Expander
TAR	yes			Should be decompressed on host/server
TXT	no	X	X	ASCII (text) file readable on any computer
WK*	no	X	X	Lotus 1-2-3 files usable by spreadsheet programs
WP	no	X		Word Perfect file
Z	yes			Should be decompressed on host/server
ZIP	YES	X		PKUNZIP, UNZIP, WinZip, Aladdin Expander

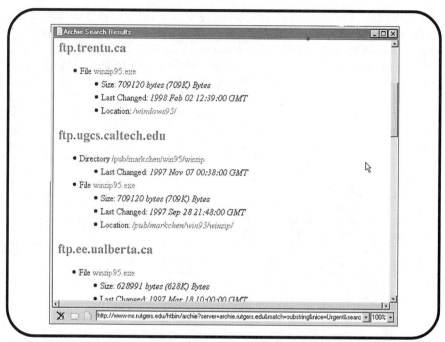

Fig. 7-4: Search results from the Rutgers University *Archie* server Web interface names the server first, then the directories, and finally the file information for matches to the search.

Finding Files Using Archie

Archie and FTP go together. *Archie* scours a constantly updated index of databases and archives for any "hits" on key words you provide for files that are accessible via FTP. What *Archie* returns to you is a list of directories and files whose names contain the word(s) you have given and can be retrieved via FTP, usually software. It is important to keep in mind that *Archie* is not a general search tool but only used for files specifically available for FTP. Nor will it access generic keywords such as "jpeg."

The listing of those files and directories is organized by host site. Below the name of each host site is a list of the directories and files whose names match your query. *Archie* indicates whether the matching object is a file or a directory, then reports full path information for getting to the directory or retrieving the file by FTP. Web interfaces to *Archie* search engines may be found at:

- http://www.ucc.ie/cgi-bin/archie
- http://www-ns.rutgers.edu/htbin/archie (gives instructions and different site options)

- http://marvin.physik.uni-oldenburg.de/Docs/net-serv/archie-gate.html

Each of these sites gives you options for selecting which *Archie* server you would like to do the work for you. The last site, in Germany, allows you to select your *Archie* server by nation. The Rutgers University site includes a brief but helpful set of instructions for using *Archie*.

Archie performs searches for specific files. You need to know the file name (or part of the name) first, and that is the name you give to the *Archie* search device. When *Archie* completes the search, you receive a list of files and directories matching your search terms, grouped by server names. *Archie* searches may be case sensitive. The report contains several tiers of information. The first tier reports the anonymous FTP host site. The second and third tiers report the exact name of the file and the directory path leading to the file that registered the hit.

Words of Caution

When you download text or software, you should keep several things in mind. First, remember that much of the material on Internet is copyrighted. With software, shareware programs put you on your honor to pay for them if you decide after a reasonable trial period that you like a program well enough to use it. Freeware is, as the name implies, free, but is still copyrighted. Other programs are in the public domain, which means that nobody holds the copyright.

Still other programs available in Internet archives are software in some state of testing. During testing periods, users are encouraged to report software bugs to the authors in exchange for free use of the program.

Whatever the situation, it's up to you, legally and ethically, to know the terms under which the software is distributed. Generally there is some type of notice provided with each program, often in the "README" file or the opening screen.

Finally, some software on the Internet may contain viruses that can damage your computer. You should only download software from reputable sources that you feel you can trust.

Jewels in Gopherspace

Before the creation of the World Wide Web, the Internet connected universities, scientists, scholars, libraries, government agencies, and research institutions that might benefit from sharing information. At that time, the Internet consisted mainly of larger mainframes and minicomputers. (Users of personal computers would use Telnet to log on to these larger computers.) These larger computers worked with a text-based interface as opposed to the graphical point-and-click approach now standard on personal computers.

Not surprisingly, then, in the early 1990s, just before the Web exploded in popularity, a text-based client/server application that could help people access files from across the Internet was developed. This service was called Gopher, because users of Gopher clients could "burrow" through the Internet to find information stored on Gopher. While the Web has largely superseded Gopher, there is still good information on Gopher servers. Moreover, Gopher has four other characteristics that recommend its use: 1) the mechanics behind delivery of Gopher information, 2) the way Gopher information is organized, 3) the stability of the Gopher protocol standard, and 4) the relative credibility of Gopher documents.

One of the great strengths of Gopher is its text-based delivery. That makes delivery of Gopher documents faster (all other conditions being equal) than a graphics-laden Web document. If what you need is words, you can access Gopher with the simplest of computers using the slowest of

Fig. 7-5: Web browsers display Gopher menus by adding the title "Gopher Menu" and indicating links to other menus with a folder icon. This is the top menu at the University of Minnesota's Gopher.

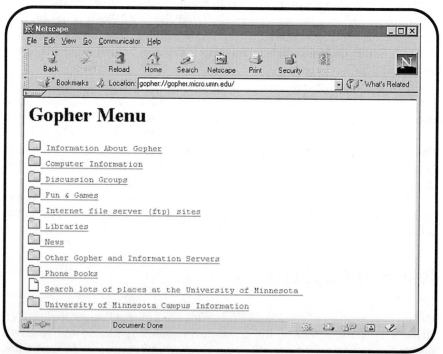

modems, and you won't have to wait forever. Text files are small, compared to graphics files, and they move relatively quickly over the Internet. Some Gopher clients can display graphics files, but that is not Gopher's strength.

Documents and folders on Gopher servers are organized into hierarchical menus. There is a direct, linear path from a top (or root) Gopher menu, through logical choices "down" to a document at the bottom of the menu tree. For people accustomed to working with the way libraries organize information by related topics, Gopher menu system seems familiar.

Furthermore, the Gopher protocol has been around since 1991 and has been well established since 1992. The Gopher standard for storing and delivering documents is not changing rapidly, in the way that HTML is. The net results are one has fewer problems with systems crashing or network hang-ups under the Gopher standard.

Finally, some people feel that documents stored on Gopher servers are often more credible and reliable than those found on some Web sites. It is extremely easy to post documents on the Web. The result is that a lot of material available is from people having no particular credentials, no experience, no special authority, or understanding of their topic. Anyone can claim to represent anything and place credible-looking documents on the Internet. Because of the popularity and the ease of World Wide Web access, many spurious documents turn up in searches.

Theoretically, the same thing could happen in Gopherspace. In practice, it rarely does. As an older technology, a less flashy one, and less widely documented, Gopher servers tend to exist exclusively at universities, government agencies, and serious research facilities. Thus, the relative number of entirely spurious documents in Gopherspace is much smaller, and persons deliberately trying to execute a Net charade face a more complicated task with Gopher.

Working Gopher

As with many other Internet services, Gopher sites can often be accessed using your Web browser. There are also some specialized Gopher clients for personal computers. Or you can Telnet to a mainframe or minicomputer that has a Gopher client.

A good place to get a taste of Gopher resources is through the University of Minnesota main Gopher server. If you want to access it through your Web browser, you enter gopher://gopher.micro.umn.edu in the address line or "open location" command. That takes you to a directory with 10 subdirectories. If you click on the subdirectory "Other Gopher and Information Services," you will be taken to a listing of "All the Gopher Servers in the World." By clicking on different servers, you can get an idea of what

Gopher has to offer. Unfortunately, you will find that many Gopher servers have been taken offline or have not been updated over the years.

To help find Gopher-based documents and directories, a pair of search engines was developed. These search engines went by the names of Veronica and Jughead. Veronica services are still widely available.

Washington and Lee University maintains a resource called the *Web Directory of Veronica Servers* that will help point you to Veronica servers around the world. The directory is available at gopher://liberty.uc.wlu.edu/ 11/gophers/veronica. Some other Veronica servers include:

- gopher://veronica.psi.net:2347/7
- gopher://veronica.sunet.se:2347/7
- gopher://veronica.unipi.it:2347/7
- gopher://veronica.utdallas.edu:2348/7
- gopher://veronica.uib.no:2347/7
- gopher://veronica.uni-koeln.de:2347/7
- gopher://gopher.umanitoba.ca:2347/7
- gopher://quasar.tach.net:2348/7

Conclusion

Although the World Wide Web has become the dominant way to post and retrieve information on the Internet, the Web itself is not the Internet. The TCP/IP protocol that defines the Internet includes three basic services—e-mail, which is still probably the most heavily used service on the Internet, Telnet and File Transfer Protocol (FTP). Although Telnet is now less widely used because there is less need to log on to larger computers to access the Net, it still has its applications. FTP has been partially absorbed into the Web. But there are still many situations in which it is necessary for journalists and journalism students to understand the mechanics of transferring large files across the Internet. Gopher is an older precursor to the Web itself. Though generally obsolete, there are still some good resources that a determined reporter can find.

Journalists should not make the mistake of thinking that the Web is synonymous with the Internet. Familiarity with beyond-the-Web resources will increase the number of tools available for doing story research.

Evaluating Net Information

By now this story is legend. A science writer for a prominent U.S. daily newspaper was looking for information on predicting earthquakes. The reporter searched the Internet and found what seemed to be treasures of information. But following the dictum of the old Chicago City News Service to "check it out," the reporter dug deeper into the information. What initially looked like a lot of good material on closer investigation turned out to be based mostly on astrology.

The Internet has made more information more available more readily to more people than any other medium. There is a lot of great, reliable, credible information out there on the Internet. But there is also a lot of junk. One of the strengths of the Internet is that anybody *can* put stuff up on the World Wide Web. One of the problems is that is seems as if everybody *does*. There's no clearinghouse through which information must pass before being posted. There is no guarantee that people who post information on the Internet have any expertise in the areas in which they are offering information. Nor is there any assurance that people who post material to the net share the same concern for accuracy that good reporters do.

For good reporters, the challenge is this: How do you know when you have trustworthy information? How can you evaluate the quality of information you pull off the Net?

Reporters must develop strategies to evaluate information found on the Web. In this chapter, readers will

- understand how to evaluate the production quality of a Web site,
- learn to use domain checks for information ownership verification,
- understand how to assess confidence levels for site ownership,
- employ the Whois database to authenticate site ownership,
- know the MIDIS system to weigh integrity of data found on the Internet,
- comprehend protocol "weight" and other internal document checks, and

- be reminded not to abandon traditional tools of journalism to check the credibility of Internet based information.

Understanding the Problem

If you visit a Web site or correspond with someone by e-mail, you generally have no way of knowing who the person at the other end really is. In some ways, the situation is similar to relying on the telephone. Until you develop some kind of tested relationship, you do not know the distant person's credentials or even if the person is who he or she claims to be. However, if you placed the call, you are working with some confirming evidence. The phone number you dialed and how the phone was answered provide you with corroborating (or undermining) evidence that you reached your intended party. If you make repeated calls over time, you begin to develop tested relationships with the distant people and you even recognize voices of the people you talk to.

However, when you are working with the telephone, you have confirming evidence, which is taken for granted because the telephone is such a commonly used tool. First, before you can place the call, you must obtain the phone number. When you dial that number, the manner in which the phone is answered may corroborate or undermine the notion that you have reached your intended source. For example, if you expect to talk to a vice president of a company and the line is not answered in a businesslike fashion, you may question whether the phone number you have is correct. If you make repeated calls over time, you begin to develop tested relationships with the distant people and you even recognize voices of the people you talk to.

In a similar fashion, when you visit a Web site (or any other Internet resource), the address—like a phone number—gives you some preliminary clues about who owns the information being served. And other clues unique to the Internet help to provide evidence about both the origins of the information and its relative veracity. Over time, you may develop trusted relationships with Internet sources just as you do with other sources. First, learn from experienced online journalists.

Production Qualities

One of the first pieces of evidence you may wish to consider when evaluating the credibility of information on the Web is the quality of the Web site on which it is found. One of the first lessons journalists learn is that misspelling a person's name is a cardinal mistake. Misspellings cast doubt on the accuracy of the entire article. Along the same lines, if a Web site is poorly constructed, it may be an indication that the information contained has been poorly developed as well.

In September 1997, a group of journalists assembled at the Poynter Institute for Media Studies in St. Petersburg, Florida, for a seminar titled "Reporting with the Internet." Under the direction of Poynter Library Director Nora Paul, seminar members developed a set of criteria for journalist-friendly Web resources. The criteria addressed document and site sourcing, ease of navigation, and searching.

Reporters developed a document titled "Wish List . . . for Web page developers." The list can be simplified and organized it into three groups of recommendations. It suggests information that should be found on 1) the home page, 2) all pages in a site, and 3) somewhere in the site.

The *home page*, (also known as top page or splash page) in a friendly, credible Web site should have a clearly marked link to "about us" information, including e-mail, phone, and address of people who produced the site content and other owners of the site. This information can be useful in verifying ownership and validity of information. Seminar members also suggested that complete site navigation information (generally called a site map) be provided on the home page. A site map provides a quick overview of a Web site, indicating how extensive it is. More extensive sites require a greater commitment from the provider of the information

All pages of a Web site, the group concluded, should include the date the page was last updated. All pages, they suggested should be free from gratuitous graphics, excess advertising, and other clutter. The panel suggested that all links in a site should be annotated. That is, there should be a description of where the links will take you. For ease of moving about the site, there should be consistent icons for links, searches, and help. Finally, they concluded that all pages should be simple, and uncluttered.

Apart from the top page, and all pages designation, the Internet reporters argued that *somewhere* in the site should reside a search capability for the site and printable help files for the search dialog. There should also be a description of how the database was created and what it covers. Statistics in a site should be made available in text or other standard formats and not limited to Portable Document Format (Adobe Acrobat .pdf) files.

Many very good sites for journalists fall short in some area or another, but the best sites will tend to incorporate most of the characteristics. In fact, most journalists, readers, and viewers intuitively apply the same kind of criteria to traditional media. For example, a news program on the public access cable channel is generally seen as less credible than CNN, in part because CNN is more professionally produced. A photocopied newsletter does not generally carry the same weight as the local newspaper.

While you do not want to dismiss information out of hand simply because it is not on a professional Web site, certainly you should demand that any site you plan to use provide you with enough "about us" information that you can evaluate who is behind the site.

Domain Checks

Beyond "about us" files, many clues about Internet site ownership and credibility are intrinsically tied up in the sites domain name and to some extent the protocol used. The Internet domain portion of the Internet address may reveal useful corroborating evidence about the owners of the information you have "discovered."

The domain naming scheme adopted by the Internet Society (ISOC) may help you partially verify ownership of information you find online. Internet domain names were discussed briefly in Chapter 2. First, by way of reminder, top level domains (TLDs) are assigned during Internet domain name registration according to the type of institution that reserves the domain. Traditionally, the InterNIC, which is manage by the company Network Solutions, controls domain name registrations. Currently five companies including Network Solutions can assign and register domain names.

The seven traditional TLD assignments are: .com for commercial enterprises; .edu for educational establishments; .gov, government agencies; .int, international bodies; .mil for military establishments; .net, a network; and .org, a not-for-profit organization. Many sites include in their domain names the two-character ISOC country code for nation of origin. Seven new TLDs were approved in 1998 but were still not implemented more than a year later.

Just as the area code and prefix of a phone number provide clues to the phone's physical location, domain names provide clues to the location and the type of organization behind a Web site, e-mail address, or other Internet resource. If someone with whom you are corresponding represents himself or herself as a university professor, you would expect his or her e-mail address, Web and other Internet resources to be maintained at an address ending in .edu in the United States or .ac.uk in the United Kingdom. If it does not, you ought to find out why. Similarly, government officials and their resources will be found at .gov addresses. The answer you receive may affect your source's credibility.

Some TLDs are more reliable as ownership predictors than others, in part because some of the domain naming policies are more restrictive than others. A kind of confidence index can be developed around domain names.

Measuring Confidence in Site Ownership

Ownership of some top level domains is more restricted than others. To register as an educational, governmental or military Web site, the owner must meet certain criteria. There are few criteria to qualify as a commercial site with a .com suffix or as a .net site.

Because certain TLDs indicate specific criteria to qualify have been met, a Site Ownership Confidence System (SOCS) develops. For example, you will have a very difficult time securing a military TLD if you represent any group other than a clearly recognized military organization such as the Royal Air Force or the United States Navy. Thus, if a site bears a .mil TLD, you can with a high degree of confidence assume that the site is owned by a military establishment. Similarly, .gov addresses are tightly controlled; you can be fairly certain that e-mail messages or Web sites bearing a .gov address in fact originate within governmental bodies.

In a like manner, a very small handful of truly international organizations, typically of quasi-governmental nature secure .int domains. Thus NATO online resources reside at the domain nato.int and the European Union holds forth at eu.int. However, the United Nations uses the domain un.org.

At the opposite end of the spectrum, the .net domain tells us very little about the owner. The .net domain is reserved for networks. However, many network owners engage in Web hosting services, have become Internet service providers (ISPs), or in other ways open their domain to the world at large. For example, Staci Kramer, an independent journalist based in suburban St.Louis., Missouri, maintains an account with Concentric Network. She pays a monthly fee. For that fee, she receives Internet access, an e-mail address (mailbox) at concentric.net, and 5 megabytes of space to post her own Web pages. Whether you send mail to her at cris.com or concentric.net it is the same. Like Staci, thousands of other subscribers from all walks of life and all parts of North America have concentric.net addresses. The .net portion of the address tells us nothing about the owner. And Concentric Network is not unique. Dozens of other networks offer .net addresses to anyone who pays a nominal subscription fee.

Slightly better, the .org domain promises us that the owner is affiliated with a not-for-profit organization. Beyond that, we don't know whether the organization is

- a philanthropic foundation (such as the W.K. Kellogg Foundation at wkkf.org),
- an activist group (Institute for Global Communications, igc.org),
- a research institute / think tank (like the Hudson Institute, hudson.org),
- an educational operation (like National Public Radio, npr.org),
- a professional interest group (like Investigative Reporters and Editors, ire.org), or
- a public information consortium (disasterrelief.org).

The difficulty is that nonprofit organizations come in all stripes. The .org domain will confirm for us that the owner is a nonprofit, but no more.

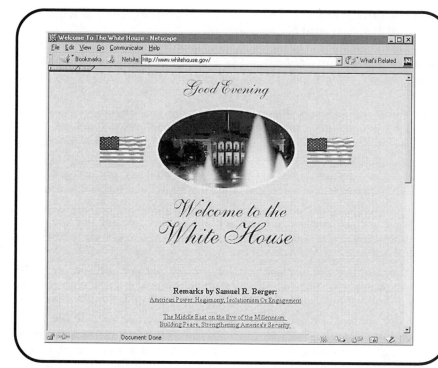

Fig. 8-1: The genuine U.S. White House site uses the domain whitehouse.gov. A group of satirists owns the whitehouse.org domain and occasionally has a splash page that closely resembles this one. The whitehouse.com site is given over to pornography.

For a reporter hoping to understand who or what is behind information residing at a .com address, the message is mixed. On the "not helpful" end of the spectrum, much that was said about .net addresses can be said about .com. Internet service providers by the barrel issue to their subscribers addresses ending in .com. Two commercial services offering customers Internet access—America Online and CompuServe—count between them more than 10 million subscribers. Add to this hundreds of thousands of commercial enterprises with their own domain names, and you have a sense of the vast range of individuals, businesses, and organizations that could be included under the .com address.

The good news is that high profile companies, and those with trademark names have precedence in securing .com addresses. Thus a journalist receiving e-mail from someone or visiting a Web site with an ibm.com address can be relatively confident that the originating source belongs to the large computer company, IBM. In the case of trademark names, then, if the trademark name or abbreviation precedes the .com TLD, confidence of ownership increases.

However, the issue of "cybersquatting" continues to be a problem. Some enterprising people have registered the names of some well-known companies with the idea of selling the domain names back to the companies for a hefty profit. The companies claim that they own the right to their names. There are several proposals circulating to solve disputes over cybersquatting but an acceptable balance between large companies and individuals who may have a perfectly legitimate need for a specific domain name has not been resolved. Consequently, you cannot always be certain that a domain name is linked to an obvious company or institution.

Moreover, some people will try to use the name of a well-known institution with a .net or .com suffix to attract unsuspecting visitors. For example, http://www.whitehouse.gov/ is the URL for the U.S. White House. But http://www.whitehouse.org/ is a satire site, and http://www.whitehouse.com/ contains pornography.

A fair level of confidence generally may be assigned to .edu addresses. Customarily, schools and research institutions are the only organizations that receive .edu addresses. Thus Harvard University serves up information at harvard.edu. Harvard serves as a good example to show how the domain names work for many universities. A generic Web address for a great majority of universities in the United States would follow this pattern: http://www.*name_or_initials*.edu in which you insert the name or initials of the university in question. Thus Stanford University is found at www.stanford.edu; University of Maryland at www.umd.edu, Ohio University is at www.ohio.edu, and so forth. The system gets sticky when you have two or more schools with similar names or initials.

For example, in the United States, both the University of South Carolina on the east coast and the University of Southern California on the west coast answer to the initials, "USC." On the Internet, only one may be usc.edu. That nod went to Southern Cal, so the Gamecocks in South Carolina took sc.edu. It is even more complicated with OSU, three state universities going by those initials: Oklahoma State, Oregon State, and Ohio State. Their domain names are okstate.edu, orst.edu, and osu.edu respectively. There are four Loyola colleges or universities in the United States: Loyola College in Maryland is loyola.edu. Loyola University in New Orleans is loyno.edu, Loyola University in Chicago is luc.edu and Loyola Marymount in Los Angeles is lmu.edu.

This *name-or-initials* .edu system works best with schools in the United States. Other nations may adopt slightly different schemes.

In the United Kingdom, university domain names conclude .ac.uk, with no .edu. Thus University of Cambridge adopts the address cam.ac.uk, after the river for which Cambridge was named. Similarly, Oxford University is ox.ac.uk. In London, City University is city.ac.uk, and University College is ucl.ac.uk. Australia's system is similar to the United States— just add .au to the .edu. Thus Queensland University of Technology is

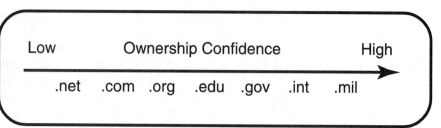

Fig. 8-2: Top-level domains suggest relative confidence for site ownership. The .mil designation is tightly controlled; you can be confident that the owner of such a site is in fact a military agency.

found at qut.edu.au, University of Sydney is usyd.edu.au, and University of South Australia is unisa.edu.au.

From the perspective of assessing source credibility, there is a problem with the .edu top-level domain. The difficulty with .edu addresses is that universities and grade schools alike receive the same TLD. Thus unless you have a clearly recognizable university, you could be dealing with material created by some grade school class.

Moreover, many universities have tens or even hundreds of Web servers running. For example, the new media center at Loyola College in Maryland has the address nmc.loyola.edu. Students often post information on the site. Even though the site is sponsored by a university, you must investigate who actually posted the material even if the TLD is .edu

One other complication is that a handful of "non-school" research organizations use the .edu domain. For example, the Brookings Institution think tank uses brookings.edu, and the National Academy of Sciences nas.edu. A quick, cursory reading of a site or e-mail address may not be enough.

In sum, a hierarchy of confidence emerges regarding the use of domain names as an indicator of site and information ownership. At one end of the confidence scale are .mil and .gov addresses. With these addresses, we can feel confident that the owners are military or government agencies. At the other end are .net addresses. Overall, confidence level for Internet site ownership can be summarized by the Figure 8-2.

Using the Whois Database

The ownership confidence scale is a "quick fix," a first impression check on site ownership. As the telephone area code tells us that "yes, indeed, we are calling someone in Omaha," the domain name gives us a light check on ownership for any site we are viewing or e-mail we are receiving. There exist on the Internet several utilities that probe domain name ownership

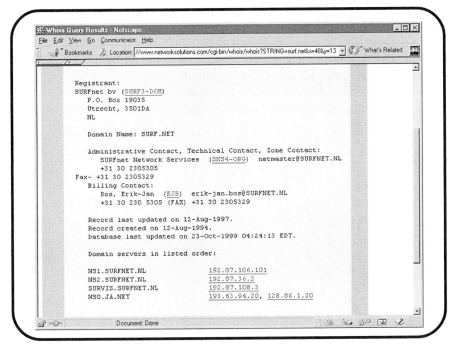

Fig. 8-3: Queries to the Whois database tell you basic information about the ownership of domain. Here, a query on "surf.net" reports mailing and e-mail addresses, phone numbers, and the name of contact people in the Netherlands.

databases and report ownership, providing the name of the organization, usually the name of two individual contact persons, and telephone numbers. At the heart of all these utilities is the Whois database.

Network Solutions, Inc. of Herndon, Virginia, manages InterNIC domain name registrations. You get access to their database and to other related databases at http://rs.internic.net/cgi-bin/whois. The site presents a form into which you type the domain name for which you are seeking information. The page also provides links to more specialized look-up sites. One of these, http://www.arin.net/whois/ permits you to insert the IP (numerical) address of an Internet site for which it reports the same information as the InterNIC Whois.

The basic Whois service at internic.net works only on .com, .org., and .net addresses, primarily in the United States. To search for European site ownership, use http://www.ripe.net/db/whois.html. For Asia Pacific addresses, use http://www.apnic.net/apnic-bin/whois.pl. For U.S. military site information try the Department of Defense database at http://www.nic.mil/cgi-bin/whois. To search the U.S. federal government database, try http://www.nic.gov/cgi-bin/whois.

Weigh Data Integrity Using MIDIS

Journalists have different uses for information. For example, information found on the Web might be for background only. In those cases, the level of integrity is not as crucial as for other uses.

The coin in trade for most reporters is credible, quotable information. Credible information is information that either the reporter believes is true or that the source of information believes is true and the reporter believes the source is in a position to know. Quotable information is credible information that the reporter wants to present as coming directly from a source.

To evaluate whether information is quotable, Stephen Miller, Assistant to the Technology Editor of the *New York Times*, has developed a system for weighing the integrity of data found online. TLDs are at the center of the system, which he calls the Miller Internet Data Integrity Scale (MIDIS). Whereas SOCS suggests criteria for developing confidence in the ownership of sites and of e-mail addresses, MIDIS addresses the relative reliability in data found there. Significant overlap marks the two systems.

Miller observes that "too much faith has been placed in information generated by computers." He notes that people are behind all information (and data) found on the Internet. He further observes that the world is occupied by "good people who tell you the truth" as well as "bad people who tell you lies." Most of the world is somewhere in the middle, Miller suggests. His MIDIS scale is designed to help reporters determine whether information pulled from the Net can be trusted.

Highest on Miller's list for trustworthiness are government sites. He observes that U.S. federal sites use the TLD of .gov. "While you might personally question the data, you are safe in quoting from it," Miller observes. He includes among his most-trusted government sites, those of municipal and state governments in the United States. State government URLs follow the pattern, http://www.state.*statecode*.us in which the word *statecode* is replaced by the two-character postal code for the state in question. Thus, the address for the official state government Web site for Michigan is http://www.state.mi.us/. City government sites also follow a pattern: http://www.ci.*cityname*.statecode.us/ in which you use the same, two-character state code as you use for state Web sites. The "cityname" portion of the address is a little less consistent. You'll find Atlanta at http://www.ci.atlanta.ga.us/; but Los Angeles is at http://www.ci.la.ca.us/; New York is at http://www.ci.nyc.ny.us/; and Chicago is at http:// www.ci.chi.il.us/. Where city and county government addresses may be less than intuitive, the official servers are often available through state servers, which do follow a consistent addressing pattern.

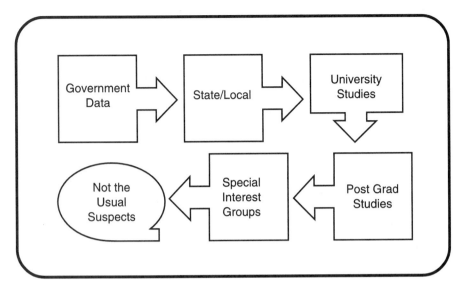

Fig. 8-4: Stephen Miller's Internet Data Integrity Scale (MIDIS) attributes the highest level of integrity to government data, "which, in any case, is quotable." University studies are next, and so on.

Next on Miller's "trust meter" are university studies that have been peer reviewed. They are found, typically at the .edu addresses of the university in question. "Quoting from these studies is also a safe bet with attribution," Miller asserts. "In addition to professors at universities, doctoral candidates often publish ongoing research on the Net. Much of this is also peer reviewed."

Third level of trust goes to what Miller calls "Special Interest Groups." He writes, "Even though we know that these groups have a political agenda, it does not follow that their data is flawed. It's also safe to use the data since it is attributable."

At the bottom of the Miller scale is the rest of the Internet. Miller characterizes his "other" category as "information published on someone's home page. Since anyone can put anything on a home page it's a coin toss as to whether the data has any validity. The one saving grace of personal/vanity home pages is that there is usually some information about the owner and a way to reach them, either by e-mail or by phone."

Protocol Weight and Other Internal Checks

Stephen Miller's MIDIS system uses organizational sources to weigh data reliability. Another indicator of data reliability is the protocol used to serve up the data. One of the biggest reasons for questioning reliability of data on the World Wide Web is that literally anybody can build a Web site. Hundreds of Internet Service Providers not only offer customers free disk space to create Web sites, but they also provide utilities to help people make those Web sites. Every day more people with no particular expertise add more noise to the World Wide Web.

But the World Wide Web is not the entire Internet. The Internet was "born" in 1969. The Web was conceived 20 years later and did not become a popular Internet environment until the latter half of 1994. In Chapter 2, we described the Web as that portion of the Internet governed by a protocol called HTTP or HyperText Transfer Protocol. Before HTTP standards developed, universities, research organizations, government officials, and large businesses were sharing information on the Internet using other protocols. Much data and information is still available through such other protocols as Telnet, FTP, and Gopher. Access to servers delivering up information in these formats is more restricted than access to the Web. That access tends to be limited to people who are more serious about research and collaboration. This more limited access on the server side of information endows that information with a higher degree of relative credibility.

Less-Used Protocols Add Credibility

Protocols enjoying the highest levels of credibility include WAIS, Telnet, and Gopher. The WAIS environment was created specifically to serve the research community. WAIS databases index resources at government servers, very large corporations, universities, and other research institutions.

Telnet protocol is native to the Internet—that is, it is built in to the TCP/IP protocol that governs communications among computers on the Internet. Telnet today is very much the same as it was when the first Internet connections were made. It gives a person access to computer resources at some distant point. It is as though you are sitting down at one of their computer terminals. Herein lies the key to Telnet's increased level of credibility. The people at the host site built a set of computer resources for their own use, and they are letting you tap into their system.

A library card catalog system is a good example. Library administrators catalog library resources for their own benefit and for the benefit of their patrons. On the simplest level, the online card catalog gives a user several ways to identify and locate holdings of a library. Books may be found by title, author, or subject. Audio recordings, artworks, or movies might also be located by genre. Other kinds of resources might be listed. More advanced library systems offer access to other library catalogs and some specialized databases. Some offer abstracts of books and magazine and journal articles. The point is that trained professionals who care about the system and the information it contains have created the system, and they are making portions of the system available to the world. Telnet resources tend to have a high degree of credibility.

Gopher was the first Internet browsing sytem released upon the world. The University of Minnesota relased the code for Gopher late in 1991, more than two years before widespread attention focused on the World Wide Web. Universities, government agencies, and a number of information keepers embraced the Gopher protocol enthusiastically, formatting large sets of data in Gopher's specialized text environment. While Web browsing has superseded Gopher, many resources are still available in Gopher format. Internet Service Providers do not routinely offer subscribers the opportunity to serve information in Gopher format. The result is that Gopher resources tend to be maintained by universities, government agencies, and large research groups. Their data tends to be among the more reliable on the Internet.

FTP servers are best known today for the software they dispense. Some government agencies and other organizations choose to use FTP servers to deliver archived text and data files. Federal Election Commission campaign contribution records, for example, are available as dBase files from FTP servers. Many public FTP sites exist, and data and information found in FTP areas is less reliable than WAIS, Telnet, or even Gopher. But generally, information and data served by FTP comes from people with a studied interest in the information they are serving. They may have an interest because they have a slant or bias, but at least they speak with some authority.

Newsgroups versus Discussion Lists

Usenet Newsgroup postings are less authoritative because anyone can and does file information. They do so with no particular authority and persons posting to newsgroups traditionally post under contrived nicknames. Thus Usenet postings may be seen as the rough equivalent to urban graffiti or random interviews with people on the street. URLs for Usenet Newsgroup postings follow the pattern "news:alt.politics."

E-mail discussion lists tend to be somewhat more reliable than Usenet news for several circumstantial reasons. The histories and traditions of the two protocols separate them. Usenet has tended to be a place where anybody can spout off on any topic. Insulting or derogatory remarks in the form of "flames" are common, and civil communication is not necessarily valued. Messages are posted on a virtual bulletin board where they might be read by the curious. Those who post to newsgroups often have no other contact with each other.

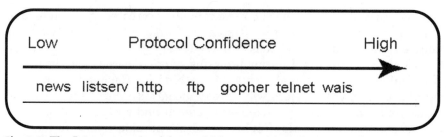

Fig. 8-5: The Internet protocol from which you retrieve data may also serve as a confidence indicator for the credibility of the data. Under this scheme, newsgroup postings are at the bottom of the heap while Telnet and WAIS generally get high marks for housing reliable information.

E-mail discussion lists, on the other hand, developed on the academic Bitnet where scholars gathered to collaborate on research and to debate research issues. Generally, real names, not nicknames, are used in sending messages that go directly to the mailboxes of list subscribers and presumably are read. Subscribers to the lists tend to be colleagues who know each other—at least by reputation—and might well meet together at association gatherings. The environment historically has encouraged thoughtful communication among respected peers.

These distinctions between newsgroup postings and discussion lists represent generalizations based upon historical traditions. In practice, you will find communities of sincere individuals exchanging useful information in newsgroups. In practice, you will also find spurious communications and junk e-mail online. Since the demise of the Bitnet as a separate educational network in the middle 1990s, discussion lists have proliferated to cover broader ranges of topics and to include people of all stripes, not just academics. Still, the cultures that defined communications in each protocol (newsgroups and e-mail discussion lists) tend to influence the kinds of communications engaged in today. In both cases, people post messages as individuals. The positions they take are not subject to company or other peer review. Again, they score lower on the protocol confidence scale.

WAIS databases tend to be maintained only by university scholars and serious research institutions. They tend, therefore to house credible information. WAIS databases are accessible on the World Wide Web, by Telnet, and by Gopher.

Taken as a whole, a new scale develops that provides the journalist with another measure by which to assess credibility of information found on the Internet.

Traditional Approaches

Working in a new media environment does not mean that journalists should abandon established journalistic traditions and practices. As a reporter, you need to know your beat. Sources need to be nurtured in the physical world, and they need to be cultivated in the online world. When you locate what appears to be a good source of information for your beat, spend some time "getting to know" the resource and bookmark it.

When you locate unique sources making unusual claims, you need to take appropriate action. Information needs to be verified through independent sources. Your experience and common sense should be brought to bear as you explore new resources in the online world.

Stand back from the trees and look at the forest. If information you find on the Internet doesn't match up with the rest of your life experience, you ought to doubt its credibility. Employ all the tests described in this chapter (SOCS, MIDIS, protocol weight, Whois) to assess credibility from new angles. Don't hesitate to use the telephone or printed resources. Credible Web sites will provide contact information for owners of the site.

A wise and ethical practice for news reporters is to confirm all critical claims through multiple sources. This is especially important if the claims you are reporting could damage someone's reputation or challenge conventional knowledge or provide your viewers and readers with information upon which they might take personal or professional action. If you find stunning information at one Web site, look for similar claims, *arrived at independently*, in other Internet resources. Use discussion lists and Gopher sites, Telnet, and other resources. Again, verify with telephone calls and/or printed resources.

Conclusion

As Stephen Miller notes in describing his MIDIS system, the world is occupied by "good people who tell you the truth" as well as "bad people who tell you lies." There are people who want to use journalists to further their own selfish ends. There are also people who don't really know what they are talking about. All these folks have the power to post information on the Internet.

Advocacy groups often adopt names associated with widely held ideals. "People for the American Way," in the United States for example, borrows prestige from the widely esteemed generality, "the American Way" to promote liberal social and political causes. At the other end of the spectrum, the John Birch Society graces its magazine with the name, *Public Opinion*, suggesting that the views expressed by the society are those held by a broad cross section of the American public.

In the online world, anybody can claim to be "Scientists for Colonizing Space." They don't have to be scientists, and they don't even have to have an organization. They can serve up documents to the world, pretend they have done research, and make their "research" available. It is your responsibility to use every tool at your disposal to verify source material.

Chapter **9**

Network News–Web Publishing

In the fall of 1998, Journal Publications launched the *Orem Daily Journal*, a daily newpaper with a projected circulation of 7,500. One of three Utah county newspapers published by the company, the *Orem Daily Journal* was to compete with the *Daily Herald*, a 33,000-circulation daily in neighboring Provo.

The *Orem Daily Journal* lost the competition. In July 1999, its publisher announced that the newspaper would cease distributing a print edition in August. It would, however, continue to be published online. Observers believe it was the first daily newspaper to move exclusively online.

The World Wide Web has followed cable television as a new technological platform for journalism. Increasingly, established journalists are moving back and forth between traditional "old media" and new media publishing ventures. Michael Kinsley has long been a star of inside-the-beltway Washington punditry. A former Washington columnist and then editor of the *New Republic*, Kinsley's face became recognizable nationally as Pat Buchanan's liberal adversary on the show *Crossfire* on Cable News Network. But in 1996, Kinsley suddenly left CNN and Washington, D.C. He was named editor of *Slate*, a new online magazine about politics and culture, funded by the Microsoft Corporation. When Hugh Downs retired as the host of the television news magazine *20/20* in 1999, he announced that he would work with iNEXTV, a division of Ampex Corp. dedicated to bringing online television to the Web. Downs was slated to work with Inextv's Executive Branch TV, which covers the activities of agencies of the federal government. After Lou Dobbs, host of CNN's popular *Money Line* business news program, clashed with his boss, he left to join a Web venture dedicated to reporting news and information about space exploration. Dr. George Lundberg followed his tenure as editor of the *Journal of the American Medical Association* with a position as editor of *Medscape General Medicine*, an online journal for doctors.

The street runs both ways. On the surface, Mike Riley seemed to be following the career path of a typical online journalist. After serving as a correspondent and bureau chief for *Time*, he headed up CNN's *Allpolitics.com* Web site, a primary source of political news on the Web. He then moved to new media ventures for *Congressional Quarterly*. But his next stop was to take the editor's chair at the *Roanoke Times* in Virginia.

And then there is Matt Drudge. Drudge won fame and notoriety as a purveyor of gossip and news scoops on the Internet through the *Drudge Report*. His reward, a show on cable television and then on ABC Radio.

New technology creates new vehicles to disseminate news. The great revolutions in newspapers in America in both the 1830s and the 1880s were made possible in part by improvements in papermaking and printing technology. Color photography contributed to a huge expansion of general interest magazines like *Life* and *Look* in the 1940s and 1950s. In those years, the movie newsreel was an important news medium. After World War II, television became the most powerful news medium. With developments in videotape, satellite broadcasting, and cable technology, cable television helped reshape and expand the range of news coverage. The Internet is the next new technology.

As well as a useful tool for reporters, the Internet, and particularly the World Wide Web, is emerging as a significant new medium for news. Companies large and small are scrambling to establish a presence on the Web. Publishing on the Web ranges from the lonely crusading writers in the best tradition of pamphleteers like Thomas Paine to the largest media conglomerates in the world like Time Warner.

This chapter will

- explain why the Web as a publishing medium has exploded,
- look at a range of news media initiatives on the Web,
- consider the challenges posed by online publishing, and
- describe the opportunity Web publishing offers journalists.

Why Online Publishing Has Exploded

Online publishing represents one of the most dramatic adoptions of new media technology in history. Compared to the penny press revolutions of the 1830s and the 1880s, or even the spread of radio in the late 1920s and early 1930s, television in the early 1950s and cable television in the 1970s, more people have gained access to the World Wide Web in a shorter period of time than have adopted any new media technology in any prior period.

The concept for the Web was first outlined in the late 1980s. By the late 1990s, more than 76 million people had access to the Web in the United States via their schools, places of work and at home. Moreover, the use of the Internet was expanding rapidly in Europe and around the world. The

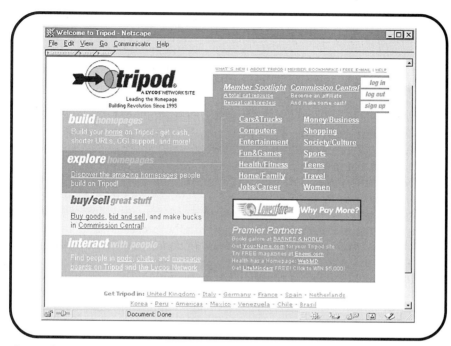

Fig.9-1: Sites such as *Tripod* (http://www.tripod.com) and *Yahoo!*'s *GeoCities* (http://www.geocities.com) that offer free space for Web pages and help in creating them have contributed to an explosion in Web publishing.

World Wide Web was the first international channel of communication widely available across national boundaries.

As important as the growth of a potential audience on the Internet has been the ability for very small publishers, and even individuals, to become online publishers. With television, for example, during most of the 1950s through the mid-1960s, many locations received only two or three channels. The introduction of UHF broadcasting increased that number to enable viewers in large cities to receive seven to ten stations.

Cable further increased the availability of programming. But, by the late-1990s, even state-of-the-art cable systems offered only about 75 to 100 channels. So, while cable television has developed a mass audience, only a relatively small number of companies develop programming for television. The cost to produce professional quality television programming is just too high, and the skills required are too specialized for many companies or organizations to fund the development of compelling programming.

To become a print publisher is also a risky venture. The cost of building circulation, printing the publication, then distributing it means that, in most cases, only companies with experience, expertise, and sufficiently deep pockets can afford to launch new ventures. While hundreds of new magazines are launched every year, most fail. No new major daily newspapers have been successfully established in the United States for many years.

The Web, however, has completely altered the publishing equation. First, because everybody with a Web browser can theoretically access any Web site (Webmasters can close their sites to the public should they choose), even the smallest online publisher can potentially reach the entire international online audience. Moreover, small publishers can register their sites with search engines and directories, assisting people who may be interested in the information they have to find their pages.

Second, the cost of building and maintaining a simple Web page can be extremely low. Many Internet service providers and large Web communities sites such as *Tripod* at http://www.tripod.com/ and *Yahoo! GeoCities* at http://www.geocities.com/ allow individuals to create their own home pages for free. And many service providers charge only nominal rates to host Web pages with up to 50 megabytes of information, which is substantial. This makes available a complete professional Web site with its own direct access to the Internet, running on its own server, for a minimum investment.

Economic Incentives

Adding to the incentive to explore Web publishing, the cost of distributing the information via the Web is fixed, no matter how much information is available on the Web site. To publish more information, newspapers and magazines have to print and distribute more copies, adding to the cost. With the Web, the distribution cost does not go up as you increase the amount of information available.

Given the economics of Web publishing, it is not surprising that all sorts of enterprises have been willing to experiment with this new medium. As they also were when radio was first introduced, daily newspapers have been ready to explore this new medium as well. By 1999, according to Chip Brown writing in the *American Journalism Review*, there were almost 5,000 newspapers online, with around 2,800 in the United States. According the trade magazine *Editor & Publisher*, around 2,350 daily newspapers in America had online editions. Revenue for the online newspapers grew from $21 million in 1996 to $203.7 million in 1999, according to the market research group Dataquest.

Newspapers are not the only traditional publishing medium to plug in online. Radio stations, television networks and television stations are also plugging in. Scores of affiliates of National Public Radio, for example, have created Web sites. Links to those stations can be found at the National Public Radio home page at http://www.npr.org/. And many commercial

Fig. 9-2: Traditional broadcast outlets have found the Web suited to their needs for several purposes. *BBC Online Network*, judged Best General News provider in the 1999 NetMedia Online Journalism Awards, offers audio and video, as well as still photos and text with their news stories.

radio stations not only have Web sites but also broadcast via the Web. Radio broadcasters are no longer limited to a specific geographic area but now can attract a national audience. Some companies are now broadcasting audio exclusively via the Web. Finally, nationally syndicated radio shows such as the *Rush Limbaugh Show* and *Dr. Laura Schlessinger* are broadcast via the Web.

Currently the Web is not as viable a medium for video as it is for audio. Consequently, few television stations are broadcasting extensively via the Web, though many are posting shorter clips. Virtually all the major networks and television news programs as well as many local television stations have created Web sites. Links to public television stations can be found at http://www.pbs.org/. An idea of how extensively radio and television has embraced the Web can be found at http://www.broadcast.com/, which serves as a Web broadcasting center for many radio stations and shows.

But perhaps the greatest stampede to the Internet has been by magazine publishers. Not only have Time, Inc., Hearst, and other major magazine publishers invested heavily in developing Web sites, many

Fig. 9-3: Magazine-style Web publications, called "e-zines" or just "zines" both flourish online and take advantage of new media possibilities. One leader in this new media field is HotWired at http://www.hotwired.com/.

small, entrepreneurial online magazines, often called e-zines (or just zines), have been launched. Perhaps the first Web-based magazine to capture widespread public attention was *HotWired* (http://www.hotwired.com/), the Web venture of *Wired* magazine, which, in the mid-1990s attempted to serve as the fresh, sassy voice of the online community. Online ventures such as *Slate* at http://www.slate.com/ and *Salon*, at http://www.salon.com/ have become viable players in the national political dialogue. *TheStreet.com* at http://www.TheStreet.com/ has earned a good reputation in financial reporting and *Feed* at http://www.feedmag.com/ is an interesting new literary magazine.

The Web is bubbling with innovative magazine-like efforts. Indeed, when a research team led by Kathleen L. Endres and Richard Caplan entered the word "zine" into the Yahoo search directory as long ago as 1996, they found the term listed in 1,146 categories. Ultimately, they sampled every tenth zine they found, building a database of more than 500 zines.

People Are Reading Online

While nobody knows exactly how many people use the World Wide Web, it is clear that the Web and online publications are being read. When special prosecutor Kenneth Starr's report on impeachment charges against President Bill Clinton were posted on news-oriented Web sites in 1998, their usage tripled. The number of page views at Fox Online reached 2.2 million at the height of the impeachment scandal. The *Washington Post* has reported that the page views of their Web site rose from 25 million a month when the Clinton scandal started to nearly 70 million a month when the scandal came to a close the following year.

A page view does not represent a reader. *Washington Post* officials calculate that 70 million page views translates to an unduplicated audience of 2 million users a month and nearly 300,000 a day.

The response to online publications has been strong enough that some are now charging people to subscribe. In the mid-1990s, the *Wall Street Journal* pioneered the effort to charge people to access online publications. In less than a month, it had signed up 30,000 paying customers, who paid either $29 or $49 for an annual subscription. Less than 40 percent of the subscribers to the Web site also subscribed to the print version of the *Journal*. The site was being visited by 32,000 to 40,000 people daily, the *Journal* reported. TheStreet.com has also charged for access, and set a target for 100,000 subscribers by the end of its first year as a publicly held company.

Media that attract readers also attract advertisers, who then may fund ongoing growth for the media. In 1995, researchers estimated that companies spent approximately $42 million for advertising on the Web. In 1996, reliable sources indicated that advertising revenues could jump more than 700 percent to $312 million. In the year 2000, advertising on the Web will have exceeded $5 billion, according to some projections. Mass media in the United States generate about $175 billion in advertising revenues a year, according to the market research company Veronis, Suhler and Associates.

In addition to promising increased advertising revenue and potentially serving as an alternate source of subscribers, Web publishing also offers media companies access to new readers. A survey partially funded by *Parade* magazine, the Sunday newspaper supplement, conducted to assess the attitudes of American teenagers about newspapers and online information sources, found that while 35 percent of teenagers between 13 to 17 never picked up a newspaper in a given week, 78 percent indicated that online information was fairly or very important in their lives. Online sources are rapidly growing as a familiar way to deliver information. The Web users, of course, are potential new readers for the newspaper. On the other hand, some readers of the *Times* may someday give up their subscriptions to the print edition in favor of the Web version, which is free.

Publishing Parameters

Despite widespread activity, online publishing, particularly on the Web, is still in its infancy. In fact, some pundits argue that the industry is still in its pre-history because a lot of the technology that will help the Web develop its own distinctive character is still under development.

As you know, many Web browsers still need additional "plug-ins" to play back delayed or real-time audio or video. Most browsers also do not yet automatically support multimedia material, fixed format documents (such as those demanding a PDF viewer), or three-dimensional images (which are developed under VRML or Virtual Reality Modeling Language). As these and other types of tools become more available, the content of Web publishing will change significantly.

But the browser is not the only technology which will improve. Java, Visual Basic, and ActiveX programming tools will allow Web developers to create new kinds of media and information applications to be delivered over the Web. The hype around Java and ActiveX (which allows developers to send small computer programs through the Web from server to the client where they perform their tasks) began to build in 1996. By late 1999, those efforts began to pay off, as Web sites offered their subscribers a range of specialized services such as shared calendars, personalized home pages, and low-cost video conferencing. Whether these applications will improve the quality of journalism on the Web, however, is not clear.

Between 1999 and 2005, the infrastructure of the underlying telecommunications network will be upgraded significantly. As information moves more quickly from server to client, new types of media content will be developed.

Although the best is clearly yet to come, current Web publishing ventures are extremely interesting. In this section, a sampling of different Web publishing concepts will be reviewed.

Newspaper Ventures: Large, Medium, and Small

The *New York Times* (http://www.nytimes.com/) has made an aggressive foray on the Web. Its publisher, Arthur Sulzberger, Jr., has joked that he plans to deliver the news through whatever medium is appropriate, including "mind meld," he told an audience sponsored by the Columbia Graduate School of Journalism. Although the opening page has the *New York Times* classic look and a late news update, the Web page does go beyond the print version.

First, the front page of the online edition carries up-to-the minute information from the major stock exchanges. If you own stocks, you can enter their symbol as well for a price update. Moreover, the front page has a feature that allows readers to search the entire site for the information they are seeking, which may be an easier method for finding specific stories than flipping through the newspaper. The search feature can identify

Fig. 9-4: Newspapers have been quick and aggressive in their ventures into Web publishing. The *Guardian* in London's *News Unlimited* site offers live coverage of sporting events, impossible for printed media.

articles from the current edition or selected articles from the past. There is also an archive of all the articles from the past year that you can search for free. But accessing entire articles costs $2.50 each.

In general, the Web site is divided into the same sections as the print version of the newspaper. But in addition to breaking news, the *New York Times on the Web* sometimes carries special sections not found in print. For example, in the summer of 1999, the business section of the *New York Times on the Web* carried a cluster of information about the nation's central bank, the Federal Reserve Board. The cluster contained past articles from the *Times* as well as background information, biographies of the Federal Reserve Board governors, testimony from Fed officials to different agencies and Congress and links to economic research.

The Business Links section reveals a trend that the Web may facilitate—the acknowledgement that many people rely on many sources of information, including several different newspapers. Through the *New York Times*, readers can get to the *Wall Street Journal, Barron's Online, Business Week, Money* magazine, and many others sources of information that are viewed as competitors in the traditional print world. It is

Fig. 9-5: The *New York Times Online* (http://www.nytimes.com/) presents a newspaper-like top page but includes a wide range of content to present stories in the site.

hard to imagine a story in the pages of the *Times* telling its readers to now refer to *Business Week* for more information. But the *New York Times on the Web* provides the functional equivalent.

In another twist, news stories on *Times on the Web* sometimes supply audio clips. When a fire at Rockefeller Center in New York injured a dozen people, the story in the *Times on the Web* included an audio clip from New York City's mayor, Rudolph Giuliani.

The Raleigh *News & Observer* (http://www.nando.net/) and the *San Jose Mercury News* (http://www.sjmercury.com/) are both mid-sized newspapers which were among the first newspapers to aggressively launch online initiatives. The founder of the *News & Observer's Nando Times* later went on to establish a company to make tools for programming for the Internet. Serving the Silicon Valley, the *San Jose Mercury News' Mercury Center* is an online showcase for Knight-Ridder, a large media company— it owns the *Miami Herald* and the *Philadelphia Inquirer* among other newspapers—which has invested heavily in new media technology.

Broadened Coverage

Both the *Nando Times* and the *Mercury Center* have used the Web to broaden their news coverage. For example, on a random day, the *Nando Times* had a story about an effort of composers in Romania to prevent their songs from being used in the election campaign and another about the support artists in India were giving to a painter who faced criminal charges for presenting a Hindu goddess in the nude. The *Nando Times* also carries a wide range of columnists and op-ed writers in its "Voices" section.

The *Mercury Center* supplied in-depth coverage of the Seybold Conference, an insiders' conference about multimedia publishing. The Seybold Conference was the type of event which used to pose a problem for daily newspapers. It was of deep interest to a small subsection of the readership. The Web page could satisfy the needs of industry insiders without stealing valuable news space for material of a more general interest.

The *Arizona Daily Star's StarNet* (http://www.azstarnet.com) has taken another approach to broadening its news coverage. In its News Links section, stories written by the newspaper's reporters are linked to related information. For example, a story about the legal troubles of former Arizona governor Fife Symington was linked to a section which included the full 23-count indictment charging him with criminal wrongdoing, a profile of the governor, an archive of past stories, and other links to information about Symington.

On a lighter note, a notice about a promising new jazz singer, Kitty Margolis, who was scheduled to perform in Tucson during the weekend, was linked to her home page. And, a story about the death of the designer of the G.I. Joe doll was linked to the Hasbro toy company's home page which displayed the entire G.I. Joe line.

The use of links to Web sites like Hasbro's has sparked a debate among some journalists. They question whether their news stories should be connected to Web sites which are essentially advertising and marketing ventures. It is an interesting question which surely will be the subject of ongoing debate as online reporting and publishing develops.

Magazines Climb Online

Unlike online newspapers, which have been primarily funded by existing newspaper companies, the Web has been a place of experimentation both for existing magazine companies and start-up ventures. The form, format and rhythm of Web publishing, which still depends primarily on text, graphics,

Fig. 9-6: In three years online, *Slate* has moved away from publishing original reporting and sees itself as providing summaries of events, dialogs, and shorter feature stories.

and periodic updates, compares closely to traditional magazine publishing routines.

There are several differences in print and online magazines, though. Unlike their print counterparts, Web magazines can be "published" incrementally as different sections are updated or changed. A weekly or monthly magazine may be changed virtually every day or even several times a day. Moreover, magazines can experiment with different types of information such as audio and video. Finally, since print magazines generally carry longer articles than newspapers, online magazine publishers seem to have been bolder in experimenting with new methods of gathering and reporting information.

Nevertheless, established magazine publishers have had to experiment extensively to find a winning formula on the Web. For example, Time Inc. launched one of the first and most ambitious online efforts in *Pathfinder* at http://pathfinder.com. *Pathfinder* served as the central home page for four Time Inc. magazines including *People, Money, Sports Illustrated* and *Entertainment Weekly*. The page also promoted *CNN Online* and *CNNfn* (a financial news service created in conjunction with *Fortune* magazine), as well as maintaining a link to *AllPolitics*, a political news service created by several major media players.

The presentation of *Pathfinder* was almost like a television set with 12 or 15 channels running at the same time. A viewer could choose any channel to watch or in which to participate. The site had chat rooms for real-time, live interaction and bulletin boards through which readers could express their opinions. You could also send letters to the editors of different Time Inc. publications.

Pathfinder was an attempt to fully embrace the Web as a new medium. But it failed. After an investment of tens of millions of dollars—an industry joke claimed that Time spent more money on its *Pathfinder* project than NASA spent on its mission to Mars of the same name—Time began to dismantle *Pathfinder* and allow each of its magazines to establish its own identity on the Web. And they have. In an online issue of *Entertainment Weekly*, for example, *EW* writer Ty Burr wrote a witty review of the Web sites of the major movie studios, of course with links to the sites themselves. There was also an article about the online buzz for Christian Bale, who starred in the movie *Little Women*. The article noted that there was four times as much talk about Bale on America Online as there was about Mel Gibson. The article supplied links both to Bale's home page and a Usenet newsgroup discussion.

Developing Unique Style

Like their print counterparts, the online magazines are developing their own style and approach. Among the most stylish, sophisticated, and intriguing new online publications are *Feed* (http://www.feedmag.com), *Salon* (http://www.salon.com), *Word* (http://www.word.com) and *Slate* (http://www.slate.com/). These online magazines are pioneering new ways to present journalism.

Slate and *Salon* demonstrate two of the many different directions online publications concerned with politics and culture have taken on the Web. *Slate* was launched in 1996 by Microsoft and edited by Michael Kinsley. In the first several issues, the Web publication posted long articles from leading political journalists. It has since moved away from original reporting and sees itself as providing summaries of events, dialogs, and shorter feature stories. The publication focuses a lot of attention on commenting on other publications and commenting on commentary found elsewhere. The publication has approximately 400,000 visitors who use its free areas. Interestingly, *Slate* is deeply integrated into Microsoft's MSN portal Web site, a portion of which runs along the bottom of Slate's opening page.

Salon was founded in 1994 with seed money from Apple Computer Corp. More visually appealing than the free areas of *Slate*, *Salon* sees itself as a "smart" tabloid on the Web. It won national attention in 1998 when it broke the story that the chairman of the House Judiciary Committee that indicted President Clinton for lying about his affair with Monica Lewinsky had also conducted a long-term extramarital relationship 29 years earlier. Many print publications had declined to carry the story.

Salon, which has about 500,000 visitors a month, is free, though it does offer what it calls "memberships" that cost $25. Members have a special area to chat with each other, receive discount prices to participate in The Well, a long-established online community that *Salon* purchased, a CD-ROM, a T-shirt and other benefits.

Salon and *Slate* demonstrate the challenges magazines on the Web face. Each has a distinct personality. Yet neither seems to have fully captured the dynamic possibilities offered by the new medium.

One of the more interesting experiments in trying to adapt the magazine format to the Web can be found at *VerticalNet* (http://www.verticalnet.com/). In essence, *VerticalNet* sites, though they are dubbed as online communities, are professional trade magazines for specific industries. But the sites have added Web features such as online auctions and e-commerce opportunities to supplement their editorial content. As many sites do, they also distribute e-mail updates to their content on the Web.

Television, Radio, and the Web

While it is not hard for publishers working within a traditional print model to see the potential of online media products, the scenario is different for radio and television journalism. First, the economics of production and distribution are far different for broadcasting than for print. In most cases, producing a professional television show is much more costly than a print product—why bother with smaller Web projects that will probably not attract as great an audience? Second, the distribution infrastructure for broadcasting is largely in place. Broadcasting more hours of programming does not affect the bottom line in the same way that increasing the print run of a magazine would.

As significantly, television and radio deal in high-quality video and audio. The telecommunications network infrastructure is not yet in place to easily distribute that type of programming. It is simply not yet really feasible to watch a half-hour of high quality video or audio via the Web. So, while it is innovative for a print publisher to include a 15-second video clip with an article, the same combination can be seen as a step backward for a television broadcaster, whose entire broadcast consists of video.

Despite the different parameters, television and radio networks such as Cable News Network, National Public Radio, and CBS are all experimenting with products on the Web, as are individual radio and television stations. Not surprisingly, CNN is running one of the most aggressive online ventures, *CNN Interactive* at http://www.cnn.com/.

Fig. 9-7: The *CNN Interactive* Web site content is enriched by associations with several other providers. The main site is connected to specialty sections for sports, for business, and for political reporting.

In addition to an ongoing breaking news service, *CNN Interactive* links readers to sections that deal with different areas of programming covered by CNN including U.S. and world news, weather, sports, entertainment, science, technology, and fashion. The home page also links to three related services. The first is *CNNfn*, a business news-oriented Web site created in conjunction with *Fortune* magazine. The second is *CNNsi*, a Web site for sports news created in conjunction with *Sports Illustrated*. The third is *Allpolitics*, a Web site for political news created by the CNN news operations.

The *AllPolitics* page demonstrates nice features with which the Web can liven up news coverage. After the vice presidential debates in 1996, *AllPolitics* provided a full transcript of the debate, highlight clips, and a poll for Web visitors to record who they thought won. Moreover, there was a contest for people to try to win a free T-shirt. And, for people who were really interested, there was an interactive, online game in which people could make their own strategic decisions guiding the campaigns of different presidential candidates. The *AllPolitics* Web site significantly increased the potential for interaction among users.

Many broadcasting efforts on the Web can be categorized in one of three ways. Like *AllPolitics,* there are attempts to increase interaction.

WJHU in Baltimore, Maryland (http://www.wjhu.org), invites listeners to respond to its talk show hosts via its Web site. Second, there are attempts to archive information. At the National Public Radio Web page (http://www.npr.org), for example, viewers can access transcripts and sound clips of past programs as well as to listen to its hourly news update. Finally, broadcasters use Web sites to distribute their schedules. WCPO, the ABC affiliate in Cincinnati, maintains a programming schedule as well as offering news capsules, transcripts and an archive of its investigative journalism at its Web site.

New Journalism on the Web

Although large and small companies have embraced the Web, perhaps the most intriguing element of this new medium is the potential for a single journalist to create a site that could make a difference. In the tradition of Thomas Paine, I.F. Stone, George Seldes and other pamphleteers and newsletter writers, a single person can publish on the Web, and perhaps make a difference.

For example, "The Consortium" (http://www.consortiumnews.com/) bills itself as an investigative zine. Published by Robert Barry, a former reporter for the Associated Press, *Newsweek,* and PBS Frontline, the Consortium for Independent Journalism was established in November 1995.

Stories covered by The Consortium include the reports that the U.S. Army's School of the Americas taught torture and assassination techniques to military officers from Latin America—a practice later renounced by U.S. Secretary of Defense William Perry. It has also published an interesting account of former Iranian president Abolhassan Bani-Sadr's allegations that the Ayatollah Khomeini had negotiated with a representative of then Republican presidential candidate Ronald Reagan about the release of American hostages in Iran prior to the 1980 U.S. presidential elections.

New Media Challenges

In the middle of the presidential campaign in 1996, a reporter for *HotWired* wrote a column concerning President Clinton's ethics. The piece had a link to a Web site which purported to detail Clinton's ethical failings. A White House staffer called to cry foul and the editors of *HotWired* agreed. They removed the offending link.

Publishing on the World Wide Web allows journalists to combine different kinds of information in new and different ways. But not every combination may be appropriate. Should movie critics link their reviews to sites designed to promote the movie Web sites? Should political correspondents

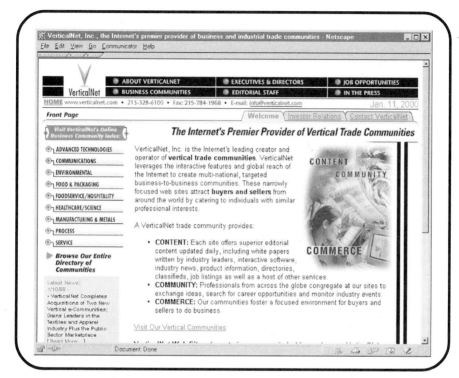

Fig. 9-8: *VerticalNet* sites are interconnected professional, trade magazines for specific industries. The sites have added Web features such as online auctions and e-commerce opportunities to supplement their editorial content. They also distribute e-mail updates to their content on the Web.

link their stories to the Web sites created by different political campaigns, candidates, or officeholders? Can journalists vouch for the credibility of the information on other sites which may be related to stories on which they have worked? Should they be required to verify all the information on linked sites?

The criteria for linking sites points to a second challenge for online journalism. How can journalists maintain the difference between online ventures which offer legitimate journalism and sites which are basically geared for marketing and promotion?

The issue and problem of clearly delineating journalism from advertising and public relations in media products has a long history. In the early penny press, advertising material was published in the news columns in exactly the same format as news items. In the early 1900s, reporters would sometimes freelance as publicity agents and place laudatory articles in the news columns of their newspapers. With the explosion in the number of cable television channels, infomercials—paid advertising which looks like a television show—have become popular.

Currently, in most cases, advertising and non-advertising is clearly marked in each traditional medium. On the World Wide Web, the potential to blur the differences between news and advertising and public relations is clear. With hyperlinking, journalists can easily connect a news report to a promotional or advertising site. Exactly where a journalist should draw the line in integrating links into stories is not clear.

A third challenge the new news media presents journalists is the issue of convergence. In the past, different news media have had slightly different mandates and have jockeyed to find their own niches. For example, most radio news consists largely—though not entirely—as an hourly headline service. Television reports news stories fit primarily into half-hour or hour formats. And, as the public increasingly received breaking news via broadcast, newspapers have offered more news analysis and trend stories. Each medium reports news in ways that utilize the technological strength of the media.

The Web combines attributes of the existing media with Web-specific characteristics such as interactivity and the ability to easily archive information. The convergence of different media on the Web presents a challenge to journalists to learn how each medium can be used most effectively.

At the same time, as the media converge in this new medium, will—for the first time—one medium completely lose its audience over time? Historically, one of the most notable features of communication has been that a new communications medium has never eliminated an older one (if you view facsimile as an updated version of the telegraph). After all, people still gather regularly for face-to-face meetings. Will computer-mediated communication be the first to drive an older medium from the news field?

Of all the media mergers which have taken place, online publishing has more examples of news operations with expertise in one media collaborating with operations with expertise in another. At some point, perhaps one of the underlying components will no longer be needed.

Or will online publishing develop its own voice, conventions and formats? Will publishing on the Web find its own niche in the news arena, leaving other niches to other forms? It generally takes a period of time for a new medium to find its form. The current form of the newspaper, for example, emerged in the late 1800s, after mass newspapers had been around for more than 50 years. In the early days of television, newscasts consisted of people reading the newspaper on the air. Only after videotape became widely available did television journalism truly create its own idiom.

In most cases, online journalism still consists of combining elements common in other media. News as a medium on the Web has not yet developed a style or voice of its own. Perhaps it won't until tools like the Java, ActiveX, and XML programming languages have had time to develop.

Finally, convergence poses another serious problem for journalism. If virtually anyone can publish online, what makes one site "news" or "journalism" and another site "entertainment" or "advertising?" Because the form is still in flux, what characteristics identify and distinguish the work of journalists and journalism from other content producers on the Web?

For example, before Microsoft launched its Microsoft Network online, it assembled a large newsroom to create news content to distribute. A few of the journalists working for Microsoft then tried to join one of the online discussion lists created for use by working journalists. The attempt set off a fire storm. Were journalists working for Microsoft legitimate or not? Would Microsoft Network news be real news or not? Viewed another way, what is the point of reporting about a professional football game online if viewers can go directly to the National Football League's Web site for scores and highlights?

Conclusion

In the past, journalism has represented one of the most competitive job markets in the economy. Many people were competing for few jobs. That led to low wages. Moreover, many entry-level journalists had to work for years for obscure and small newspapers and magazines before they could get an opportunity on high profile publications. Many talented journalists simply left the field.

The emergence of the Web as a publishing medium has changed that. First, the sheer number of jobs has increased dramatically. Moreover, news media have to compete in a broad arena to attract people with skills in creating Web sites. Consequently, Web journalists command higher salaries than many of their print counterparts. For example, in 1998, an entry level reporter in Carlsbad, New Mexico, could expect to make under $20,000 a year. An entry level online editor could earn twice that amount.

Finally, more experienced journalists do not have an advantage over younger journalists when it comes to Web publishing. As a result, online publications provide a great chance for young journalists to work for high profile publishing platforms early in their careers.

Of course, there is risk as well as reward in starting a career in online journalism. First, many of the entry level jobs consist of reformatting information reported by others for posting on a Web site. Secondly, in the same way that broadcast journalists sometimes find it hard to transition into print journalism, it is not clear that the skills used in online journalism would be appropriate training for journalism intended for other media. Nevertheless, online journalism is still in its infancy. As in print and broadcast, the pioneers are often richly rewarded.

In the news media, technological change has always led to great challenges. It also leads to great opportunity. With the emergence of the World Wide Web, journalists have an entirely new medium in which to practice their craft and their art, a medium unfettered by many of the constraints of other news media. The investment needed to launch a new daily newspaper is so great that few ever try. While there has been an explosion of news programming on television, it is mainly financed by large networks or television stations.

The World Wide Web is the first international communication medium which can be successfully used by companies of all sizes and individuals as well. And, the Web is still in its infancy. The opportunities it offers journalists seem to be virtually limitless.

With the Web, journalists are only limited by their own initiative, creativity and desire. Like television in the 1950s and 1960s, new forms for journalism are being developed. And, like television from that period, when people look back at the online world today, undoubtedly they will see a golden age.

Chapter **10**

Law, Ethics, and the Internet

In 1998, one man reporting from his cramped one-bedroom apartment in Los Angeles shocked the world by posting on his Web site that *Newsweek* magazine was prepared to publish a story that the President of the United States had conducted a sexual liaison with an intern serving in the White House. With that posting, Matt Drudge burst into the public view, considered by many to be the first quintessential cyberjournalist. While the leads for his first stories purportedly came from the trash cans of the gift shop at the CBS studios where he once worked, Drudge now does the majority of his reporting from his home, where he is plugged into the Internet, watches television, and has a satellite dish. Informants also send him rumors, which he then posts on the Web.

Reporting rumors without verifying them can be dangerous for journalists, however. In fact, in August 1997, the *Drudge Report* carried a story that Republican political operatives were planning to spread a rumor that White House aide Sidney Blumenthal had beaten his wife. Blumenthal protested that the report was false. And although Drudge retracted the information and apologized the next day, Blumenthal slapped him with a $30 million libel suit. Blumenthal also named America Online, Drudge's Internet Service Provider, in the suit. And while the charges against AOL were dismissed, the case against Drudge was allowed to proceed, a substantial burden for a person with a reported net worth of less than $20,000.

The Internet and computer networks in general are not outside the boundaries that generally govern speech and communications media in America. But, precisely how the Internet will be regulated is still being debated. Computer communication networks, including the Internet, represent new media for expression. Because messages are usually written, computer-based communication functions much the same as print media. Because information can be widely distributed via networks providing one-to-many communication, conceptually it also functions to some degree in the manner of cable television. Because some messages appear to be private and because the federal government has played a large role in establishing the network infrastructure, the Internet itself can be seen as something akin to the post office or to the telephone system before it was deregulated. Because information can appear on people's computers in their homes without their having requested it, some computer networks resemble broadcast networks. And, because children can access and use computer-based networks relatively freely, these new media may face added scrutiny from the courts, which have a special mandate to protect children from certain categories of speech, including indecent language.

Ithiel de Sola Pool noted in his book *Technologies of Freedom*, that different media are regulated differently depending on the environment which existed when they came into prominence. Despite the simple phrasing of the U.S. Constitution's First Amendment, television has a different level of First Amendment protection from print media. And cable television is regulated still differently. Neither came into prominence until long after the First Amendment was written.

The regulatory landscape for computer-based communications is in the process of being charted. The legal and ethical rules are not yet established. For journalists, computer-based communications have several functions. Computer networks serve to gather and to report information. They are also vehicles for expression.

This chapter will

- look at regulation concerning the Internet as a medium of expression relative to obscenity, libel and copyright issues,
- review three areas in which the Internet is used as a tool for reporting—confidentiality, freedom of information, and open meeting laws,
- touch on other issues involving free speech and computer-based communication, and
- examine some of the ethical dilemmas reporters using electronic communications resources may face.

The objective of this chapter is not to issue definitive legal or ethical opinions. Those will be worked out in practice and in court. Instead, it is intended to raise some of the key questions journalists, lawyers, publishers, students, and citizens confront as they incorporate this new communication medium into their daily work routines. The law cited in this chapter is primarily law as it exists in the United States of America, in many ways the most liberal nation regarding journalistic freedom in the world. The principles discussed apply as well—if not more fervently—to journalists in other nations.

Free Speech and the Internet

In February 1996, as part of a sweeping reform of the telecommunications industry, the United States Congress passed the Communications Decency Act. Drawing from language used to regulate television broadcasting, the bill banned the use of the Internet to transmit or display "indecent" or "patently offensive" material to children under the age of 18. Violators could be fined or sent to prison for up to two years, or both.

The legislation set off a storm of controversy. Proponents of the bill argued that there was a need to safeguard children from sexually explicit material readily available via the Internet. Outside cyberspace, they argued, there are laws to restrain the display of sexually graphic pictures in public places and the selling of pornography to children.

Opponents countered that the public must be able to use the Internet to access any information they desire. Because users must proactively search for and request what they want to appear on their screens, the proposed regulations would not only prevent children from getting the questionable material, but adults as well would be denied access to information to which they were legally entitled. Material that was perfectly legal in print would be banned from the Internet. As one attorney put it, Congress "cannot ban 'indecent' speech among adults and cannot do so on the Internet as well." Opponents also argued that the law was unenforceable and that parents, rather than the government, should be responsible for controlling their children's access to undesirable material.

To challenge the law, a coalition of 37 organizations joined a lawsuit. The coalition included online information services such as CompuServe and America Online, Internet Service Providers such as Netcom, computer companies, including Apple Computer and Microsoft, civil liberty organizations, and professional groups, including the Society of Professional Journalists and the American Society of Newspaper Editors.

In 1997, the U.S. Supreme Court ruled that the provisions of the act were unconstitutional. In the majority opinion, the Court argued that speech on the Internet could not be restricted to what could be acceptable for children, and the provisions of the Communications Decency Act would unduly burden adult-to-adult communication. Government regulation of speech on the Internet would interfere with the free exchange of ideas in society, which the First Amendment was created to protect.

With that ruling, the Supreme Court gave the Internet broad First Amendment protection, similar to the protections enjoyed by newspapers and print media and more extensive than those associated with broadcasting. But the full extent of those protections have still to be determined.

For example, in Portland, Oregon, a Web site was created to oppose abortion. Among pictures of damaged fetuses and dripping blood, the site had a list of doctors who performed abortions. Doctors who performed abortions who had been killed were crossed off on the list. The names of those who had been wounded were shaded in gray. The site also contained photographs, home and work addresses, phone numbers, and other information about doctors performing abortions.

Some of the doctors involved and Planned Parenthood of America sued the Web site operator, claiming the site violated the Freedom of Access to Clinic Entrances Act of 1994, which made it illegal to intimidate by force or threat of force people involved in providing reproductive health services. The Web site operator claimed the information reflected political speech about the issue of abortion and was protected by the First Amendment. The jury agreed with the doctors. The site was taken offline.

Libel Considerations

Clearly, anybody can say whatever he or she wishes online. As with print and broadcast media, there are restraints against libel, copyright and misappropriation violations, obscene speech, and privacy violations.

Libel laws are perhaps the most significant for journalists. The overwhelming majority of news reports name people. Sometimes published information contains false information that may damage reputations of people. Libel laws specify the criteria defining when journalists can be punished for publishing false information that may hurt other people.

In the landmark 1964 *New York Times v. Sullivan* case, the U.S. Supreme Court ruled that the news media could not be punished for libel for reporting false information about public officials unless plaintiffs demonstrated that the journalists had acted with "actual malice." The court defined actual malice as a reckless disregard for the truth. The court reasoned that American democracy depended in part on a vigorous press, but a vigorous press was bound to make mistakes from time to time. Therefore, the press needed "breathing room" in which it could make mistakes without being punished.

Since then, the court has issued a series of rulings in which it refined the *Sullivan* decision. In *Sullivan* and in subsequent cases the court has maintained separate libel standards for public versus private figures. In *Gertz v. Robert Welch Inc.* (1973), it ruled that the *Sullivan* standard applied to public figures who had thrust themselves into the forefront of public controversies or had involuntarily been thrust to the forefront. The *Sullivan* standard did not apply to private figures who had neither thrust themselves nor had been thrust into the public arena. For private people, the states are free to develop their own standards for libel as long as they do not impose liability without fault.

In the 1989 *Harte-Hanks Communications v. Connaughton* decision, the court opined that the media exhibited "actual malice" if the reporters or editors most likely knew that the information they planned to publish was false, and they deliberately avoided acquiring the knowledge that would have confirmed the probable falsity of the information. In 1990, the court decided, in *Milkovich v. Lorain Journal Co.*, that "opinion" did not necessarily fall into a separate category regarding First Amendment protection. If an opinion column contained information that was demonstrably false and damaging to a person's reputation, the reporter and publication or broadcast company could be punished for libel.

Finally, in 1977, the Second Circuit Court of Appeals decided in *Edwards v. Audubon Society* that reporters and publications could not be punished for libel if they published attributed information from sources which they believed were reliable and credible, even if that information ultimately proved to be false and harmful.

The rules of libel, of course, apply to all journalists. But reporters using the Internet and other electronic communication networks have to be particularly sensitive to potential problems. The first potential pitfall is the notion of a public figure.

What Is a Public Figure?

In some ways, computer-based discussion lists and network newsgroups are new types of public forums—forums in which individuals can be as vocal as they choose. Unlike other types of public forums, people on computer networks do not need a particular expertise to be recognized by people with authority, such as the moderator of a public meeting, to express their views.

As you monitor discussion lists and newsgroups looking for leads or sources of information, the names of people who regularly participate may quickly become very familiar to you, more familiar than perhaps other well-known individuals. People who aggressively post to an online discussion may become a source or a subject of a story for you.

It is not clear, however, that people become public figures simply because they are active in online discussion groups. From one vantage point they have clearly thrust themselves into public view (at least regarding the issues they are discussing). From another perspective, they have not. Legally, it is still not even clear whether the Internet should be considered a public forum.

On the other hand, at least within the context of a chat room or online discussion, the distinction between public and private figures may no longer be relevant. Private figures are afforded greater libel protection than public figures, in part, because they cannot respond to false information about them as effectively as public figures. Within a chat room, of course, people can respond.

Nonetheless, no court has yet accepted the idea that the ability to respond makes everybody communicating on the Internet a public figure. In fact, reporters should not believe they are protected by the *Sullivan* rule if they choose to report on people they have encountered online.

Does Net Culture Encourage Libel?

The question about who is a public figure is more vexing because of the developing culture of the computer networks themselves. In many online discussions, despite admonitions against it, many participants will "flame" (violently disagree with) other people's messages, using intemperate, hostile, and vituperative terms. The great majority of newsgroups (Chapter 7) are unmoderated. That means anyone can post anything. Moreover, from time to time, "flames" may be reposted to other discussion lists, to newsgroups, or may even be stored in databases.

While people who "flame" others may believe they are exercising their right to free speech, what they post could be libelous. That is, the flames could consist of verifiably false information that damages the reputation of the person who has been flamed. Unless there are very compelling reasons, reporters generally should not look at flames as useable, legitimate information.

In most cases, reporters looking for information will monitor the discussion lists and newsgroups looking for leads then contact people privately. Nevertheless, they should be aware that almost all individuals participating in those discussions should be treated as if they are private individuals for the purposes of libel. Because different states have different libel standards for private individuals, reporters must be even more careful to avoid reporting damaging, false information.

The best defense against accusations of libel in the United States is provable truth. Reporters should treat information they find online, particularly information about people, as critically as they treat information they receive from other sources. Veteran computer users have a long- standing rule of thumb: garbage in = garbage out. That applies to information found on the Internet and other places as well.

Service Providers and Libel

While people who utter or publish libelous materials clearly are legally responsible for their actions, one wonders if the Internet Service

Providers who host the chat rooms or Web sites on which the libel takes place can be held responsible as well. The courts have returned conflicting opinions on this issue.

In the case of *Cubby v. CompuServe*, which was decided in New York in 1991, Cubby Inc., which intended to publish an online gossip sheet, claimed that false statements about it were published by a rival on CompuServe's Journalism Forum. The court ruled that because CompuServe had no legal relationship with the people who published the material and had no opportunity to prescreen the material or exercise editorial control, the service itself could not be held responsible.

However, in the 1995 case of *Stratton Oakmont v. Prodigy*, the online service Prodigy was held to be responsible for statements made by the moderator of its Money Talk forum. The court ruled that the moderator, in fact, was acting as an agent of the service. The distinction made in the two cases was this: (1) In Cubby, CompuServe was seen simply as a distributor of information and did not have knowledge of the libelous material; (2) in *Stratton Oakmont*, Prodigy was seen as a publisher of information.

In 1996, the Communications Decency Act, whose provisions restricting indecent speech on the Internet were struck down as unconstitutional, also had a section that immunized Internet Service Providers for materials originating with a third party. In 1997, false messages were repeatedly posted on America Online, directing people to call Kenneth M. Zeran if they wanted to purchase T-shirts that bore tasteless information about the bombing of the Federal Building in Oklahoma City. Zeran argued that AOL did not remove the defamatory messages quickly enough, failed to post retractions and did not screen adequately for more defamatory messages. A U.S. district court ruled that the Communications Decency Act protected services like AOL, both as a publisher and distributor of information, from charges rising from material posted by third parties.

Copyright

Copyright law is often poorly understood by journalists. In short, copyright law is intended to give holders of the copyright the exclusive right of use to what they have created. Generally, that copyright covers the expression of an idea via one of several media. The United States Copyright Act of 1976 created seven categories of authorship, including: literary works; musical works; dramatic works; sound recordings; audiovisual works; pantomime and choreographies; and pictorial, graphic and sculptural works. International copyright treaties extend similar guarantees across national boundaries.

The creator of a work does not have to take any special action to obtain a copyright. As soon as the expression is "fixed," in a medium—that is, published—the work is protected by copyright law. Consequently, journalists should start with the idea that everything on the Web is copyrighted.

Works falling into most of the categories outlined by the Copyright Act can be distributed via computer networks. Consequently, copyright laws are important for journalists in three areas. First, what are the restrictions on the use in their stories of information they have found online? Second, what are the copyright issues involved in creating a Web site? Finally, what rights do journalists have to their own work which may be distributed by a publisher online either via the Web or through an electronic database?

An infringement of copyright is judged by three factors: the originality of the work, the proof of access to the copyrighted work, and the similarities of the works compared.

Using Information Found Online

Because most journalists attribute the information they publish to a source, the key questions for reporters when they wish to use information they have found or received online is how much of the material they have found can be quoted verbatim and how much of the work can they use in general? A common scenario for online journalists occurs when they see an interesting message in a network newsgroup or discussion list and want to quote it directly, crediting the source. Many journalists see newsgroups and discussion lists as analogous to public meetings. If people speak during business sessions of a public agency at a public meeting, of course, reporters can quote them.

But the analogy fails on two levels. First, online forums are not public agencies conducting public business for the public good. Second, postings to discussion groups are not spoken words; they are original works of authorship fixed in a tangible medium of expression—in this case electronic—which can be "perceived, reproduced or communicated either directly or with the aid of a device," to use language close to that of the copyright statute. Consequently, when someone posts something to a list or newsgroup, that posting is presumed to have copyright protection. The person who holds the copyright legally controls how that posting can be used. If the person does not want you to quote the posting, he or she legally may be able to prevent you from doing so.

Copyright, however, only protects the specific expression of an idea and not the idea itself. Consequently, if you do not directly quote information you find electronically but only use the facts contained, you may be able to avoid copyright infringement.

Misappropriation

Misappropriation is the legal expression of the notion that people should not be allowed to compete unfairly by using the work or property of others, particularly if they claim the purloined work is their own. The 1918 Supreme Court case *International News Service v. Associated Press* is a classic example of misappropriation.

William Randolph Hearst, who owned the International News Service (INS), admitted that he pirated stories from the Associated Press using a variety of tactics. Sometimes INS editors would rewrite the stories—sometimes they wouldn't—before transmitting them to its clients. Hearst claimed that, because AP did not copyright the story (the copyright law was somewhat different then), and nobody can copyright the news itself, the information was in the public domain. The Supreme Court decided that, although AP did not have copyright protection, the INS actions unfairly interfered with AP's operation at precisely the moment when it would reap the profit from its efforts.

Misappropriation could emerge as a significant issue for people using online services. On the Internet, for example, many people now publish their own "news services." There are many, perhaps hundreds, of electronic journals circulating; and some print magazines are publishing electronic versions on computer networks. If journalists use these news wires and journals as sources of information, they have to be very careful about how they report the information. It is very easy, and tempting, to download information in an electronic form and cut and paste it into an article. That could put the reporter at risk of claims of infringement or misappropriation.

Misappropriation was the issue when a Web site called *TotalNews* began using frames technology to surround material from major newspapers with ads it had sold. *TotalNews* did not actually copy any material from the newspapers' Web sites. It just programmed its site so the material would show up in one frame and the ads would be displayed in another frame. The newspapers argued that *TotalNews* had misappropriated their material.

Implied License

Copyright laws and the risk of misappropriation, however, do not mean you can never quote information from the Internet. There are two exceptions when copyrighted material can be freely used without the permission of the creator. The first is called "implied license." The second is known as the fair use doctrine.

An implied license is the idea that some people publish work with the idea that it will be republished or circulated by others without their specific permission. For example, when you send a letter to a newspaper with the salutation "Dear Editor," the editor can safely assume that you intend for the letter to be published in the newspaper.

Along the same lines, if somebody posts a message to a discussion list and another person copies part of the message in the response, that may be a technical violation of the copyright but is probably protected by the notion of implied license. People expect their messages to be copied, and perhaps even forwarded to other discussion lists, without their permission. An implied license can only be granted by a copyright holder. So if a third party has forwarded a message to discussion list, there is no implied license for participants in that discussion.

Fair Use

The 1976 U.S. copyright law also included provisions for what is known as "fair use" of copyrighted material. The fair use provisions allow others to use portions of copyrighted material without the permission of the copyright holder under certain conditions. The criteria by which fair use is evaluated include the purpose and character of the use, including whether the material is used either for nonprofit educational purposes or for-profit ventures; the nature of the copyrighted work itself; the amount of material used relative to the total amount of material; and the effect of the use upon the market value of the copyrighted work. Perhaps the two most important criteria are the nature of the copyrighted work itself and the effect of the use on the market value of the material.

In one episode, *The Nation* magazine published an excerpt of the memoirs of former President Gerald Ford without the permission of Harper & Row, who held the copyright. In the 1984 case *Harper & Row v. Nation Inc.*, the U.S. Supreme Court observed that a critical element of the work is whether it is published or not. The scope of fair use is considerably more narrow for unpublished works.

In 1991, the Second Circuit Court of Appeals underscored the importance of protecting a creator's right to control the first public appearance of the expression of a work in *Wright v. Warner Books Inc.* Nevertheless, it allowed Warner Books to publish a biography of novelist Richard Wright, even though it included small portions of his letters and journals stored at the Yale University library and not yet published. Because posting something on a discussion list that may be read by thousands of people is like publishing, the scope of fair use for material found in electronic sources is broader than for things like unpublished personal letters. Electronic messages that have been publicly circulated are probably open for fair use.

A Work's Market Value

The second criterion that should help protect journalists if they choose to quote from newsgroups or discussion lists is the impact on the potential market value of the material. In *Salinger v. Random House* (1987), the Second Circuit Court of Appeals decided that biographer Ian Hamilton's use of unpublished letters in a biography of the novelist J.D. Salinger was not allowed because, in part, appearing in Hamilton's book could have an impact on the future commercial value of the letters. The panel ruled, however, that the biographer could use the factual content of the letters.

This ruling is significant because most of the postings on discussion lists and newsgroups probably have no future market value. Newsgroup postings often are not archived at all; they simply vanish. Consequently, journalists usually will not have to worry about hurting the market value of the postings they quote from electronic sources.

Nevertheless, if you want to quote material directly from the electronic sources, you should keep these limitations in mind. Nearly all of the information you find via electronic sources has copyright protection. Electronic journals, news wires and electronic versions of print material have the same copyright protection as material that has been traditionally published. You should also work under the assumption that information posted to newsgroups and discussion lists is copyrighted.

Therefore, you should limit the amount of material you quote directly as much as possible, particularly if you think that information either has not been published (you have been forwarded a copy of a private e-mail message, for example) or if you think the material may have market value in the future. In general, for published material, including material published electronically, fair use allows for the verbatim quoting of no more than 300 words of a work and those 300 words can total no more than 20 percent of the total work. (In other words, you can't quote a 200-word poem entirely and claim fair use protection.) The best alternative is to secure the permission of the creator of the work you wish to quote.

Some observers believe the need to secure permission from copyright holders to use specific material can have a chilling effect on robust debate in America. Nevertheless, in *Harper & Row v. Nation Inc.*, the Supreme Court specifically ruled out a First Amendment defense for copyright infringement. In that decision, the Court declared that *Nation's* interest in reporting the news as quickly as possible did not outweigh President Ford's right to control the first publication of his memoirs.

Fair use has emerged as a contentious issue on the Web. For example, a Web site called the *Free Republic* routinely posted news stories from the *Los Angeles Times*, the *Washington Post*, and other newspapers on its Web site and encouraged visitors to comment on the story. The newspapers filed a copyright infringement suit against the Web site, whose operator argued that the use of the articles was covered by the Fair Use doctrine. The stories were only posted to stimulate conversation, he argued. Moreover, since he did not generate any revenue at his site, he did not realize any commercial value from using the news articles.

Copyright and Web Sites

Journalists must keep in mind that, if copyrighted material is posted to a computer bulletin board or Web site, the copyright itself has not been affected. A journalist cannot use material posted online with impunity. Furthermore, people who are creating Web sites cannot freely use material from other Web sites. Access providers to the Internet may also be at risk if copyrighted material is posted on a computer for which they provide access to the Internet.

In a well-publicized case in 1995, the holders of the copyrights to the published and unpublished works of the founder of the Church of Scientology, L. Ron Hubbard, sued Dennis Erlich, a former minister of Scientology and now a vocal critic, for publishing portions of the writings in the Usenet newsgroup alt.religion.scientology. Erlich used Netcom to gain access to Usenet. The copyright holders sued Erlich as well as Netcom after they refused to act on notification of copyright violation.

The plaintiff's arguments were that, because Netcom maintained the system which copied and distributed the works in question throughout the Internet worldwide, it was equally responsible for the copyright violation along with the person who had posted the material and the owner of the BBS on which it first appeared. Netcom responded that, while it maintained the system, the plaintiff's theory would make the operator of every Usenet server in the world liable for the copyright infringement.

A northern California court indicated that it did not believe that Netcom, the Internet Service Provider, could be held responsible for direct liability, but perhaps could be guilty of contributory libel for not acting after it was notified of the infringement. The court's opinion, however, was at odds with the Working Group on Intellectual Property Rights, a federal committee reviewing the issues of property rights in relationship to the National Information Infrastructure, which has proposed a stricter standard.

In the same case, the court reflected on people who simply read unauthorized copyrighted material online. The court argued that browsing the Internet is the functional equivalent of reading and is consequently fair use—much the same way as when a person in a bookstore browses through a book, then decides not to buy it.

Overall, the issue of the responsibilities of Internet access providers and others concerning copyright infringement is not clear. Legislation has been introduced in the United States Congress which would add legal burdens to technology managers monitoring material on the Internet. Simon and Schuster and other publishers reportedly are carefully monitoring the Internet for copyright violations related to the books they have published.

It is clear, however, that people cannot post copyrighted information on their Web sites without permission. They can, however, insert pointers from their pages to other Web sites containing copyrighted material, allowing their viewers easy access to material.

Copyright Protects Creators

On one hand, journalists and Web site creators have to be careful about using copyrighted materials in an unauthorized fashion. On the other hand, copyright protects their work from being distributed online without their permission. For example, in 1993, eleven writers sued the New York Times Co., Time, Inc., the *Atlantic Monthly*, Lexis-Nexis and others for illegally sublicensing their articles to electronic databases. Lexis-Nexis provides electronic archives of the articles of a wide range of newspapers and magazines. The publications contended that they had the right to provide the material to the databases without compensating the authors.

In the spring of 1996, *Atlantic Monthly* reached a settlement on the suit in which it agreed to pay the authors for the use of their material and to negotiate for electronic rights in the future. *Harper's* magazine, the *Washington Post*, and the *New Yorker* magazine agreed to pay for electronic rights and to additionally compensate authors whose material had been used. In 1999, the Second Circuit U.S. Court of Appeals ruled in *Tasini et al. v. New York Times et al.* that the reuse of freelance work on databases without the author's express permission constitutes copyright infringement.

Journalists and authors must carefully scrutinize the contracts and agreements they sign with publishers. If they do not sign over the electronic rights to their work, they retain those rights. If their articles then appear online or in an electronic database, they probably have the right to additional compensation.

E-mail

For most of the life of the Internet, e-mail has been the most heavily used application. Currently, billions of e-mail messages regularly travel via the Internet all over the world. Because e-mail often is used for one-to-one communication, many people think that the same rules that govern regular mail and telephone usage apply to e-mail. That is not the case.

In short, e-mail users should not assume that their communication via e-mail has the same protection as the communications via more traditional channels. In short, your e-mail provider, particularly if it is the company for which you work, has the right to review your e-mail. Indeed, companies often establish guidelines for e-mail use and punish people who violate those guidelines. Moreover, companies can bar people from sending e-mail to them. Finally, Internet Service Providers often will open their e-mail records to law enforcement or other government officials.

Most large companies routinely set policies governing the use of e-mail and violations of that policy can be severely punished. In 1999, for example, Edward Jones & Co., a stock brokerage company, fired 19 people for failing to admit that they sent pornography or off-color jokes via its e-mail system. A spokesperson noted that company regulations made it very clear that it was not acceptable for employees to use e-mail for nonbusiness purposes.

For journalists, the fact that companies routinely monitor e-mail has two implications. First, you should not assume that sources with whom you are communicating via e-mail can be fully candid. While e-mail can often be an effective way to get quotes, for sensitive issues, a face-to-face interview at a neutral location may still be the most effective approach. Secondly, when you use e-mail to communicate with a source, the company will have a record of that interaction.

Indeed, companies have the right to fully control their e-mail systems. America Online has aggressively moved against senders of junk e-mail, also known as spam, to its members, winning a series of victories in court. For example, AOL was awarded damages after it sued LCGM Inc. for sending spam for pornographic Web sites. The court also ruled that LCGM's attempts to evade AOL's filtering technology could be considered fraud.

The corporate control of e-mail systems goes beyond junk mail. In California, a judge ordered a disgruntled former Intel employee to stop sending mass e-mail to the company. The judge ruled that the e-mail, which accused Intel of a wide range of misdeeds, amounted to trespassing on its computer systems.

Finally, journalists should know that Internet correspondence does not seem to have the same protection as reporters' notebooks. While 29 states and the District of Columbia have laws that shield journalists from being compelled to disclose unpublished materials, those laws generally do not mention digital information. Furthermore, a lot of e-mail is very easy to trace. For example, in 1999, when the Melissa virus was released via e-mail, investigators were able to locate the originator of the virus within two days.

Confidentiality

Journalists working online must also be aware that they are working in a new medium. Some of the protection they may enjoy using traditional methods may not apply when they are online. Two of the most important ways in which online communication differs from other media is in the confidentiality of the information journalists gather and store electronically and in the emergence of speech codes governing online behavior in some settings.

Reporters have long fought to establish the principle that they can keep confidential the information they gather and the names of the sources from whom they gather it. The reasoning is that, without that protection, sources may not be willing to share with reporters important information that the public should know. The U.S. Supreme Court, however, has not accepted journalists' arguments about the need for a shield from law enforcement. In *Branzberg v. Hayes* (1972), the court decided 5–4 that the First Amendment did not absolve journalists from their responsibilities for testifying before grand juries and responding to relevant questions.

Since then, some states have passed shield laws to limit the way law enforcement officials can force journalists to disclose information; some state courts have recognized a limited privilege for reporters based on the First Amendment; and several U.S. circuit courts have acknowledged that information gathered by reporters should have some limited protection under specific circumstances. Still, there is no federal shield law rooted in the First Amendment. Nor has Congress chosen to pass a federal shield law.

The lack of a shield law could be more problematic for journalists working online. Typically, if police believe that a reporter has information relevant to a case, they subpoena the reporter to testify and to produce his or her notebooks. If need be, the police will issue a search warrant and physically gather notebooks and other information. In those types of situations, journalists working with what was known to be sensitive information could take precautions against being forced to disclose it. They may not tell their editors the names of their sources. They may hide their notebooks or not write down important facts. And, they can take a principled position and refuse to testify when called before the grand jury or into court. Several reporters have gone to jail rather than disclose confidential information. In many cases, their news organizations have supported them legally and financially in their efforts.

Online journalists do not have the same type of control over their information; nor can they necessarily count on the support of the computer system or company providing online access. By definition, online journalists initially gather information in an electronic format. At some point, that information is stored electronically on a hard disk or tape. As Oliver North (former National Security Council aide to President Ronald Reagan) found out, just because you delete something from a hard drive does not mean the information has been removed. When you do delete something, the information itself does not disappear until new information is written over it. Several software programs can retrieve deleted files.

Erased Files—Not

Law enforcement officials know that computer hard drives can still retain information that the user intended to delete. Hard drives are now subpoenaed in the course of criminal investigations. Law enforcement officials will often confiscate the entire hard drive with all the information on it.

Consequently, if you capture or store sensitive information that you do not wish to disclose, you should not store it at any time on a hard drive. Moreover, if you store sensitive information on a hard drive that is shared with other users, you are putting all of the information on that drive at risk. A law enforcement agency could conceivably confiscate the entire computer and there would be little that an individual reporter could do about it.

People accessing the Internet through a university-based connection could not rely on the support of the university if law enforcement agencies demanded the information. A university might be disinclined to lose an entire hard drive full of information employed by many users just to support your interpretation of the demands of a free press.

Of course, many reporters never are asked to surrender confidential information to law enforcement agencies because it is relevant to a criminal or civil proceeding. But, this extreme case raises a more common and troubling issue for online journalists. The information stored on a shared hard drive is not private or secure. In almost all cases, if you are accessing electronic information through a network, the system administrator can gain access to your files and can monitor your e-mail traffic. You have to conduct yourself accordingly.

And, while people who use the Internet like to believe that they also own it and should be able to establish the rules which cover its use, they don't and can't. The computers that are linked through the network are each owned by an organization or person. Those owners have the right to establish rules that govern their use. For example, Lawrence Livermore National Laboratory discharged workers for using its computer system to access pornographic sites on the Internet. Moreover, companies like America Online have made it clear they won't protect the confidentiality of their subscribers in the case of criminal and perhaps civil investigations. Journalists should be fully aware of the rules governing use of the computer systems they use and be careful not to violate them. Nor should journalists necessarily expect that Internet access providers will defend their free speech rights vigorously should a dispute arise.

Speech Codes

In fact, owners of computer-based communications networks have to be sensitive to more than just free speech concerns in controlling what is posted on their computers. In the fall of 1994, Santa Rosa Junior College reached a settlement with the U.S. Department of Education in which the college agreed to pay three students $15,000 to settle sex-discrimination charges related to men-only and women-only online computer conferences conducted by the school.

The students charged that the single-sex conferences violated a federal law that prohibits sex discrimination in schools that receive federal funds. The computer bulletin board, which was launched by a professor of journalism and hosted more than 100 online conferences, was seen as an educational activity of the school and, therefore, subject to what are known as Title IX regulations.

Federal investigators found that derogatory remarks about two women posted on the men-only conference were a form of sexual harassment creating a hostile educational environment. The Department of Education's Office of Civil Rights argued that computer bulletin boards do not enjoy the same level of First Amendment protection as the campus newspaper. The office has proposed banning comments that harass or denigrate people on the basis of sex or race.

The school's lawyer argued that the online conference should have been protected by the First Amendment. Nevertheless, the college felt compelled to settle the case.

Along the same line, in 1995, Jake Baker, a student at the University of Michigan, posted a story to the newsgroup alt.sex.stories. The story was a rape fantasy and used the name of one of Baker's classmates. Baker also sent e-mail to a friend indicating that the story expressed his real feelings. When the story and the e-mail became known, Baker was criminally charged with threatening the classmate whose name had been used. Although the criminal charge was dismissed, Baker was ultimately expelled from the University of Michigan.

Open Meetings and Freedom of Information

Journalists are not the only community group taking advantage of computer-based communications networks. Public officials and government agencies are also incorporating new technology into their work. Their activities raise two vital concerns for journalists. First, "Are open meeting laws being circumvented through the use of computer networks?" Second, "How much of the information collected by governments should be available to journalists in an electronic format and how much should that information cost?"

Since the mid-1970s, many states have passed what are called Sunshine or Open Meeting laws. The purpose of these laws is to ensure that public business is conducted in the open where the public can see and hear what happens. Except under specified conditions, members of many school boards, local government commissions and other agencies cannot conduct official business without first notifying and inviting the public to observe or participate. As new forms of communication become available, the definitions both of meeting and public access to meetings have come under pressure. Can officials "meet" online or via a video conference to conduct business? Does inviting the public to a video or online conference fulfill the spirit and letter of the open meeting laws?

Sunshine laws vary from jurisdiction to jurisdiction. Journalists must be on guard to ensure that agencies do not try to use new communication technology to conduct public business in a covert or hidden fashion.

Along these lines, public access to government computer files has been a significant issue for several years. The question has three important aspects.

1. Are electronic records considered "records" under freedom of information laws and therefore must be made available on request?

2. Must government agencies provide information to journalists and the public in an electronic format?

3. How much can government agencies charge for access to electronic information? Can agencies give exclusive rights to information to private data providers who, in turn, can charge whatever the market will bear for the data, even if the pricing makes it prohibitive for smaller publications and individuals to purchase?

Once again, these questions are being decided at all levels of government. Journalists must stay aware of the deliberations that will resolve the questions, as they could have profound influence on the practice of journalism.

Access for Online Journalists

As the number of people publishing online increases, the issue has emerged concerning who constitutes a "legitimate" journalist and thus should be allowed entry to locations such as the press gallery in the United States Congress and other restricted venues. The question of access frequently dogs journalists working in a new medium. For example, newspapers tried to bar radio reporters from certain locations in the 1930s. And, television cameras are routinely banned from criminal and civil courts, although newspaper reporters are allowed in. In most places, judges have broad discretion when it comes to televising, or even photographing, trials.

In February 1996, Vigdor Schreibman, the publisher of the Federal Information News Service (FINS), was denied admission to the United States Senate and House press galleries. FINS is published only online and is regularly read, according to Schreibman, by thousands of people. A subscription costs $2.95 a year, but the newsletter can be read free—and has been posted to different newsgroup discussion sites.

According to the head of the congressional periodical gallery, who is a working journalist, Schreibman was rejected because his publication was more of a hobby than a commercial venture. And, while representatives of online publications such as those created by *National Journal* will undoubtedly be recognized as legitimate journalists, the proliferation of online journalism will raise the question of how to make distinctions. As Alan Fram, the Associated Press correspondent who heads the executive committee of the daily press gallery for Congress, remarked to the *Wall Street Journal*, "If we are going to admit such critters, how do we avoid opening the barn door to anyone with a home page?"

Obscenity and Other Free Speech Issues

As participants in the robust debate protected by the First Amendment, journalists should also be aware of free speech issues that may not have a direct impact on the way they do their jobs. They include the ability of one jurisdiction to impose its standards for speech in another jurisdiction and the ability networks give journalists to circumvent international press law. As in other media, obscenity serves as the flash point of one locality imposing its standards on another. In its pivotal ruling in *Miller v. California* (1974), the Supreme Court decided that local community standards should be used to evaluate whether material was obscene.

In the summer of 1994, the city of Memphis won a decision against a computer bulletin board operator in the San Francisco Bay area for distributing obscene pictures. Law enforcement officials had actively requested that the material on the bulletin board be sent to them. The court ruled that because people had to subscribe to access the pornographic material, the operators of the bulletin board should have known that their material could not be distributed in Memphis.

In the same way that computer networks may be avenues for circumventing restrictions on the distribution of pornography, they may also provide ways to circumvent national press laws in other countries. As we reported about the Karla Homulka case, Canadians used network newsgroups to spread information about a grizzly murder case, even though the judge in the case had imposed a news blackout.

In many cases, people will be applauded for circumventing press laws. They will be seen as defying the heavy hand of censorship. But, people who do violate those press laws could have to pay a heavy price. The judge in the Karla Homulka case threatened to shut down specific computers suspected as the vehicle for violating his gag order. Journalists who receive information that has been distributed in violation of national press laws must keep in mind that somebody may have to pay a price for making that information available. It should not be published frivolously.

Online Ethics

Consider this scenario: You are walking along a road and you come across a knapsack. You stop, pick up a book that has partially fallen out of the knapsack, and open it. The first page states that the information is to be read and used only by people who have purchased the book.

At that point, is it unethical to read on, if only to see if you can find the name and address of the person who owns the knapsack? If, in looking for the person's name, you read something which could be of value to you, is it wrong to use that information? If you read the entire book, then return it to the knapsack and leave, have you stolen anything?

As you use online information, you will likely come across information that was not intended for your eyes. As a reporter, you may join a list without the other list members knowing the focus of your interest. They may think the discussion is just among specialists in a narrowly defined area. A private e-mail message might be posted or forwarded mistakenly or maliciously to a discussion list. Navigating through the maze of computers on the network, you may find a back door to a commercial database open only to those with paid subscriptions. In other words, from time to time, you will find a knapsack with an open book on the road.

Online journalism promises to open a whole new arena for discussions of media ethics. And the ethical boundaries—what journalists morally should or should not do online—will only be worked out over time as more journalists use electronic services and more journalists debate their use. Nevertheless, all journalists should adhere to certain ethical guidelines.

Three Rules Hold

First, journalists should almost always identify themselves as such if they plan to use information from discussion lists or network newsgroups. In most cases, journalists have the ethical obligation to allow people to choose to go on the record or not. Using hidden cameras is very controversial in standard journalism. To lurk on a discussion list, then quote people who did not know that what they wrote would be used in a different context is as deceptive as posing or going undercover to report a story. While, from time to time, in traditional journalism the benefit of posing to reveal a significant social wrong may outweigh the deception involved, that probably will not be the case in most instances in online journalism. In almost all cases, journalists have an obligation to let the people with whom they interact know that they are talking to a reporter.

Second, journalists must identify the source of their information in their reporting. Attribution is an essential element of journalism. If you don't know definitively who the source of information is, you must be very careful if you choose to use it. Widely published journalism codes of ethics frequently warn that journalists should verify all information. At the same time, you should not claim credit for information that somebody has published on a network without crediting that source.

Third, journalists have to respect the limitations of the information they gather online. Online information should be treated in the same way as information gathered through any other technique. Creators of Web sites also can face ethical problems. For example, anybody can create a link that points to any other Web site. But as computer columnist Lawrence Magid noted in the magazine *Information Week*, he would be outraged if his Web site was linked to the Web site of the American Nazi Party. Moreover, it is possible to incorporate copyrighted material, particularly graphics, into Web sites without technically copying them. Consequently, without violating the letter of copyright law, you can violate its spirit. The question is—should you?

Beyond the Rules

Ethical rules will not, and cannot, cover every situation. For example, was Daniel Ellsberg justified in stealing the Pentagon Papers in the early 1970s? Those papers laid out in vivid detail the way the United States government had misled and lied to the American people about its policies in Vietnam. Were the *New York Times* and the *Washington Post* justified in publishing that information, even though the information was both classified and stolen? Whatever you feel, Ellsberg could not have passed the Pentagon Papers along to the *New York Times* and the *Washington Post* as easily if photocopying—a new communications technology at that time—had not been invented.

Like photocopying—and radio and television before it—computer-based networks are a new communications technology. Legal and ethical controversies will only be decided in action, as people like you try to decide the correct course of action in the complex situations that will arise in the future.

Conclusion

The freedom of speech and freedom of the press are essential features of democratic government. But exactly what constitutes freedom of the press and what constitutes abuse by the press is continually reinterpreted. The introduction of new communications technology, such as the Internet, complicates the interpretative process.

Consider the issue of privacy. The concept of privacy was first developed legally in the 1890s as a reaction against an intrusive press. Harvard professors Samuel Warren and Louis Brandeis, the latter of whom later became an associate justice of the U.S. Supreme Court, were appalled that photojournalists would print photos of society events—including the wedding of Warren's daughter—without permission. They theorized that each person had a legal zone of privacy in which neither the press nor the state could intrude.

With the Web, there are many possibilities for journalists to potentially invade that zone of privacy. They could track people's paths through the Web, for example, or discover their shopping habits. On the other hand, some people have set up Webcams to record every aspect of their lives. If somebody makes his or her life public by broadcasting via the Web, how much of that person's zone of privacy has been relinquished?

Many legal observers agree that First Amendment law has not yet caught up with the Internet. But people do agree that speech on the Internet is not freer than print speech (though it is freer than broadcast speech). Journalists must be careful to fully adhere to the same legal standards that apply to traditional print media.

Chapter

11

Chapter

Getting More out of Your Browser

Leonard Bernstein is the state editor for the *Los Angeles Times*. He supervises reporters, edits stories, consults with other editors and deals with a host of distractions, all at the same time. At any moment he is simultaneously meeting with somebody, talking on the telephone and working on his computer. Multitasking is his life.

The Internet and the World Wide Web are two more tools Bernstein has thrown into his mix. The faster and more efficiently he can use those tools, the more work he can get done faster and better. Working faster, smarter and better is the prime challenge for journalists working on a 24-hour news cycle.

In Chapters 3 and 4, you learned the basic operations of the two key pieces of Internet client software, the Web browser and the e-mail client. The browser is designed to allow you to do just that—browse the Web by selecting links and with no need to type any commands, then you are browsing. As you know, the two most popular World Wide Web browsers are Microsoft *Internet Explorer* (*IE*) and Netscape *Navigator* (*NN*). Both *IE* and *NN* use graphical interfaces.

But current browsing software is capable of doing many things beyond just calling up Web pages and letting you click on words and other page objects. Many people use only the basic features of the browser and their e-mail clients, as described earlier. But browsers and e-mail clients are rich with features. The purpose of this chapter is to show how journalists can use advanced features to work more efficiently. In this chapter, you will learn how to

- personalize your browser to do routine tasks for you and to manage mail when you are on the road,
- apply keyboard shortcuts to save precious time online,
- use the browser search function to find keywords in a long document,

- distinguish among popular browsers and e-mail clients,
- use "plug-ins" to extend browser functionality, and
- effectively collect and organize bookmarks.

Browsing software is developing rapidly. Both Netscape and Microsoft add new features and refine old ones constantly. As new versions of each package are released, not only are new features added, but old ones often get moved to new "places" in the program. Most of the specific references in this chapter are to Netscape *Navigator* 4.7 and *Internet Explorer* 5.0, the current versions of each browser in general release at the time of this writing. It is likely that future versions of each program will continue to support all the functions described in this chapter, but that access to some of those functions—especially customizing features—may be moved to other places in the program as the software evolves.

For the 22 million subscribers to AOL and CompuServe online services, we have included a short section near the end of this chapter that speaks to concerns unique to those services and their proprietary browsers.

Both Netscape and Microsoft offer their browsers in suite with an e-mail client. Consequently, this chapter will discuss features of Netscape *Messenger*, Microsoft *Outlook Express*, and Qualcomm's *Eudora*. These clients are tightly integrated with Web browsers. Moreover, e-mail clients also can serve to read Usenet messages (Usenet was described in Chapter 5).

Many people use the Internet software provided by their employer, school or Internet Service Provider. But you do not have to be limited by their choices. Although *Internet Explorer* and Netscape *Navigator* dominate the market, a third browser, *Opera*, also will be briefly described because it has a few unique features that make it worth mentioning. The choice of which browser to use ultimately becomes a matter of personal preference. It will depend on how you work and what traits you value most in your browsing software. Your choice of e-mail packages may impact your browser decision. Many people start with whatever program was installed on their computer and they stay with it because that's what they learned. But you don't have to be so restricted.

Personalizing Your Software

Because different people have different wants and needs, the publishers of Internet client software have enabled end-users to control different aspects of the operation of the programs. You can adjust the way the software looks on screen. You can select the Web page that opens when you initially start up the browser. You can determine how the browser manages bookmarks and other advanced features. You can designate a preferred search engine; how to manage e-mail and newsgroups; and which "helper" programs to use to read specialized information. You personalize your browser software using the configuration options and browser preferences command sets.

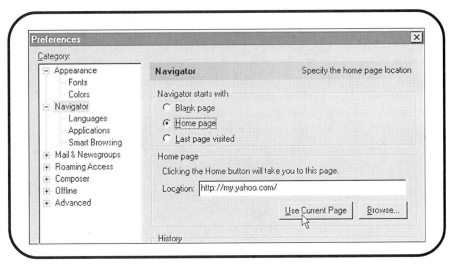

Fig.11-1: One of the easiest (and often most efficient) ways to personalize your browser is to select your own home page. While this image shows the process in Netscape *Navigator*, all browsers make the process easy.

When a browser is first installed, you are generally asked to supply basic profile information on yourself—things like your name, your e-mail address, and the company you work for. The browsing software may get some of this information from your computer's operating system, but usually it will ask you to confirm its data at the time your browser is installed or first launched. Some of the preference settings are specific to the World Wide Web while others are specific to e-mail or Usenet newsgroups. You can alter most of this data by editing browser preference settings. Furthermore, both *IE* and *NN* support the maintenance of several profiles. This is especially useful in a public laboratory setting or a newsroom where several people share the same online computer. A browser so configured generally asks you to log on at start-up, so it can retrieve your profile.

Choosing a Home Page

One of the easiest and most convenient preferences you can select is determining which Web page opens when you first launch your browser. By default, each browser opens at the home page of the company that publishes the software. *Explorer* opens at microsoft.com, *Navigator* opens at netscape.com, and *Opera* opens at opera.com. At universities as well as news companies, systems administrators often reset the home page to the company or school home page.

However, you can just as easily select your own home page. That home page may be a personalized page you have created at a portal site like *Yahoo!* or *Excite*. It might be a page you created yourself—perhaps a customized bookmarks page you or someone else has created in *Navigator* or some similar page created using an HTML editor.

One way to reset the home page of your browser to a page of your choosing is to first open the page in your browser. With the page of choice displayed in your active browser window, follow this procedure:

- In *Navigator*, select "Preferences" under the Edit menu. In the Preferences window, select Navigator, and then check the radio button next to "use current page" in the "Home page" section of the Navigator dialog. Click on "Okay" twice to save the setting.
- In *Explorer*, select "Internet Options" from the Tools menu, select the General tab and "Use Current" in the "Home page" box, then click on "Okay" to save the setting.
- In *Opera,* select "Set Home" on the Navigation menu, and under "Global Home Page" click on "Use Active." Click on "Okay" to save the setting.

Now, any time you start your browser without clicking on a hyperlink displayed in another program, the page you have selected will be the first page displayed. This page may be a page on the Internet, one on your Local Area Network, or an HTML file on your computer. Some journalists carefully build their own bookmark files complete with custom descriptions (see the bookmark section later) and set that to be their home page.

If you are working in a public laboratory setting, you may want to carefully consider whether it is appropriate to reset the default home page. While students from the Chicago area may be delighted to have the *Chicago Tribune* as the default home page, students from Chattanooga may find it annoying.

Setting Your Mail Identity

As noted earlier, Internet client software comes in a suite of programs including Web browsers and e-mail clients. In the Netscape *Communicator* package, *Navigator* is the browsing client software, and *Messenger* is included as an e-mail client. For *Explorer*, the default e-mail client at this writing is *Outlook Express*, distributed freely with *IE*. *Opera* incorporates a limited client for sending mail, and the publishers plan to include a full client with version 4.0.

The most popular stand-alone mail program is Qualcomm's *Eudora*, which comes in a free version called "Light" as well as the "Pro" version. When you purchase *Eudoro Pro, Internet Explorer* is included in the package. Other e-mail clients include *Pegasus Mail*, a freeware product, the

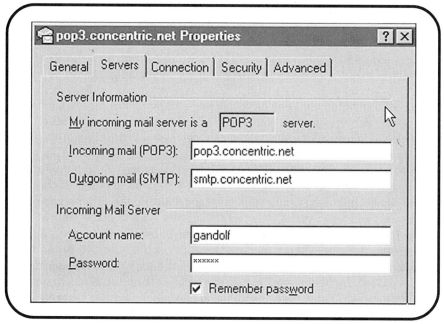

Fig. 11-2: To configure a browser to send mail or to configure an e-mail client, you need to know at least the names of your mail servers, your username, and password. This is the server configuration tab for *Outlook Express*.

University of Washington's *Pine*, widely distributed on mainframe systems but also available for desktop computers, and Forté's *Agent* and its freeware version, *Free Agent*. Generally e-mail clients do double duty, permitting you to manage Usenet newsgroup postings.

In all the browsers, and regardless of which e-mail client you use, you need to tell the software the names of your incoming (typically a POP or MAPI) and outgoing (SMTP) mail servers. Think of it this way: When you send a letter via U.S. mail, you drop the letter into a large mailbox. When you receive a letter, it generally is placed in a small mailbox near your home. SMTP servers are the large, outbound mailboxes. POP and MAPI are your personal, incoming mailboxes.

Often your company or university information technology specialists configure your software for you. However, if you travel on reporting assignments (or in some other way you have to change computers), you will be obliged to do some minimal configuring of mail software. In addition to knowing the names of the mail servers, you will have to know at least your e-mail address and your account username and password. Using this information, you may be able to configure mail clients on public machines to access your mail.

If you configure a public computer to read your mail (regardless of the specific mail client), there is always the danger that other persons may use your mail account when you are done. If the machine you are using keeps track of mail accounts by establishing profiles that require you to log on, then all you may need to do to protect your e-mail security is to log off and follow system instructions (which may require you to drop your network connection when you are done). If the public computer you share does not require you to log on with your own private account, you inevitably need to reverse what you have done by removing the server, username, and password information you provided or by deleting your profile.

Outlook Express (the e-mail client that comes with Internet Explorer) routinely accommodates multiple profiles under the "Accounts" portion of the Tools menu. Select the "Mail" tab, and a listing of accounts will be displayed. If your account is not there, you will need to add it. If there are multiple accounts listed, you may consider deleting the other accounts. At minimum, you will want to use the "Set Order" tab to move your account to the top. The reason for both actions is the same. When you tell *Express* to "Send and Receive" mail, it goes through each account in order, top of the list to the bottom. If your account is at the bottom, then your mail is retrieved last. If you are working from a public computer, then chances are the other accounts represent people who used the computer before you but forgot to delete their account information when they were done getting mail. By deleting the other accounts listed in *Express*, you are doing them

Fig. 11-3: In Netscape *Communicator*, mail identity and server settings are entered under Mail & Newsgroups section of the Edit | Preferences dialog.

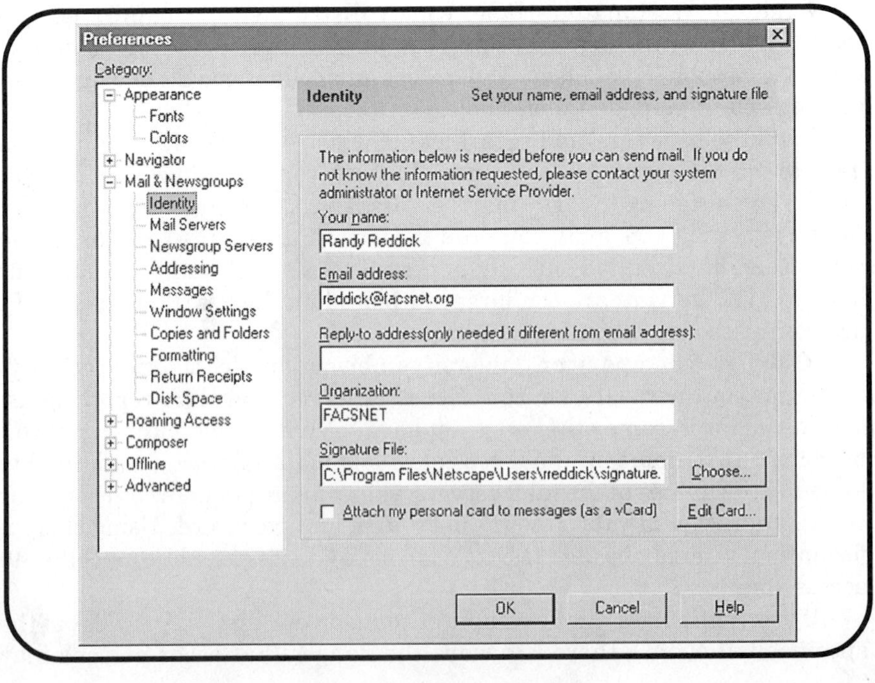

and yourself a favor. You are helping the owners of the other accounts by assuring that no one else gets their mail or uses their account to send mail. You help yourself by assuring that you have less chance for confusing clutter as you do your mail.

In Netscape *Messenger*, these preferences are specified under "Preferences" on the File Menu. Under Preferences, you select "Mail and Newsgroups" and then provide the server information, your e-mail address, and password.

In *Eudora Light*, you set these (and most other) parameters from the "Tools" menu under "Options." Basic account information is managed under the Personal Info and Hosts dialogs. If you enter the information there, it should show up automatically under "Getting Started."

Remembering Your Password, Automatic E-mail Checks

Your e-mail software can remember your password, if you do not want to type in the password each time you get mail. It's a small thing, but it will save you a few seconds each time you get mail. Be aware, however, that if you set your client to remember your password, then anyone who uses your computer may have access to your mail unless you are forced to log on each time you use the computer.

Another potential time saving setting is to tell your client to automatically check for your mail every 15 minutes or so. All complete mail programs discussed here will check for mail in the background and then alert you when you have new mail. On the other hand, some people do not want to be bothered by constant e-mail alerts.

In *Outlook Express*, you tell the software to remember your password by selecting Tools | Accounts | Mail | Properties | Servers. You can set *Express* to automatically check your mail by selecting "Options" from the Tools Menu, and then selecting the "General" tab. When you check the box next to "Check for new messages every," you then have the option of setting the frequency of checking. The default is 30 minutes.

Messenger stores all these settings under "Preferences" in the Edit Menu. To have *Messenger* remember your password, first select "Mail Servers" under "Mail & Newsgroups." The "Incoming Mail Servers" box lists all the servers for which your copy of *Messenger* is configured (often there is only one server listed). Click on the "Edit" button, and under the "General" tab are check boxes for both options, remembering your password and automatically getting your mail.

Eudora Light accepts these parameters under the "Checking Mail" dialog in the Tools | Options Menu. All three programs will check for mail while the program is running in the background. That is, as long as the program is configured to check your mail automatically, it will do so whenever it is running, even if you are presently working in another program (such as your word processor). All three programs have options for notifying you with a distinctive sound when the program finds new mail.

Netscape *Messenger* is completely integrated with *Navigator*. If you configure *Messenger* to remember your password and to automatically check and download (two separate functions in *Messenger*) mail every 10 minutes, it will do so even if you are only running *Navigator* to browse the Web. *Messenger* will then notify you that you have mail, even though you did not start *Messenger*, per se. This can be a nice feature if you like it. If you would rather be free to browse the Internet without having your messages checked and downloaded, then choose the configuration that fits you best.

Automatic E-mail Signature

In the ink-on-paper world, you sign all letters you send out. In the digital world, you tell your e-mail software that you would like it to include your signature (which may include your physical address, telephone, and other contact information) at the bottom of each letter. You set the signature and the signature parameters once, and then the software takes care of "signing" all your e-mail letters for you. This can be a great time saver.

Messenger and *Eudora* like to have your signature in a small, isolated text file. By default, *Eudora* stores your standard signature in a file called "Standard.txt" in the "Sigs" folder. *Messenger* simply asks you to tell it where the file is. *Eudora* wants you to actually enter your signature text into a window it provides. The program then stores the signature in either a standard or alternate text file. *Express* will let you specify a file or enter your signature into a dialog box.

For *Express*, the Signatures Tab is one of nine on the "Options" portion of the Tools Menu. For *Messenger*, signature options are offered at the bottom of the Identity dialog box. In *Eudora*, the Signatures tab is available directly from the Tools Menu. In *Opera*, you choose "Mail" from the Preferences Menu, and you name the file in which your signature resides.

Managing Bookmarks Wisely

Most reporters have a trusted network of sources. For example, during political campaigns, reporters will check in regularly with a group of consultants, academics, pollsters and other observers. Police reporters routinely cultivate sources throughout the department. In some ways, Web bookmarks

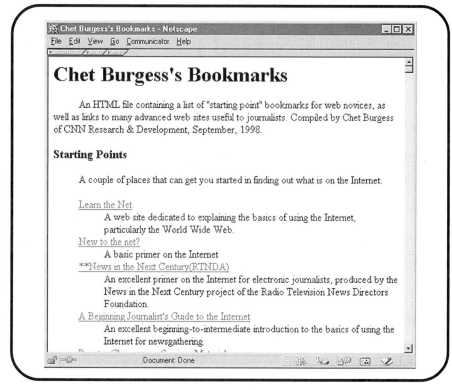

Fig. 11-4: Netscape bookmark files may be edited in *Navigator* and then displayed by any browser. Chet Burgess takes advantage of the bookmark description property to build meaningful sets of bookmarks.

or hotlists are the cyber-equivalent to trusted sources. Reporters find themselves checking in regularly with a fixed set of information sources.

When Mark Schleifstein of the *Times-Picayune* spoke at the annual meeting of Investigative Reporters and Editors in New Orleans in 1998, he shared with his journalist audience a diskette containing his bookmarks of environmental sites on the Internet. Later the same year, Chet Burgess of CNN gave to reporters attending his classes at the annual meeting of the Radio and Television News Directors Association in San Antonio a diskette containing bookmarks on a wide range of topics. David Milliron, first at Gannett News Service and then with the Atlanta *Journal-Constitution* has for years maintained a set of bookmarks of sites useful to his reporters. Rich Meislin created a set of bookmarks listing starting points for reporters and editors at the *New York Times* that became so popular the *Times* Website now serves up a modified version to the general public, under the title of *CyberTimes Navigator* at http://www.nytimes.com/library/tech/reference/cynavi.html. *Brill's Content*, a magazine that covers the world of journalism, routinely reports the entries on top journalists' hotlists.

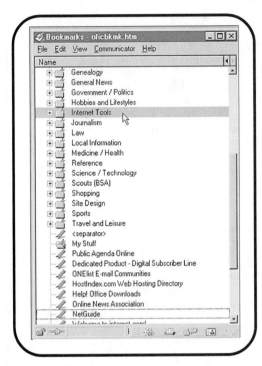

Fig. 11-5: One way to organize your bookmarks is through "drag and drop." In *Navigator*, you first open the Bookmarks editing window (Ctrl-B). Using your mouse, you select the bookmark in question, then pressing the left mouse button all the time, you drag the selected listing to the folder or the place in the list you want the bookmark to reside. You drop it in place by releasing the left mouse button.

The Web browser makes it very easy to create lists of useful Internet sites. These lists are called "favorites" in *Internet Explorer*, "hotlists" in *Mosaic* and *Opera*. Most other browsing software, including Netscape *Navigator*, has used the term "bookmarks." The term "bookmarks" can also be used generically to be interchangeable with "favorites" and "hotlists." The following description of bookmark management techniques primarily describe bookmark management in *Explorer* and *Navigator*.

Adding bookmarks to your list is simply a matter of choosing the Bookmarks or Favorites Menu and selecting "Add." The keyboard shortcut for both *Explorer* and *Navigator* is Ctrl-D. If all you do is place a bookmark on a site, the site listing is added to the bottom of your list of bookmarks. It is not placed alphabetically nor is it dropped into a folder.

Placing bookmarks is so easy that most journalists (who by nature tend to nurture a wide range of interests) new to the Web find they soon have an extensive mass of bookmarks that is more confusing than helpful. Many reporters complain that a day or two after setting bookmarks, they have a hard time remembering what many of the items are. Others complain that their lists of bookmarks are too large or otherwise so disorganized that they have a hard time finding listings for sites they know they have.

Four procedures will help to tame the bookmark information tide.

1. Organize your bookmarks into folders.
2. Edit site titles and descriptions.

3. Learn to be very selective in choosing bookmarks so they are meaningful to you.
4. Where appropriate, use multiple bookmark files.

Bookmarks and Their Folders

Financial journalism has emerged as a growth beat in the 1990s. Financial journalists regularly use a wide range of information sources. They consult research reports published by brokerage and investment banking houses. They review regulatory filings. They track the financial markets minute by minute. They may monitor chat rooms. And they study the announcements of specific companies. Many financial journalists may quickly build a list of 200 Web sites. Grouping those bookmarks in folders is a method to make sure you can access the site you want quickly.

Grouping bookmarks in folders accomplishes two ends. First, you organize related sites into limited sub-lists so that you can find a particular site more easily when you want it. Second, when you open a folder, you see lists of related sites that may serve as reminders of other resources that could be of help on your current project. If your sites are listed with descriptive titles, then you will have an easier time making sense of what you have as you scan through your list of bookmarks.

Navigator, *Opera*, and *Explorer* come with a default set of bookmarks and bookmark folders. In all programs you have the option to place bookmarks directly into the appropriate folder or to move the bookmark into its folder later. The process for moving bookmarks already created and for creating new folders for bookmarks begins the same. In *Navigator*, you want to select "Edit Bookmarks" from the Bookmarks Menu. In *Explorer*, you want to select "Organize Favorites" from the Favorites Menu. The keyboard shortcut is Ctrl-B in either program (Cmd-B on a Mac).

In *Navigator*, selecting the "Edit Bookmarks" choice (or typing Ctrl-B) produces a directory window much like other program windows. The "Edit Bookmarks" window has its own "File, Edit, View . . ." menu choices. You use this menu to create new folders. Once your folder is created, you place bookmarks in it by dragging them to the folder. As an alternative, you can select "Bookmarks" from either the Communicator Menu or from the Location Toolbar and select "File Bookmark." You then are presented with a list of all your bookmark folders from which you select the folder into which you want the new bookmark to go. *Navigator* then places the new bookmark at the bottom of the list of bookmarks in that folder.

The "Organize Favorites" option on the *Explorer* Favorites Menu (shortcut Ctrl-B) produces a dialog with a listing of your Favorites accompanied by four action buttons: "Create Folder," "Rename," "Move to Folder," and

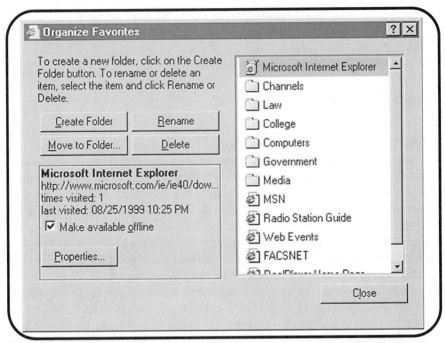

Fig. 11-6: In *Internet Explorer*, you may drag and drop bookmarks either in the "Organize Favorites" dialog, shown here, or by displaying Favorites along the left side of your browser and moving them there.

"Delete." You have the option of dragging and dropping favorites into their folders or of selecting a favorite and clicking "Move to Folder." *Explorer* enables another approach to organizing your Favorites through the "Favorites" folder icon on the Standard Buttons toolbar. Click on it once and a Favorites frame pops up in the left-hand portion of your browser window. The frame displays your Favorites folders and any individual favorites that you have not placed in folders. Two icons give you the options of adding the current page to your list or organizing the list you have. You can hide the Favorites frame by either clicking on the Favorites folder icon a second time or by clicking on the close button (X) at the top of the Favorites frame.

Through the "Edit Bookmarks" screen in *Navigator* and the "Organize Favorites" dialog in *Explorer*, you can create folders, rename them, and group related site listings into folders that are meaningful to you and the way you work. Having your bookmarks organized according to a scheme you select can significantly increase the efficiency of the time you spend online. With the newer versions of browsing software it is possible to place your new bookmarks into the appropriate folders in the first place so that you don't have to do so later, when you may have forgotten key information about recently placed bookmarks.

If you limit your folders to 12 to 15 listings each, then your list remains manageable. If you drag all your bookmarks into folders, then when you click to get the bookmarks list, you will see only a list of folders until your mouse passes over a folder, revealing its contents. If you place 12 to 15 bookmarks in 12 to 15 folders, you can reasonably manage more than 200 bookmarks. As with all directory structures, you can also place folders within folders for more detailed organization. Your goal should be to be very selective or you may defeat the purpose of all your careful cataloging of bookmarks.

Edit Site Titles and Descriptions

When you place a bookmark, the site is listed by the title of the page upon which you are placing the bookmark. Sometimes a document is without a title, and you have a nameless bookmark. Often, the title is no more instructive than "Welcome to Net Center." Fortunately, you can edit the titles that are displayed when you show your bookmarks. And more than that, at least in *Navigator* you can add descriptive commentary to help you remember just what the bookmark location contains.

The first step in this process is to make a note of the page title before you place it. The title is displayed in the Title Bar of the active browser window. If the page you wish to add to your bookmarks has a descriptive title, then you have no need to change. If it has no title or the title is not distinctive, you need to either provide the title or edit the existing one. For either *Explorer* or *Navigator* you start the bookmark customizing process by typing Ctrl-B (Cmd-B on a Mac). *Explorer* presents you with four buttons, as we described earlier, one of which is to rename a Favorite.

In *Navigator*, you have more options for your bookmarks. When the "Edit Bookmarks" window appears on your screen, select "Properties" from the Edit Menu. The dialog you receive gives you options to change the title, the URL, and to offer a description. The description is not routinely displayed when you are viewing bookmarks from the bookmarks button on *Navigator*. It can be seen from the "Edit Bookmarks" window when you inspect the bookmark's properties. If you open the bookmark file (by default it is called bookmark.htm) in your browser, it will display your bookmarks, linked by titles, and with the descriptions you have provided accompanying the title. *Navigator* has a special kind of bookmark folder called the "Personal Toolbar Folder." Any folders or bookmarks you place in this folder will be displayed on the Navigator Personal Toolbar immediately below the Location Toolbar. This gives you the ability to place six to eight carefully chosen folders that will be immediately available and appear on their own, separate from the bookmarks folder.

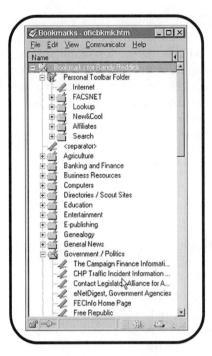

Fig. 11-7: Bookmarks and folders placed on the Personal Toolbar portion of Netscape *Navigator* will show up on the top of the browser itself.

Multiple Bookmark Files

Duff Wilson at the *Seattle Times* keeps a set of bookmarks for each project he is on. *Navigator* permits you to keep multiple bookmark files and to switch among them. Wilson has a core set of bookmarks of general sites useful on a wide range of projects. He has compiled those into his "Home Page." He has posted his home page, the *Reporter's Desktop,* for all the world to share at http://www.seanet.com/~duff/. Using the search and catalog tools on his home page, and any other appropriate sites, he begins building a new set of bookmarks for the project at hand.

The safest way of maintaining multiple bookmark files in *Navigator* is to make a copy of your existing bookmark.htm file and then to delete the bookmarks from the copied file. Let's say you copied your bookmark.htm file and called the new file "Projects.htm." From the "Edit Bookmarks" window, you can select "Open Bookmark File" from the Edit Menu. Select the new file you have created (Projects.htm), click "Open," and it will be loaded as your current bookmarks file. The title bar of the Edit Bookmarks window carries the name of the file you are using. You can select the top bookmark or folder you want to delete, then holding the shift key down, select the bottom one. All bookmarks and folders in between will be selected. You then merely hit the delete key, and they are all gone. You might want to keep the "Personal Toolbar Folder."

Because *Navigator* keeps its bookmarks in one flat file it is very easy to maintain multiple bookmark files and to share bookmarks with colleagues.

Save Time with Keyboard Shortcuts

Since the introduction of the Macintosh computer and Windows 3.1 in the early 1990s, the dominant way to interact with a computer has been to point and click with a mouse. Indeed, the use of the World Wide Web exploded with the introduction of a point-and-click interface. For a journalist working against a deadline to assemble notes and to write or script a story, point-and-click is not always the most efficient way to work.

Typically, journalists do most of their work in some kind of word processing or text editing program where they not only write stories and/or scripts, but often take notes as well. Every time you take your hands off the keyboard to grab your mouse and then click on something you interrupt the flow of your typing or note taking. Even some of the actions associated with navigating the Internet or managing e-mail require you to type—either entering addresses in a browser window or the text of an e-mail message. Keyboard shortcuts incorporated in browsing software permit you to execute a wide range of online motions from your keyboard, with minimum need for a mouse.

For example, if you wanted to open a new Web page, such as http:// www.nas.edu/ (home for the National Academy of Sciences), you could do so without ever grabbing your mouse. Instead of taking your hand off the

---

Fig. 11-8: Your Browser's Edit Menu (shown), View and and File menus, typically will show you keyboard shortcuts available. In the example shown, we have selected "Find In Page" from the Edit Menu, and we see that Ctrl-F is the keyboard shortcut for the operation.

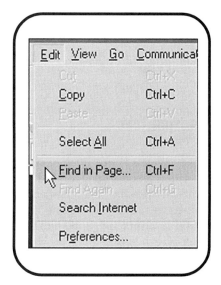

keyboard, grabbing the mouse, clicking the file menu, and selecting "Open," you could: Type Ctrl-O (Apple Cmd-O). This brings up a dialog box that asks you for the address you want. In some versions of *Navigator* or *Explorer*, you start the "Open Location" dialog box by typing Ctrl-L (Apple Cmd-L). In *Opera*, you merely hit the F2 key to start the dialog. In all browsers, you may see what the shortcut command is by using your mouse to drop down the File Menu and then read the command. Useful keyboard shortcuts may be found on the File, Edit, and View menus.

Searching within a Document

One useful keyboard shortcut permits you to do repetitive searches for words or phrases within a document in your browser window. For example, you may have located a copy of the U.S. Constitution online (available at http://www.house.gov/Constitution/Constitution.html), but all you are interested in are those sections that pertain to impeachment of the President.

With the document loaded in your browser, you start a search by typing Ctrl-F (Apple Cmd-F). In the search dialog box, you type the word "impeachment" (it is not case sensitive unless you specify the search is to be case sensitive), and hit the Enter (Return) key. Your browser will take you straight to the first occurrence of the word "impeachment." If you then type Ctrl-G (Apple Cmd-G), the browser will take you to the next occurrence of the word. The Ctrl-G process for finding the next occurrence works in Netscape *Navigator,* in *Messenger*, and in the e-mail client *Eudora. Explorer* does not support it. Instead, you are obliged to click on a "Find Next" button.

This technique can be useful in many situations where you are following up on a search done at a public search site. You may wind up retrieving very long documents but have an interest in only a narrowly defined topic. Just use the "Find" keyboard command, Crtl-F.

Copying Text

Let's say you actually were searching for the text in the U.S. Constitution that described impeachment proceedings, and you have located the relevant sentences. As a government document, the text is copyright free. All you have to do to snag the text is to select it, copy it to your operating system's clipboard, and then paste it into the document you are writing.

Selecting text in a browser window requires you to use a mouse— unless you select all the text by using the keyboard shortcut Ctrl-A (Apple

Cmd-A). Once your text is selected, you copy it to the clipboard by typing Ctrl-C (Apple Cmd-C), and you paste it into your word processing document with Ctrl-V (Apple Cmd-V). If you are familiar with the Windows or the Mac operating system keyboard shortcuts, you will recognize that these and many other keyboard shortcuts employed by browser software are consistent with shortcuts in other applications for Windows or for the Mac.

Navigating by Keyboard

Keyboard shortcuts also permit you to do a number of other useful operations. The Windows operating system has an edge here because the system and programs written for Windows are designed to have chief functions accessible by keystroke, independent of the mouse. Table 11-1 shows some of the more common keyboard shortcuts.

Staying Connected on the Road

When CBS's Dan Rather wanted to cover the civil war in Afghanistan, he donned a native costume and traveled to that country. CNN's Bernard Shaw was in Baghdad when the Gulf War erupted in 1991. Indeed, since before Horace Greeley hired Karl Marx to report on events in Europe, journalists have traveled to where the story is.

Whether the story takes you across state or across the globe, the challenge for the contemporary journalist remains to stay connected to the Internet. To stay connected, you can:

1. Use an Internet service provider (ISP) that has points of presence (POPs) in the cities to which you travel.
2. Forward mail to a Web-based mail manager that you access through borrowed machines.
3. Configure borrowed or public machines to access your mail.
4. Use a mobile phone to gain local access.

Telecommunication services are becoming more global. The day is not far off when you will be able to use your cellular telephone everywhere in the world. Global access to the Internet is growing as well. One Internet Service Provider recently advertised local access in "more than 300 cities" in the United States. Another boasted of POPs in the United States, the United Kingdom, and Europe, and a third proclaimed global access. The message is simple. ISPs are motivated to offer local telephone access in a large number of cities. The good news for you is that with local access points, you do not have to reconfigure your browser, e-mail clients, and/ or computer dial-up software every time you are working out of town.

Table 11-1: A listing of some of the more common keyboard shortcuts supported by browsing software

Win Shortcut	Mac Shortcut	Result
Ctrl-N	Cmd-N	Opens a new browser window (N, IE, O)
Ctrl-M	Cmd-M	Starts a new mail message (N)
Ctrl-M	Cmd-M	Initiates send/retrieve mail routine (E, OE)
Ctrl-S	Cmd-S	Save the current page / mail message (All)
Ctrl-F	Cmd-F	Starts "Find" dialog to search for text within a document (All)
Ctrl-G	Cmd-G	Finds next occurrence of text string defined above (N, E)
Alt-Left	Cmd-Left	Browser goes back to previous page (N, IE, O)
Alt-Right	Cmd-Right	Browser goes forward to next page (N, IE, O)
Dn/Up	Dn/Up	Text in display scrolls one line at a time (All)
Pg Dn/Up	Pg Dn/Up	Text in display scrolls one page at a time (All)
Tab	Tab	Move cursor between boxes in a form (All)
Ctrl-W	Cmd-W	Closes current window (N, O)
Esc	Esc	Stop page download (N, IE, O)
Ctrl-D	Cmd-D	Sets bookmark (Favorite) on current page (N, IE) In Eudora, deletes the current message
Ctrl-B	Cmd-B	Opens bookmark (Favorite) list for editing (N, IE)
Ctrl-R	Cmd-R	Starts the mail message "Reply" function (N, OE, E)
Shft-Ctrl-R		Starts the mail message "Reply to All" function (E, N, OE)
Ctrl-C	Cmd-C	Copies selected text to the OS clipboard (All)
Ctrl-V	Cmd-V	Pastes copied text from the OS clipboard (All)
Ctrl-A	Cmd-A	Selects all text, other objects in open document (All)
Shft-Ctrl-F	Shft-Cmd-F	Start search of e-mail messages for text string (N)
Ctrl-P	Cmd-P	Print current document (All)

Key: E=Eudora, N=Netscape, IE=Internet Explorer, OE=Outlook Express, O=Opera

Generally, you have only to change a phone number in your dial-up networking profile on your notebook computer to connect to your ISP in the new city. This means that you need to look up the telephone number before you leave town. ISPs routinely make lists of local numbers available in their Web sites. You get the number before you leave home, write it down, and connect when you get to the new city. The chief advantage of working this way is that all your client software settings remain untouched and everything continues working as it was before you left home. Appendix C provides a discussion of Internet Service Providers and how to select one that fits your needs.

Web-Based Mail Services

Another strategy for staying in touch while you are on the road is to use Web-based mail reading services. Web-based mail was described in Chapter 4. Dozens of such services can also capture mail from your ISP's mail server and hold messages for you at a Web site. When you want mail, you navigate to the mail server on the Web, log on, and manage your mail. Some of these services also offer Internet access at a fee or for free. The price you pay for the service is advertising at the mail processing site and perhaps one-line advertisements appended to each of your mail messages. Processing mail at a remote Web server tends to be considerably slower than downloading mail directly to your computer and using your own mail client.

A search of *Yahoo!* "Computers and Internet" resources on the phrase "free e-mail" produced a list of 95 sites in the fall of 1999. Some sites offering free Web-based mail include.

- *Excite* offers free voicemail, fax, and e-mail available from http://www.excite.com/
- *Hotmail*, a service that specializes in free e-mail at http://www.hotmail.com/
- *Juno*, a long-standing free e-mail service at http://www.juno.com/
- Netscape *Web Mail* at http://Webmail.netscape.com/
- *Yahoo!* Mail at http://my.yahoo.com/

The way that these typically work is that you sign up by visiting the site. In the process of signing up, you must give the names of your outgoing (SMTP) and incoming (POP) mail servers, your username, and password for getting mail. You may be asked whether you want the Web mail service to erase mail on the original server or leave the mail there. You also tell the Web mail service how often you want it to check for new mail.

If you have more than one e-mail account, some Web-based services let you keep multiple profiles. You can specify which ones you want to be active during any time period.

Configuring Public Browsers

Earlier in this chapter you learned how to configure the e-mail clients associated with Web browsers. The Web browsers in many public access computer labs have e-mail clients associated with them. As long as you know your SMTP and POP server names, by following the same procedures described earlier, you can configure the e-mail client to access your e-mail. If you go this route, however, you must be sure to remove your information after you finish reviewing your mail. Also, frequently your server will delete messages that you have retrieved (many people save their messages on their own hard disk drive). That means that you must be prepared to deal with the e-mail you retrieve or you may want to save messages to a floppy disk.

Wireless Access

One of the most interesting developments in the late 1990s has been the development of wireless access to the Internet. In 1999, the first generation of cellular telephones that doubled as Internet access devices were released. Indeed, AOL has announced a long-term goal to provide Internet access through a wide variety of devices such as cellular telephones.

Along the same lines, some companies are offering wireless access to the Internet directly via wireless modems in laptop or desktop computers. For example, in 1999, Metricom, based in Los Gatos, California, offered wireless Internet access in Washington D.C., San Francisco, Seattle, and selected hotels and college campuses.

Extending Browsers with Plug-Ins

The World Wide Web is a multimedia environment, capable of transmitting and displaying not only text documents but also graphics, video, static sound and streaming audio, and animation. As you learned in Chapter 3, standard Web browsers cannot display all the different kinds of media that can be transmitted via the Web. For some of these media types, your browser relies on third-party programs called "plug-ins" to deliver any medium beyond text, graphics, or simple animations. These plug-ins extend the capabilities of your browser.

The first hint that you need a plug-in comes when you load a page or click on a link pointing to a file that your browser does not recognize. In some cases, you get a dialog window that asks you what program you want to use to open the file. At other times, the browser recognizes that a specific plug-in is required to open the file, and offers to take you to a page (at the Microsoft or Netscape Web sites) from which you can select a plug-in to download. Some Web pages tell you that you will need a certain kind of plug-in, and they offer a link to take you directly to the third-party site where the plug-in resides.

In Chapter 3, you received a broad overview of plug-ins. This chapter will take a more in-depth look at some of the most popular plug-ins used with today's browsers, including Real Networks' *Real Player* for playing back streaming audio and video, Adobe's *Acrobat Reader* for displaying and printing publications formatted in Adobe's portable document format specification, and *Alexa* to aid in searching the Web.

Streaming Media

News media Web sites frequently employ digital audio and/or video clips in their news packages. Some radio stations send their broadcast audio signal out live over the Internet. Unfortunately, both audio and video files contain a lot of information, much more information than is contained in text and graphics files.

Generally speaking, most files transmitted via the Web are first received by the browser and then displayed. Many audio and video plug-ins follow the same procedure. First the audio or video file is downloaded and then played. Because audio and video files are so large, however, downloading those files can take a long time. A video file that will run for two seconds can take two minutes to download.

Streaming media is a method to circumvent the speed problems faced by audio and video. In streaming media, as a video file arrives at its destination, data are stored for a few seconds and then played back even as the rest of the file is still being received. Because the entire file does not have to be downloaded prior to viewing, viewing begins sooner, and larger files can be created.

Real Networks is the leader in streaming media, though it has competition from Microsoft, Apple, and others. Netscape bundles *Real Player* with its *Communicator* software suite. To access streaming media using the Real Networks format you need the *Real Player* plug-in, which you can download for free from the Real Networks Web site, http://www.real.com/.

Portable Document Format (.pdf)

Graphic artists and publication designers may spend hours creating a printed document. Their objective is to get the document to appear—on paper—exactly the way best suited to communicate some message. They apply their talents to produce a carefully designed interplay of type, graphics, photos, and white space. They control exactly what people see and to some extent the way people see it because it is permanently fixed by ink on paper.

The Web environment is not so rigid. Different browsers display the same documents with enough differences to inspire a sense of futility in the hearts of many document designers. And the same browser, running under a different operating system, also can display the same document differently.

Because HTML simply does not control the look of the files on the screen to a sufficient degree, people have looked for alternatives. One solution is Adobe *Acrobat* and its portable document format (.pdf) documents. These documents deliver pages and publications that appear exactly as they were created regardless of the type of computer upon which they are viewed or (within reason) the printer upon which they are printed. The *Acrobat* software package has two parts. One is a program called *Acrobat Distiller*, which converts documents into the .pdf format while preserving the look and feel of the original document.

When you encounter a .pdf file, you need a free plug-in called Adobe *Acrobat Reader* (*Acrobat Reader* also works as a stand-alone product). *Acrobat Reader* displays the document so that it looks on your computer the way it did on the document designer's computer.

While there are some advantages to this arrangement, one disadvantage is a serious shortcoming for journalists. In earlier versions of *Acrobat Reader* text in .pdf format was not searchable nor could quotes be selected and copied to your system clipboard for inclusion in stories. The *Acrobat Reader* is freely available at the Adobe site, http://www.adobe.com/.

Alexa, the Research Assistant

For journalists, one of the least-publicized browser plug-ins is also one of the most valuable. *Alexa* does not enable you to view or hear special Web content. It is an innovative research aid. Like other plug-ins, it is freely available at the publisher's Web site (http://www.alexa.com/).

Once installed, *Alexa* runs alongside your browser and monitors the pages you visit. It then creates a report consisting of information about each site you visit. The report starts with a relative traffic rating and links to reviews on the site. The rest of the report, in the *Internet Explorer* version, is divided into seven major categories.

1. "Contact Information" includes phone number and address for the registered owner of the site as well as links to a map and directions to the site's home, links to a related City Guide, and the date the site first came online.

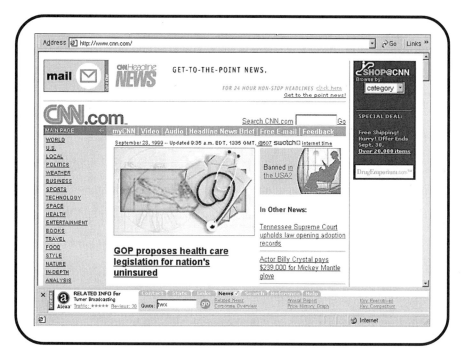

Fig. 11-9: *Alexa* installs itself as a thin strip across the bottom of *Internet Explorer*. In this form, it displays seven tabs leading to classes of information about each site you visit. *Alexa* may also configure as a vertical version along the left side of *Explorer* (see Fig. 11-10).

2. "Site statistics" includes some consumer-oriented data including notes on third-party reviews, site speed, freshness of content, links pointing to the site, pages in the site, an opportunity to vote for the site, and links to archived pages.

3. "Related Links" suggests other sites with contents similar to the one you are currently viewing. If you happen to be using a search engine, *Alexa* displays links that take your query to other search engines.

4. "News" is news related to the company that owns the site you are viewing. This includes financial information, key competitors, and company overviews on publicly held companies.

5. "Reference" is a look-up utility that allows you to use *Encyclopedia Britannica Online*, the *Merriam-Webster Dictionary and Thesaurus*, and Britannica's Web Guide.

6. "Search" facility permits you to select from six search sites and then enter a query. Used in conjunction with "Related Links," this can be a powerful tool for researching any topic.

7. "Help" includes searchable FAQs and technical support, a help file, and a tour of *Alexa* features.

Fig. 11-10: Configured vertically, Alexa plants itself along the left side of *Internet Explorer*. In this form, it gives expanding and collapsing lists linked to information about the site you are currently visiting.

If you install *Alexa* with *Internet Explorer*, the add-on plants itself along the bottom of your browser by default, displaying seven note card-style tabs. In *IE*, *Alexa* may be moved to the left side, in the frame occupied by Favorites when you click on the Favorites button in the Standard Buttons Toolbar. In the vertical arrangement, the plug-in gives you two additional links: a "one-page report" option and a link to a document that explains the source of *Alexa* data.

A different version of *Alexa* is designed to run with Netscape *Navigator*. *Alexa* 1.41 runs as a separate small window at the foot of (but not contained within) the *Navigator* window. *Alexa* 1.41 also works with *Opera*, but *Alexa* does not promote support for use with *Opera*. The free-floating version does not have all the same tabs as the *IE* version. Instead, some of the tabs are compressed and combined into a more streamlined set of choices. It has popup windows that offer links to site statistics and related links. Links on the bar offer to take you to the Encyclopedia Britannica site, the *Alexa* site, or to a cached version of the current page.

Later versions (4.x) of Netscape *Navigator* provide an alternate version of the *Alexa* service. When you click on the "What's Related" button on the *Navigator* menu bar, some of the choices you are given point to the *Alexa* services from within the Netscape *NetCenter* site. You get a select list of related sites near the top of the menu, and at the bottom of the menu you get a "detailed list" option that takes you to a page of the Netscape site provided "by Alexa." Just as you get with the *IE* version, you get options for stock quotes and news on the company behind the site. You get external search options and some Netscape-specific search options, but no link to the Britannica online encyclopedia.

Interestingly, *Alexa* has the ability to call up archived versions of Web pages that may not be available any longer. In an effort to assist users who encounter "File Not Found" messages when they click on links, the *Alexa* toolbar provides the user with the most recent snapshot the service has of a given URL. To do this, the Alexa service archives vast samples of World Wide Web pages—pages visited by *Alexa* users. The archive option is available in both the free-floating bar and the *IE* versions of *Alexa*. It is not available in the Netscape internal version.

Plug-In Cautions

Plug-ins add flair to documents and life to the Web-browsing experience. Plug-ins like Adobe's *Acrobat Reader* and *Real Player* from Real Networks permit you to view (and hear) information you might not be able to "read" any other way. *Alexa* adds depth to the research process. You will have to be the judge of whether they help you as a journalist to do the research or produce online documents you need. Experts on browsing software warn there can be a price to pay for adding plug-ins. Plug-ins can slow down the performance of your browser, even if you are not viewing files that require any plug-in.

The problem is that plug-ins, especially if you have several of them installed, add system overhead to your browser. Some of the plug-ins, like *Alexa*, may be turned off or on at will. Others, like *Real Player* tend to install themselves so that they are running in the background as soon as you start up your computer—they do not wait to be invoked by the browser. A wise course of action here is to install only those plug-ins you will definitely need.

Selecting the Best Software

With perhaps a half-dozen easily available e-mail clients and at least three browsers from which to choose, which is best? The answer, unequivocally, is "it depends." Five factors should be considered, roughly in this order: 1) which software your company or school supports (or insists you use), 2) which software works the way you work, 3) your budget, 4) your need for handholding, 5) aesthetic appeal.

If your school or company selects the software for you and insists you use the selected client, you have little choice but to learn what is provided to you. If you have freedom to choose your software, then budget is probably the lesser of the next two criteria; much of the software is available for free although many companies offer advanced versions of their software for which they charge. If you spend time experimenting with several different e-mail clients, you will find they all pretty much do the same things. What is different is the way they do those things, the way the Internet client software works with the rest of your software, and the look and feel of the program. Much the same can be said of browsers.

Distinctions among Browsers

Publishers of the two leading browsers have been so aggressive in competition with one another that computer magazines print frequent updates on what they call "The Browser Wars." Some of Microsoft's marketing practices involving *IE* became the focal point for a U.S. Justice Department antitrust suit.

The benefit to online journalists who use either browser is that the programs are constantly evolving, rich with features, and free. The downside is that as the programs have grown rich with features they have also required more computer resources. The complete Netscape *Communicator* (32-bit Windows version 4.61) package takes nearly 20MB on your hard drive during a typical install. *Internet Explorer* is even more demanding, requiring 89MB during installation and 55MB after installation for a typical install of *IE* 5.0 with "Internet Tools."

Space demands is where *Opera* really shines. The entire *Opera* program, in compressed archive format, fits comfortably on a floppy disk. The publishers of *Opera* maintain that its smaller size helps it to run faster. Moreover, *Opera* and *Eudora Light* may run on slimmed-down laptop computers when *Internet Explorer* and *Navigator* may not.

Despite their similarities the major browsers are not exactly the same. The Netscape *Communicator* suite can be distinguished from Microsoft's *Internet Explorer* in three ways. First, in *Communicator*, the *Navigator* browser and the *Messenger* e-mail client are seamlessly integrated. If either program is loaded into your computer's memory, the other program is just a couple of keystrokes away. Moreover, Netscape *Composer*, an HTML editor that lets you create Web pages, is included as well.

The second distinction is that *Navigator* saves bookmarks in one, flat HTML file that any other browser can read, and *Navigator* can switch to a new bookmarks file with just a few keystrokes. It makes sharing bookmarks with others or dedicating a set of bookmarks to a project an easy matter of copying one file. For the same reason it is easy to copy

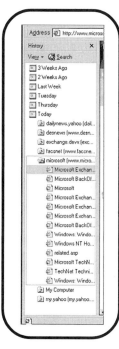

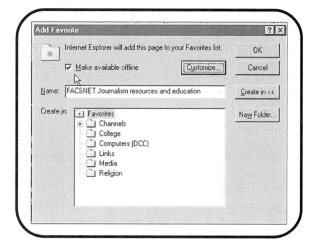

Figs. 11-11, 11-12: *Internet Explorer* maintains a history file of places you have visited that can span over several weeks (left). *IE* also permits you to save bookmarks for reading offline (above). When you do so, you save pages down several levels in a site.

bookmarks to your laptop or to move your bookmark files back and forth between the office or school and home.

A third distinction is that the browser contains one-click icons that switch you into the mail mode, HTML editor mode, or news reading mode. In fact, there are keyboard shortcuts for switching among the *Communicator* elements.

On the other hand, *Internet Explorer* is more tightly integrated with programs in the Microsoft *Office* suite of programs. For example, *IE* relies on *Outlook Express* as its e-mail client. If you have Microsoft *Word* on your computer and the full *Outlook* program, you can make *Word* your e-mail editor. Moreover, although *Internet Explorer* does not store its bookmarks in one HTML file that can be read by any browser (and a host of other programs), its "favorites" are accessible to programs belonging to the *Microsoft Office* suite.

Another feature that sets *IE* 5.0 apart from *NN* 4.6 is *Explorer's* History panel. The program tracks all the places you have visited for several weeks. When you ask for a display of history, *IE* opens up a panel alongside your main browser window and gives you a list of folders representing the Web sites you have visited today, other days this week, last week, and so forth. You open the appropriate day, and within the day are folders representing each site and then listings of the pages you visited. This can be handy for revisiting a page you failed to note in other ways.

Another interesting feature in *Internet Explorer* is its ability to save sites for offline viewing. When you add a favorite to your list in *IE*, you have the option to check a box that says "Make available offline." This saves the current page to your computer's hard drive. You may also save pages below the page you are saving as a favorite. When you click on the "Customize" button, you select how deep into the site you want *Explorer* to save. The advantage to this is that you can review significant portions of Web sites offline, say, on an airplane. The disadvantage is that you can very quickly use up a large amount of disk space on your hard drive.

The look and feel of *Opera* are so different from the other two browsers it would be unique if only for its appearance. *Opera* by default uses your entire screen. Within the main *Opera* window, the program opens three browser windows in the main part of the screen and two bookmark windows on the left. Bookmark folders appear on the upper left frame. Contents of whatever folder is selected in the upper frame appear in the lower bookmark frame. Like the left frame History display in *Internet Explorer*, the left frame in *Opera* may hide hotlists. The hotlists frame

---

Fig. 11-13: *Opera* is distinctive among browsers in many ways, including its appearance. By default it starts up with three browser windows open to separate documents. You have the option of returning to any group of windows you like every time you start up. *Opera* comes with a deep set of bookmarks (shown here at the left) aimed at the research-oriented.

may be "undocked" from the left frame and displayed as a floating window that you can specify stays on top of all other windows or falls behind the active window. This makes *Opera* very friendly toward journalists who work a lot from their bookmarks.

Opera has several features that allow you to manipulate the images on the screen. Zoom, found in a drop-down window at the right of the address bar, permits you to select page zoom settings from 20 percent to 1,000 percent of normal size. Toggle buttons at the left of the address bar let you turn off images (graphics) or turn them back on with one click. Turning graphics off speeds up the rate at which Web pages are loaded and displayed.

The program in its current version (3.60) has limited built-in e-mail capabilities. It will permit you to send mail from within the program, but not to receive mail. It will, however, hand off mail functions to other programs if you specify that choice. While you may download a trial copy for free, you are obligated to register the program ($35 U.S.) if you use it for more than 30 days.

Distinctions among E-mail Clients

E-mail clients today offer spell check utilities, the ability to include graphics, use various typefaces, and attach binary documents. They support automatic mail retrieval and notification while you are working on something else, and their address books accept nicknames to aid your memory and speed the process of addressing mail. They will even read the address books from other programs. However, the programs do have different nuances.

All three programs support nicknames, a trait that lets you type a short name into the address field and the software fills in the address. Netscape *Messenger* has also implemented the "Look Ahead" feature that the two main browsers support when you are typing Web site addresses to open. As you type the person's name or nickname into the "To" field, *Messenger* monitors each character you type, looking for the unique combination of letters that will separate one addressee from all others. It reports to you constantly until you either tab out of the field or hit the Enter key. If you have a large address book, it will probably start by reporting, "<Multiple Matches Found>." As soon as you type the defining character, it reports to you the person's name and e-mail address. Because it gives both the name and the e-mail address, you have double assurance that you are sending to the correct person. And all this requires no mouse action; the entire process takes place from the keyboard.

In contrast, *Eudora* accepts the nickname but does not report back to you any confirming full name and address. *Outlook Express* does support "look ahead," but it does not display the e-mail address itself. In some cases, this requires you to click on the "To:" button and to search your address book if you seek confirmation that the correct address is selected.

Managing Attachments

Each e-mail client program manages attachments differently. *Eudora*, by default, removes attachments from the e-mail message and places them in a separate directory. It adds a line to the e-mail message telling you the name of the attachment and where Eudora placed it (by default in an Attachments folder). The name is linked, so all you have to do is to click on it to start the process of viewing or saving the attachment. This can be handy because you always know where to go for the attachments and it saves you the trouble of manually retrieving the attachment. The down side is that it is easy to forget that attachments are being placed in the folder all the time.

Messenger places a paper clip button at the top of the message to give you an alternative click point for retrieving the attachment. *Outlook Express* informs you that you have an attachment by placing a paper clip icon in the header information area, and it can be easy to overlook the icon and miss the fact that you have an attachment. Text attachments are not displayed in line, but must be viewed separately. If you get discussion list messages in digest format, then *Outlook Express* tends to treat each message in the digest as a separate attachment that must be opened one at a time. This slows considerably the process of monitoring discussion list digests.

Stationery and Mail Themes

E-mail over the Internet was once purely text without any formatting. Today, e-mail clients routinely support creation and delivery of e-mail messages as colorful and varied as pages on the World Wide Web. *Eudora* and *Outlook Express* come with stationery options that permit you routinely to include with your e-mail background images, logos, designs, and everything else you might include on paper stationery. *Messenger* suggests that you create templates for frequently used message types. Typically, such messages are sent in rich text format (RTF) or in HTML, the language of the World Wide Web. Both formats are text based; yet they support document formatting. *Outlook Express* supports both rtf and HTML mail. It comes with a sampling of stationery, and generally is much easier than the other mailers when it comes to setting up and using stationery. If you want to add flair to your e-mail, this is the program.

If you employ stationery or do text formatting in your mail, all the care you have taken to prepare a pretty document may go to waste if the person at the receiving end has a text-only e-mail reader. Some universities force folks to manage their mail through *Pine* software on a host computer. Some corporate systems managers prefer the relative security of a text-only messaging system.

Even if people at the receiving end of your messages have mail clients that give them the ability to read HTML and/or rich text messages, you can't always be sure they are seeing the message at their end the way you formatted it at your end. If you are not sure your addressees can read the HTML or rich text format message the way you expected, the safest route is to configure your mail client to send text only.

Concerning AOL and CompuServe Browsers

America Online gained preeminence as an online service by mass distributing its own software, packaged with a number of free hours of online time. As AOL evolved into an Internet Service Provider, it continued its tradition of providing its own software. CompuServe (now owned by AOL) has followed suit. Both AOL and CompuServe offer to their 22 million plus subscribers proprietary versions of Microsoft *Internet Explorer* specifically designed to provide easy access to their services.

The AOL and CompuServe browsers do not look the same as their general marketplace siblings. They have a different menu structure and different program icons, and they do not respond the same way to the keyboard shortcuts described in this chapter. For example, you may wish to place a bookmark on a Web site you like by using the keyboard shortcut Ctrl-D. The shortcut works for the general marketplace versions of both *Internet Explorer* and Netscape *Navigator*. However, if you are using *CompuServe 2000* software, typing Ctrl-D will disconnect you from CompuServe (and the Internet). Similarly, typing Ctrl-O in the hopes of launching the "Open New Location" dialog will produce unanticipated results. To open a new location, you will need to type the address in the address window on the browser.

The price AOL and CompuServe users pay for the convenience of the proprietary software is generally having a slower browser, extra "clutter" on the screen (special AOL and CompuServe icons and extra windows), and entirely new kinds of keyboard shortcuts. However, you can still use your AOL and CompuServe connections to run the generic *IE* and *NN* browsers.

Using Generic Browsers under CompuServe and AOL Accounts

To use generic versions of *Internet Explorer*, Netscape *Navigator*, or *Opera* while connecting to the Internet through CompuServe or AOL is a two-step process. First you connect to AOL or CompuServe through your normal procedure. Once connected, you minimize the AOL or CompuServe browser (do not close it). With the AOL or CompuServe browser minimized, you may launch any of the generic browsers and use them for Internet research. The performance of generic browsers under this condition will sometimes be slower than the performance of the same browser working through a standard ISP, yet generic browsers may still be faster than the proprietary ones provided by AOL and CompuServe.

Conclusion

The Internet software suite including Web browsing software and an e-mail client is at the heart of the online workplace. Much of the work done by online journalists is done researching stories through World Wide Web sites and corresponding with people through e-mail clients associated with or integrated into Web browsers. Browsers tend to be feature-rich programs integrated with or closely connected to e-mail functions. Browser plug-in programs extend their functionality so that they can display files they couldn't on their own.

Your productivity online can be greatly enhanced as you learn more about how your browser and associated e-mail programs work. Such things as keyboard shortcuts and internal document searching can be great time savers. If you are free to choose which software you use, you would do well to experiment with several different programs and then to select the software that works most like you do.

Chapter **12**

Net Impact on Journalism

On November 18, 1951, Edward R. Murrow sat in a control room in New York City while live images of the Brooklyn Bridge were broadcast over the Columbia Broadcasting System network. A few seconds later, the scene switched to a live image of the Golden Gate Bridge in San Francisco. It was the first live, coast-to-coast television broadcast in America.

Although the images were less than compelling—after all, the network was broadcasting images of bridges—Murrow, who became the dean of American broadcasting, marveled at the technology. He was amazed the images taken across the country could be broadcast live so effortlessly.

And Murrow was right to be amazed. Within half a decade, television was on its way to being the dominant mass medium in America, a perch it has held for the past 40 years. In that period, to a large degree, television has shaped entertainment, politics, and news in America.

The impact of television on journalism was just one in a long list of new technologies that have influenced the way that news is reported and distributed to the public. In the 1830s, improvements in printing technology enabled mass circulation newspapers to emerge. Entrepreneurs like James Gordon Bennett were able to establish newspapers in which the main content was news rather than commentary.

The invention of the telegraph in 1846 increased the speed at which distant events could be reported. High-speed photography in the 1880s and 1890s fueled the cult of celebrity in America. Radio and film evolved in the 1920s and brought immediacy and moving pictures to news. Television made stars out of both journalists and politicians.

And the pace of technological innovation has speeded up in the last 30 years of the twentieth century. In the 1970s and 1980s, cable television, satellite broadcasting, and cellular technology have given the world real-time news any time from anywhere. Journalists now broadcast live from the war fronts, major demonstrations in faraway lands and natural catastrophes from across the globe. It is common for senior American governmental officials to track major events around the world by watching CNN.

The Internet, and specifically the World Wide Web, represents the major new communications technology of this generation. The emergence of the Internet has led to a stampede of new companies into the news business. At the same time, major media companies have scrambled to reinvent themselves to take advantage of the opportunities offered by the Internet. A standard refrain in the conventional news media now is "for more information, check our Web site."

In this chapter you will

- review how the growth of television changed journalism,
- examine the differences in news content between Web sites and other news media,
- look at the rise of multimedia journalism,
- explore how Web-based journalism can potentially increase public debate and press accountability,
- understand how the Web has changed the economics of journalism, and
- assess the impact of the Internet on journalism.

How Television Changed Journalism

In 1960, presidential candidates John F. Kennedy and Richard M. Nixon agreed to debate each other on television. Nixon, the vice president of the United States, was confident that the appearance would tip the election in his direction. After all, he was a skilled debater and he viewed his opponent as an intellectual lightweight.

Three days before the debate, Nixon fell ill. Nonetheless, he continued to push himself at a torrid pace. Moreover, he suffered from that dreaded syndrome, the five-o'clock shadow. His beard grew rapidly during the day and by the evening, unless he shaved again, a dark stubble was noticeable on his face.

Many people believe that five o'clock shadow should not be a major issue in a presidential campaign. But in 1960, it was. During the televised debates, Nixon did not look well. He sweated openly on camera. He looked pale. His five o'clock shadow was obvious.

The result was that according to the conventional wisdom and some anecdotal evidence at the time, although a majority of the people who listened to the debate on radio thought that Nixon had "won" on substance, most of the people who viewed the debate on television thought Kennedy, who had appeared cool, calm and collected, had won. In an election that proved to be extremely close, some pundits believed Kennedy was chosen to be president of the United States because he was more telegenic.

Since the 1960 election, television completely changed political campaigns and reporting on political campaigns. In 1968, Joe McGinnis showed in *The Selling of the President* how Madison Avenue advertising techniques played a central role in Richard Nixon's successful campaign. Over time, politics became increasingly mediated by television. By the late 1980s, mainstream newspapers regularly reported on the political advertisements that candidates aired. Reporters and newspapers were no longer the primary conduit through which candidates communicated with the voters. Television captured that role.

But completely reshaping political campaigns and political journalism was only one impact of television on journalism. Television also redefined the role of the reporter. Television changed the definition of news. And television tightened the news media's grip as the gatekeeper of information for public discussion.

It is hard to imagine, but when radio and then television emerged as major mass media, news professionals who worked in that area were not considered journalists. Print journalists tried to exclude radio and television reporters from many of their professional associations and from specialized news venues. Of course, television reporters ultimately were accepted as bona fide journalists. Nonetheless, the role of the television reporter and the print journalist are often quite different.

For example, in 1998, CNN correspondent Peter Arnett reported a shocking story that asserted that despite its denials, the United States had used chemical weapons during the Gulf War in 1991. It was an explosive exposé of the actions of the United States military from a journalist who had a reputation as a hard-nosed reporter willing to follow a story to wherever it led. The military vigorously disputed the story. But in the controversy that followed, there was a surprise. Although Peter Arnett had narrated the story on screen, the majority of the reporting had been done by the story's producer April Oliver. Arnett had done little of the actual legwork or interviewing himself.

Indeed, television placed a focus on the people in front of the screen rather than on the people who actually report the stories. While Mike Wallace and the team at *60 Minutes* have won reputations for tough journalism, behind-the-scenes producers do most of the actual work. ABC News White House correspondent Sam Donaldson earned a reputation as a provocative questioner of various presidents because he was seen on camera shouting at them as they passed by, not because he had dug deeply into issues. Some observers have remarked that the difference in reporting on the Watergate scandal and impeachment in the early 1970s—a story moved forward largely through print journalism—and the Monica Lewinsky scandal and impeachment in the late 1990s was that during Watergate, reporters actually found unwilling sources and dug up new facts about what had happened. Reporting in the Lewinsky scandal consisted of talking heads on television speculating about what was going to happen next. In short, in television journalism the emphasis is placed on who appears on camera rather than the reporting that takes place off camera.

The need to meet the requirements of television, which is a visual medium, also has shaped what qualifies as news. The contours of television news are shaped by two parameters. First, a visual medium needs good visuals. That means stories that don't have compelling images are less likely to be reported than stories that tell a visual tale. A long-standing axiom in local television news (an axiom that is under hot debate) is that "if it bleeds, it leads." The axiom means that because crime scenes offer compelling visuals, they are likely to capture viewer attention and should start the broadcast. In contrast, except in extreme cases, crime is often relegated to the second section of newspapers.

The second defining parameter of television news is time. Most daily news broadcasts restrict the length of each story to less than two minutes. A 30-minute news broadcast may have only 10 to 12 stories or fewer. Even stories on news magazines run only around 18 to 20 minutes. Consequently, complex stories that may require more explanation and background than can be conveyed in 90 seconds are more difficult to report on television.

Moreover, because television news shows had to appeal to a large audience, care had to be taken to include stories that appealed to a cross section of the population. As a result, national news broadcasts include light features as well as political news and other kinds of stories.

Ironically, the technical considerations that shape television news content have spilled over to newspapers as well. Since the success of *USA Today*, newspaper editors have been admonished to publish short stories and use snappy graphics to attract the attention of generations of people raised on television. Newspapers have been encouraged to publish "news you can use" kinds of features that often worked well on television.

While television clearly reshaped the image of reporters and news content, perhaps the most significant impact of television has been on the national agenda. Network news was the first national media. For the first time information could be transmitted to the entire nation at once. Network news could define, to a large degree, what the country knew every day and what the public discussed by serving as the gatekeeper on national information.

For more than a generation, CBS, NBC and ABC largely defined the national news agenda. Other organizations could not really compete with them. The process of putting together a national network was simply too complicated. They were joined in the early 1980s by CNN, which capitalized on new cable technology to establish a news network. CNN succeeded, in part, because the networks were slow to react to cable's potential.

Setting the national agenda is a complicated process. To some degree, the network news organizations take their cues for coverage from the *New York Times* and the *Washington Post*. Consequently, the rise of television enhanced the influence of the most prestigious newspapers, sometimes at the expense of their competitors.

In summary, the technical requirements of television completely reshaped journalism over the past 50 years. News became increasingly visual. Stories were shortened. Reporters were known for their presence in front of the camera rather than for their digging behind the scenes. But even as news became shorter and snappier, television journalism claimed a major role in defining the national agenda and serving as the gatekeeper for information to the public.

The Web's Challenge to Television

The World Wide Web promises to have as dramatic an impact on journalism as television. In some ways, journalism on the Web can be seen potentially as the anti-television. Where television required short stories and flashing visuals, the Web has virtually unlimited space and the capacity to easily combine print with visuals and sound. Web sites can appeal both to mass audiences and specialized niche publics. And the Web is not bound by time. The constraints on television simply don't come to bear on the Web.

In the first five years of Web journalism, the lack of constraints has had both a positive and negative effect. First, the established media's gatekeeping role has been challenged. When special prosecutor Kenneth Starr released his interim report in his investigation of President Bill Clinton, many newspapers felt that the material in the report that related to President Clinton's sexual activities were not appropriate to be printed in mainstream newspapers. And it is very difficult to give the details of a several-hundred page report on television.

But the report was published on the Web. That meant that anybody who wanted to read the sordid details of President Clinton's misadventures could read them. And hundreds of thousands of people apparently wanted to see the report itself.

The salacious material in the Starr Report was not the only information of that kind related to the impeachment proceedings in 1998 and 1999. While President Clinton was faced with being removed from office for lying to a grand jury about his adulterous affair with a young intern, the story emerged that the chairman of the House Judiciary Committee, who was spearheading the process and pushing hard to impeach the President, had also engaged in a long-term adulterous affair when he was in his forties. Mainstream newspapers and television news shows, serving in their role as the gatekeepers of public information, decided not to publish the story. *Salon*, a Web-based magazine of politics and culture, decided otherwise and published the story. Once *Salon* published the story, traditional news organizations followed.

Network news and national newspapers can no longer define what the public sees or hears. Content dismissed or ignored by traditional media

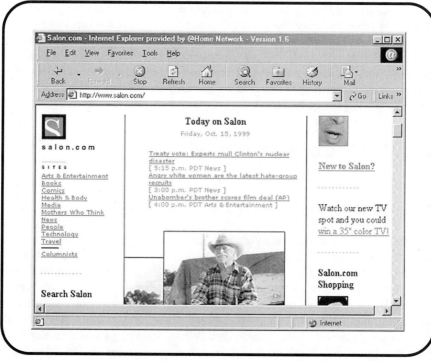

Fig. 12-1: Pushing the boundaries of journalism, Web-based *Salon* carried information about an affair the chairman of the House Judiciary Committee had had when other media at first refused to carry the story. When *Salon* did report the matter, other media had to follow.

can be easily published on the Web, broadening the scope of information that reaches the public.

In addition to news, the Internet has demonstrated that ability to reach mass audiences in other areas as well. In 1999, a handful of books and a few songs began their climb to national attention (in the case of music, it was largely through free downloads) via the Web and e-mail discussion lists. But the Web mostly works in conjunction with traditional media in bringing material to the public's attention. For example, the business newspaper *Investor's Business Daily* has a regular feature consisting of news culled from the Net. So while material that originates on the Web can make a national impact, network television and national newspapers still play a large role in defining the national agenda.

Liberation of Content and Its Presentation

Each new communications technology has shaped the content of news and its presentation. With the spread of the telegraph in the 1840s, not only could news from distant places be reported in a more timely fashion, news was often presented in short, terse bursts suitable for transmission over the wires as opposed to the more literary approaches used prior to that. Flash and high-speed photography brought a new immediacy to news reporting. Not only could people read descriptions of events, they could see photos of the events as well.

News photography was so shocking to some segments of the public that Louis Brandeis, then a professor at Harvard University Law School and later an associate justice of the United States Supreme Court, argued that people had a right to privacy. Radio and television also changed not only what is reported—radio, for example, made it possible to report directly from the scene of news—but how the news was presented as well.

The Internet and the Web is also changing both what is reported and how it is reported. Although the trend in both newspapers and television is toward shorter stories, Web-based media blessed with virtually unlimited space can carry both short and very long stories. Moreover, Web stories can be linked to supporting information such as reports, testimony, transcripts, studies, statistics and related articles. In some ways, the Web ultimately will prove to be a more complete source of information than any other news medium. That possibility is clear by the way broadcasts ranging from financial news on CNBC to NFL football games continually encourage viewers to log on to an appropriate Web site, at the risk of losing the viewer for the broadcast.

And not only can the Web carry more information, it can carry more types of information as well. Print journalism is confined to text and images. Radio is limited to audio, and television is almost exclusively an audio/video medium. The Web can carry all kinds of content—text, graphics, audio, video, animation, and more. Consequently, news stories can be presented in many different forms and in many different ways on the Web. In the first generation of online news, television news organizations would publish video clips to accompany text-and-graphics-based stories on their Web sites. As news organizations gain experience with the Web, however, they will be able to move past simply reusing existing content and be able to better integrate different media types. The result may be a much more compelling presentation of the news.

Rise of the Multimedia Journalist

When the book *Black Hawk Down* by Mark Bowden was published in 1999, it quickly became a best seller. The story of a misguided U.S. military adventure in Somalia, the book was well reported and well written. It also had appeared in a range of different media, including a CD-ROM and on *Phillynews Online* (http://www.phillynews.com), the Web site of the *Philadelphia Daily News*, as well as in the newspaper itself. Of course, it is not unusual for the same story to be presented through different media. Magazine articles are often expanded into books and books and news stories often serve as the basis for television shows and movies.

But it is unusual for the same story to be presented in different media by the same author at the same time. The story appeared both online and in print (in book form) simultaneously. The online version had several interesting features. In addition to having extensive graphics and audio, readers could send e-mail to Bowden, who responded online. He received leads to new sources of information and was asked a wide array of questions in a public, as opposed to private, exchange. The e-mail interactions were part of the overall presentation of the material.

In the past, the lines between different media were rigidly drawn. Although print journalists often moved over to broadcasting (fewer broadcast journalists switched to print), journalists in each area worked within the confines of the medium itself. Television reporters gathered audio and video content for their reports, which were given a coherent flow through the use of narrative. Print journalists wrote.

Fig. 12-2: Multimedia content with a variety of formats is one of the specialties of philly.com.

The Web is breaking down those rigid barriers. In the early days of Web journalism, reporters and editors have been called on to master new forms. Many of the entry-level positions at online publications consist of taking content prepared for broadcast or print and converting it into a Web format. Online editors and reporters must have basic HTML programming skills.

The need for HTML programming skills is the equivalent to the need for production skills in broadcast and print. To a large degree, television reporters have not been required to work the camera nor the sound equipment (although they did in the early days of CNN). In print operations, editors do now perform page layout. In many online publications, editors are expected to work in HTML.

But HTML skills are only one part of the new multimedia skills mix in journalism. One of the strengths of online journalism is that stories can contain print, graphics, photos, video, audio and other media content. A single journalist can be responsible for gathering all the material. As Web journalism matures, reporters themselves may be able to work in all media at the same time, learning to present stories in more innovative ways. Online journalism can expand the skill sets reporters have, making them more versatile and making their stories more interesting.

Increasing Debate and Press Accountability

Metabolife 356, distributed by the Metabolife Company, has been a top selling herbal product in America. It is marketed as an aid to weight loss, and sales increased from 4,800 bottles in 1996 to 22 million bottles in 1999. But as is often the case in the use of herbal products for health reasons, Metabolife 356 and the founder of the company are surrounded by controversy. Not only are the health claims made by the company not scientifically proven, the founder had earlier pleaded guilty to charges linking him to illegal drug trafficking.

On September 9, 1999, the founder of the company, Michael Ellis, agreed to an interview for the ABC newsmagazine *20/20*. Reporter Arnold Diaz confronted Ellis with a laundry list of charges. Ellis felt that he was being subjected to a deposition in a court of law.

Generally, once a company executive has agreed to appear on a television newsmagazine, the presentation of the material is in the hands of the news organization. Companies can complain about television shows, but tens of millions of viewers will see what the journalists choose to broadcast.

That is no longer the case. Worried and unhappy about what they anticipated would be a negative report, executives at Metabolife uploaded the complete, unedited video tape of the interview to a Web site (http://www.news.interview.com) and spent $1.5 million to advertise its availability across the country. In the first 15 hours, one million people visited the site.

ABC News complained that Metabolife was trying to influence its editorial process. Metabolife officials countered that if the *20/20* report was fair, there would be no problem.

Metabolife is not the first company to record an interview with a news organization and then use that video to try to get out its side of the story. In the mid-1970s, an Illinois power company heavily promoted a video it made refuting a report by CBS's *60 Minutes*. But Metabolife is one of the first companies that could use the Web to get out its message before the story was even broadcast.

Clearly, the Web and the Internet provide access for more people to larger audiences. The news media no longer have a stranglehold on information that reaches the public. Along the same lines, more people can comment on public affairs to a wider range of people than ever before.

Perhaps the explosion of public debate is best seen on financial journalism. Until the Internet came along, opinion about stocks, bonds, and the direction of the economy was controlled by Wall Street analysts and duly reported by specialized newspapers and magazines. With the growth of the Web, however, most major online financial information sources have chat rooms for individuals to comment on different companies. Oftentimes, people who frequent the chat rooms develop followings and have the ability to influence the price of stocks and companies.

The opening of public debate has its rewards and its risks. Clearly, there is a long-standing vision that truth best emerges from a multitude of tongues. Many investors find the information posted on the chat rooms very valuable. They discover information and insights that they might have missed otherwise. Indeed, that philosophy is the underpinning of the First Amendment.

On the other hand, robust debate often invites abuse as well. For example, during an investor conference the chief executive officer of HealthSouth, a multibillion-dollar rehabilitation services company, learned that messages had been posted on an online bulletin board claiming that top executives at HealthSouth engaged in swapping spouses. One poster even claimed that one top executive was having an affair with the chief executive officer's wife.

The CEO of HealthSouth decided to identify the sources of the information. It turned out that ex-employees and the spouse of someone who had been fired were posting the messages. Striking back, the CEO of HealthSouth has sued those individuals to stop the postings.

The opening of debate and the increased ability to challenge news reports potentially will change public discussion. On the one hand, the authority of the mainstream media will be open to challenge. On the other hand, people will need competent professional journalists to help them sort through information to determine what is credible and what is not.

The Economics of Journalism

In 1834, James Gordon Bennett started the *New York Herald* with $500. He worked on a single bench and did most of the work himself. He prospered. So did Horace Greeley when he established the *New York Tribune* in 1841. Greeley's success motivated Henry Raymond to launch the *New York Times*. Indeed, from 1835 to 1929, newspapers were routinely established as entrepreneurial ventures.

But starting with the Great Depression, it became too costly and too risky to start newspapers. Over the past 30 years, fewer than five new major daily newspapers have been established while scores have closed.

During the 1950s, television became an area of entrepreneurial activity. But the television market was highly regulated by the federal government. To establish a television station, an ownership group had to obtain a license from the Federal Communications Commission. Many cities could only support one or two television stations. Those licenses generally went to well-heeled investment groups. Moreover, television has been more of a medium of general entertainment than news. Since the 1970s, few new stations have been established. The barriers to entry are just too great.

Consequently, for most of the last 20 years, magazines have been the only news media that have witnessed many new entries into the marketplace. And in many cases, new magazines were directed at very targeted audiences.

The Web has changed all that. Obviously, Web sites can be established without a license from the federal government. Moreover, Web sites can be established on a shoestring. Nearly anybody can set up a Web site and anybody with media savvy can get attention for the Web site.

That combination has made online journalism the first dynamic area of widespread entrepreneurial activity in the news media for generations. Like Bennett, Greeley, and Raymond in the 1830s and 1840s, thousands of people are setting up news-oriented Web sites both to inform the public and to establish profitable businesses.

In fact, for the first time since the early 1960s, entrepreneurial media companies are able to attract venture capital and then become public companies. Access to investment capital is essential to build professional media organizations. Since they have been able to go public, news and commentary Web sites such as *TheStreet.Com* and *Salon* have been able to make creative contributions to the media mix.

Indeed, the opportunity to go public has attracted major journalists to the Web. For example, Lou Dobbs, the vice president in charge of CNN's financial news network, left CNN to join a Web site dedicated to reporting news about space exploration. Hugh Downs joined an online journalism site after retiring from ABC's *20/20*.

But the economic model of online journalism is far from clear. Most viewers resist paying to subscribe to Web sites. They expect to access the information for free. And it is not certain that Web sites can attract enough advertising to make them self-supporting. Many people think that for Web sites to prosper, they ultimately will have to sell something via e-commerce. And it is not obvious how e-commerce selling will blend seamlessly with news and information Web sites. There could be many ethical issues and potential conflicts of interests involved in selling goods via a news Web site.

The Impact of the Internet on Journalism

The Web is the newest communications medium of the generation. Its impact on journalism and the public should be as great as the impact of television. The Web has challenged the hold that large, national media have held on public discussion since the growth of the television networks. The Web promises to open public discussion to more voices using many different media content.

More importantly, the Web has recreated journalism as an area of creative entrepreneurial activity. Reporters are able to report on different kinds of stories and present them in different ways. Web sites are scrambling to attract audiences and to build big profitable business. As they do, the sites and the journalists that create them will be able to influence public life in profound and unpredictable ways.

Conclusion

In the second week of January 2000, America Online announced that it would merge with Time Warner, Inc., the largest media company in the world. The merger launched a flurry of activity in which Internet-based "new media" and print- and broadcast-based "old media" explored different ways to combine.

Driven by the growth of the Internet and the Web, the distinctions between different news media are rapidly fading. One of the central ideas behind the AOL–Time Warner deal was that the same "content" should be available to consumers through whatever medium is most appropriate for them.

Meanwhile, the concentration of the mass media into fewer and fewer hands continues. AOL–Time Warner would dwarf companies like Disney and News Corp. The challenge and opportunity for journalists will be to ensure that concentrated ownership of the media does not silence smaller players and individual voices.

Starting Places for Journalists

Theoretically, you could start anywhere on the World Wide Web and find anything else on the Web *if*: 1) you had enough time, and 2) the Web "sat still" long enough. Neither condition prevails. Nor is news static. Online directories and keyword search engines can help journalists find what they need, when they need it, to build background information and to set stories in the proper context. Here are a few carefully selected sites designed to get you started.

Keyword Search Sites

Different devices employ diverse net search strategies (robot versus human) and offer various search refinements.

> All-in-One Search Page—http://www.allonesearch.com/ | The name says it: links to search and browsing sites from many different perspectives.
>
> Alta Vista—http://www.altavista.com | Very powerful system, but must use "Advanced Search" options. Good help files.
>
> CUSI—http://cusi.emnet.co.uk/ | One form allows search of several Web engines for documents, people, and more.
>
> Deja.com—http://deja.com/ | Search for information posted in newsgroups. Several filter options under "Power Search."
>
> Dogpile—http://dogpile.com/ | Web metasearches, Usenet filings, yellow pages, maps, and more.
>
> Google—http://www.google.com/ | Has specialized searches, archives of many pages taken off the net.
>
> InfoSeek—http://infoseek.go.com/ | Annotated search results. In addition to keyword, has subject catalogs. Can search Web, newsgroups, e-mail addresses, and more.

Lycos—http://www.lycos.com/ | Search for title of documents, head-
ings, links, keywords. Note: rights to this engine recently sold.

NorthernLight—http://northernlight.com/ | For free and for fee
searches. Web plus proprietary database. May search a known
third-party site from NorthernLight.

Tile.net—http://tile.net/ | Does keyword searching for ftp sites, mail
lists, and newsgroups.

TradeWave Galaxy—http://galaxy.einet.net | Keyword searching,
subject-oriented browsing. Search Web, Gopher, Hytelnet at once.
Links to other search tools and reference materials.

Web Crawler—http://webcrawler.com | Searches by document title
and content.

Yahoo!—http://www.yahoo.com | Keyword searching as well as
subject-oriented browsing.

General Directories

Directory sites or subject catalogs follow predetermined subject trees. Pick
a subject—or related subjects—and browse for relevant information. Can
be quick.

Argus Clearinghouse—http://www.clearinghouse.net/index.html |
Topic browser with site rating system.

Internet Public Library—http://www.ipl.org/ | This site has links to
reference documents, net catalogs, and search engines.

LSU Webliography—http://www.lib.lsu.edu/weblio.html | Subject
guides organized by academic discipline.

World Wide Web Virtual Library—http://vlib.org/ | Best of the Web
vetted by experts in each field.

See Yahoo! and TradeWave Galaxy in previous list.

Hotlists and Other Journalists' Resources

These are sites where journalists have gathered—for the benefit of other
journalists—lists and catalogs of links to other sites deemed useful.

Avi Bass's NewsPlace for News and Sources—http://www.niu.edu/
newsplace/ | Separate lists for media sites, for primary source
material, and for Internet navigating help.

Duff Wilson's Reporter's Desktop—http://www.seanet.com/~duff/ |
Duff's Links to best sites for doing stories.

FACSNET—http://www.facsnet.org | A new service with many
original documents including backgrounders and reporting
tutorials. Includes beat-oriented Internet browsing resource.

JournalismNet—http://www.journalismnet.com/ | By Julian Sher: Internet tutorials and links for journalists, story tips, media criticism, government links, strong Canadian resources.
Launch Pad for Journalists—http://www.ccrc.wustl.edu/spj/ resources.html | St. Louis, Missouri (USA), chapter of SPJ, has resource links organized by topic areas.
Makulowich's Virtual Journalism Library—http://www.cais.com/ makulow/vlj.html | Wide range of resources linked here.
National Press Club Library—http://npc.press.org/library/ reporter.htm | Friedheim Library lists online reporting tools.
Nikos Markovits' Journalistic Resources—http:// www.markovits.com/journalism/ | Links to journalism organizations, research sites, media sites, other hotlists.
Scoop CyberSleuth's Internet Guide—http://scoop.evansville.net/ | *Evansville Courier* resources.

Professional Organizations

American Society of Journalists and Authors—http://www.asja.org/ | Information about ASJA, an organization promoting freelance nonfiction authors and journalists. Information on hiring freelance writers, as well as member information and events.
Asian American Journalists' Association Web site—http:// www.aaja.org/ | Organization goals, membership information, conferences, links to chapters.
California Journalism Online—http://www.csne.org/ | Joint project of CSNE, CNPA, CFAC, and APNEC. Job listings, CNPA Bulletin, salary survey, links to U.S. newspapers and to Internet resources for journalists.
CompuServe Journalism Forum—http://www.jforum.org/ | Information about and registration for the CompuServe Journalism Forum. Journalism links.
European Journalism Centre—http://www.ejc.nl/ | Focused on the European journalist, providing education and contacts. Links to a mission statement, selected publications, and event information.
Investigative Reporters and Editors—http://www.ire.org/ | Thorough listing of IRE publications, programs, activities, and special projects. Occasional pieces from IRE Journal.
Minorities in Broadcasting Training Program—http:// www.webcom.com/mibtp | MBTP is a nonprofit organization dedicated to placing multicultural trainees at television and radio stations across the United States.
National Association of Black Journalists—http://www.nabj.org/ | NABJ history and objectives, directory of chapters, and board of directors.

National Association of Broadcasters—http://www.nab.org/ |
Information about the organization, press releases, events, and
job listings.

National Association of Science Writers—http://www.nasw.org/ |
Information about the organization, membership information
(and inducements to join the organization), links to member home
pages, and information about the NASW job bank.

National Conference of Editorial Writers—http://www.ncew.org/ |
Conference information, calendar, job bank, links to other resources,
mailing lists, and discussion topics.

National Institute for Computer-Assisted Reporting—http://
www.nicar.org/ | Links to NICAR mission satement, publications,
events, and mailing lists.

National Press Club—http://npc.press.org/ | Contains information
about NPC services (including dining, etc.), publications, an
events schedule, and research tools through the Eric Friedheim
Library and News Information Center.

National Press Photographers' Association—http://metalab.unc.edu/
nppa/ | NPPA programs, publications, contests, member services,
and related topics.

New Directions for News—http://www.newnews.org/ | Institute
dedicated to fostering "innovation to help newspapers better serve
democratic society" and helping "journalists to adapt and survive
this period of rapid change."

Newspaper Association of America—http://www.naa.org/ | Confer-
ence and events calendars, NAA publications and news, and links
to newspaper sites.

Poynter Institute for Media Studies— http://www.poynter.org/ | The
Poynter Institute Web site. This site provides links to a mission
statement, bibliographies, journalism links, announcements and
activities, publications, and other files.

Radio and Television News Directors Foundation—http://
www.rtndf.org/rtndf/ | Mission statement, a list of programs
sponsored by RTNDF, staff listing, and links to radio and television news sources on the Internet.

Radio-Television News Directors Association—http://www.rtnda.org/
rtnda/ | Describes RTNDA organizations, membership, conven-
tions, Reporters' Toolbox, research, and RTNDA activities.

Society of Environmental Journalists—http://www.sej.org/ | Anno-
tated links to environment-related sites, basic information and
mission statement from SEJ, and selected publications.

Society of Professional Journalists—http://www.spj.org/ | Society
mission statement, selected publications, current topics of interest, membership information, and various mailing lists.

Other Useful Sites

A few "jumping-off" places containing exceptionally rich resources.

Awesome list—http://www.clark.net:80/pub/journalism/ awesome.html | John Makulowich's list of 38 "truly awesome" and many more merely awesome net resources.

CARL—telnet//pac.carl.org or http://www.carl.org/ | Journal and magazine articles can be located here and faxed to you (for a fee). UnCover Database.

City.Net—http://city.net | Links to city information worldwide. Mass transit maps.

Direct Search—http://gwis2.circ.gwu.edu/~gprice/direct.htm | Gary Price's extensive links to search interfaces.

FedWorld—http://www.fedworld.gov or telnet://fedworld.gov | U.S. Commerce Dept. gateway to 130+ Federal agencies.

Government by Sterby—http://users.erols.com/irasterb/gov.htm | Extensive U.S. government links, links to other world government sites.

MetroScope—http://metroscope.com/ | More cities information.

Newhouse Net Lists—http://web.syr.edu/~bcfought/nnl.html | A compendium of electronic newsletters and e-mail discussion lists of interest to communications professionals.

Choosing an Access Provider

Journalists may have Internet access from the office and students from school, but, for any number of reasons, either might benefit from a personal account providing a 24-hour Internet connection. In many regions of North America and the United Kingdom, Internet Service Providers (ISPs) offer unlimited dial-up access to the Net for less than a typical cable television subscription.

While the challenge of the past was to find a service provider, the challenge today is to select from a myriad of choices. The purpose of this appendix is to describe different types of services, to suggest guidelines for choosing one, and to provide contact information for a select few.

Commercial Hybrids versus ISPs

Commercial hybrid online services such as America Online, CompuServe, Delphi, GEnie, and Prodigy have long passed e-mail to one another and thousands of other destinations via the Internet. By 1994, most had begun to offer to their subscribers other Internet-based services, including access to Usenet newsgroups, Telnet, and, finally, World Wide Web access. One should understand that these companies have become Internet access providers second, and that their first business was to provide other services.

Commercial hybrids have always offered e-mail. They have provided various "forums" or "rooms" or "chat groups" for people to gather online and to share points of view on topics of mutual interest. They also have offered access to encyclopedias and other references to their subscribers as well as newspaper and wire service text, magazine content of varying kinds, and gateways to premium information services.

Internet access provided by these services traditionally had a premium cost attached to it, was limited in its range, and has been plagued with slow performance. They tended to charge you an hourly premium for any Internet access beyond a basic allowance for their accounts, typically five hours per month. It is very easy to use five hours a *week,* with only casual "cruising" of the Internet.

Dial-up access from ISPs dedicated to providing Internet connections was consistently more economical. ISPs offering flat rates for unlimited access abounded, so the hybrids had to adopt flat rate pricing to compete. For the journalist seeking to mine the information riches on the Internet, unlimited, flat-rate service is the first criterion you should demand from an ISP offering dial-up access.

Shell Accounts, SLIP, and PPP

Dial-up access comes in two basic varieties: shell accounts and PPP accounts. The shell-only account is rare anymore. It is less expensive (generally less than $10 per month), uses simple technology, and is text-based. Still, the shell account can provide access to many resources on the Internet. It's just that you don't see the graphics or hear the sounds on the more sophisticated World Wide Web pages as they are loaded into your computer. It is, however, possible to download graphics and audio and play them back later.

What you get with a shell account is space on and access to a Net-connected computer—typically a UNIX-based machine. This machine is your host. You use a simple communications program to dial into and "talk" with the host. When you log on, you see a system prompt, and you must type commands following each system prompt in order to make things happen. Pointing and clicking a mouse does not make things happen on the remote host for a shell account.

Most important, all the computing is done and all the programs are run on the distant computer that you have dialed into. The only thing that happens on your machine is that the communications program makes your computer emulate a dumb terminal, totally reliant on the host to do all the work of computing.

With SLIP (Serial Line Internet Protocol) and PPP (Point-to-Point Protocol) accounts, you run a dialer program that talks to the remote host and asks it to open a direct connection to the Internet. This allows you to run whichever programs you have selected on your machine. The most apparent difference is that you can use graphical World Wide Web browsers, and other client software that takes advantage of the built-in features of your computer's operating system. With Windows and Macintosh computers this means you have point-and-click convenience, the ability to copy and paste between windows or applications, and other system conveniences.

Some ISPs offer both shell and SLIP/PPP access for their flat fee. For journalists who are prone to travel much in their work, the added convenience of both SLIP/PPP and shell access can be a great boon. Consider the following circumstances.

I maintain a PPP account with a large ISP, for which I am charged a flat $19.95 U.S. per month. I also keep an account with CompuServe, one I have had for more than a decade. One of the reasons I chose my ISP is that it has local telephone access in more than 400 cities across the United States. Any major city I visit in the United States can be reached by PPP access.

When I am abroad, however, I still have local Internet access through the account's shell provision. I have this because CompuServe has local dial-up numbers worldwide. When I am in London or Geneva or Montreal or Mexico City I access CompuServe, which gives me the ability to Telnet back to my shell account, then receive my e-mail. In that way I stay in touch with my editors, my colleagues, and my family wherever I am.

Price, Features, and Free Access

Journalists desiring free Internet access have increasing numbers of options. Both juno.com and hotmail.com have provided free e-mail for some time. Users of the service accept a certain amount of advertising in their e-mail in exchange for the free access. For people who already have mail accounts, large portal sites such as *Yahoo!* and *Netscape Netcenter* offer Web-based mail accounts that will help one keep connected while traveling.

Still other providers promise full Internet access—not just e-mail—on similar terms. Hundreds of free access providers are scattered across the globe. Few coherent lists of free providers exist. However, in the United Kingdom, Jason Etheridge compiled a list of 57 free providers in mid-1999. UK providers generally pay for their services by collecting a portion of the telephone charges. Etheridge's list may be accessed at http://www.etheridge.freeserve.co.uk/freei/main.htm.

Some providers charge regular subscription fees rather than support their service through adverstising or taking a cut of telephone fees.

By "unlimited" access, we mean your provider does not care how many hours you are connected. Your monthly charge is the same whether you are on one hour per day or twenty. In selecting your access provider, you should specify that you plan to be online several hours per day and you want a "flat" rate.

Internet magazines such as *Yahoo! Life .net*, or *Boardwatch* carry advertising for ISPs. You might choose one of them, using the guidelines here described. The following lists may be of help.

Internet Service Providers

Concentric Network	800-939-4262
EarthLink Network	800-395-8425
IDT Internet	800-438-8996
NetCom/MindSpring	800-501-8649
Pipeline (PSINet)	800-379-8847
Frontier	800-463-8386
UUNet	800-488-6383

All of these providers give some kind of "unlimited" PPP access for a flat monthly fee (some restrictions on hours may apply). All have points of presence in most major cities in the United States. Many have some kind of 800 access for regions lacking a local number.

Other considerations in choosing an ISP might include the number of communities with local access, if you do a lot of traveling; whether the account also includes shell access; and, what kind of software and technical support are provided. Not all the providers listed here have presences outside the United States.

Commercial Hybrid Providers

America Online	800-827-6364
CompuServe	800-848-8199
GEnie	800-638-9636
Microsoft Network	800-373-3676
Prodigy	800-776-3449

These services are long on support, almost always have local phone numbers, have low fees for basic service, offer immediate access to many virtual communities, and provide many other attractive services.

Glossary

ADSL — (n.) An acronym for Asymmetric Digital Subscriber Line, a form of DSL (q.v.) in which bandwidth is apportioned so that download speeds and upload speads are not equal. Typical service might be 384 kilobits per second download and 128k upload.

alias — (n.) An e-mail address given as a substitute for a longer, less intuitive address. For example, a college may issue a student the address z4j28@pegasus.acs.ttu.edu. Through an alias utility, the student may get mail addressed simply to McCoy@ttu.edu.

anonymous FTP — (n.) A process allowing anyone with an FTP (File Transfer Protocol) client to access FTP servers and to retrieve files from that server. Under anonymous FTP, one typically logs on using the ID "anonymous" and one's e-mail address as the password.

Archie — (n.) A program that searches for files publicly accessible at anonymous FTP sites.

ASCII — (n.) An acronym for American Standard Code for Information Interchange, ASCII commonly refers to the set of characters used to represent text on paper. Distinguished from binary (q.v.), or computer instruction code. "Text" is sometimes used as a synonym. Most word processors allow you to save files in text (ASCII) format. E-mail, by its nature, is communication carried in ASCII format. Files that contain only text characters are called ASCII files.

bandwidth — (n.) The capacity of a network to handle data traffic. "Bandwidth" is often used to imply that online communication is a limited resource which should not be wasted frivolously.

binary — (n., adj.) Computer code, distinguished from "text" or ASCII. Binary files contain instructions that tell computers and computer peripherals such as printers how to do their work.

BIOS — (n.) Acronym for Basic Input/Output System, low-level instructions that tell the computer how to interface with hardware.

Boolean — (adj.) Applied to logic used in searching for information. Boolean logic uses terms such as "AND," "OR," and "NOT" to limit the results of information searches. A search for "defense AND policy NOT nuclear" would produce a list of files and directories containing both "defense" and "policy" in them but would eliminate from the list any such files or directories that contain the word "nuclear."

BPS (Bits Per Second) — The measure used to gauge the speed of a modem. The more bits per second a modem can transmit, the faster it is. Although slightly different, Baud rate is another term which refers to the speed of a modem.

BTW — Shorthand for "By The Way."

client — (n.) Name given to a computer or software program that negotiates with another computer (the "server") the delivery of files and information to the first computer. Sometimes used to describe the computer on which the software resides.

code — (n.) Programming instructions that tell computers (and computer peripherals) what to do. (v.) To write computer programs.

commercial information services — Commercial enterprise which provides information online for a fee. The largest consumer-oriented commercial information services are CompuServe and America OnLine. Many more services are in the planning stages. Most commercial information services also provide access to the Internet.

cyber — A combining form used generally to refer to the online world.

cyberspace — (n.) The collective environments or "places" created by computer networks. Term coined by William Gibson in the book *Neuromancer*.

database — (n.) A body of facts, usually focused on a predefined topic, and gathered together in some computer. Organized into meaningful patterns, data (facts) in a database becomes information.

discussion list — (n.) A method by which individuals can communicate easily with many people by using e-mail. People subscribe to discussion lists, then automatically receive all messages other subscribers send to the list.

DNS — (n.) Domain Name Server. A computer that uses a distributed database to translate network address names (such as pegasus.acs.ttu.edu) into numeric Internet Protocol addresses (such as 129.118.2.52) and vice versa.

domain — (n.) A naming system given to Internet nodes, or subnetworks connected to the Internet. All computers belonging to the subnetwork share the same domain name when they are linked to the Internet. A university typically has several large computers and many lesser computers under one domain. For example, "ttu.edu" is the domain for Texas Tech University. Host computers sharing that domain include UNIX machines named "Pegasus" and "Unicorn" and a VAX cluster under the generic name "TTACS."

download — (v.) To retrieve a file from a server or any other online computer.

DSL — (n.) Acronym for Digital Subscriber Line, a networking technology that permits high speed Internet access over twister pair, or regular RJ-11 telephone wire. Bandwidth of up to 1.5 Megabits per second is possible. DSL comes in both asymmetric (ADSL, q.v.) and symmetric forms.

e-mail — (n.) Electronic mail. Text messages sent across computer networks to digital mailboxes where they are retrieved and read at the leisure of the recipient.

emoticons — (n.) A grouped combination of keyboard symbols and text used to express emotions in computer communications. The best known is called a "smiley" and is formed using the keys colon, dash, and right parenthesis :-).

ethernet — (n.) A type of local area network (LAN) in which computers containing network cards are linked by cabling to other computers with similar cards.

e-zine — (n.) Electronic magazine. Refers to the content and the site of an online magazine product.

FAQ — (n.) Acronym for "Frequently Asked Questions," commonly pronounced "fak." A text file that addresses common concerns about a given subject or topic.

file — (n.) A discreet, complete set of digital information containing such items as a text document, program instructions, graphic images, or database resources. (v.) To cause information to be placed in computer storage.

firewall — (n.) A network security barrier designed to protect a local network from being accessed by unauthorized persons via the Internet. Typically, firewalls disable some of the Internet's packet sharing features to make outside access more difficult.

flame — (n., v.) Heated responses/insults directed at an individual who has posted something on the Net to which the responder is reacting.

FTP — (n.) Acronym for File Transfer Protocol, a set of instructions for moving files across the network from one computer to another. Sometimes employed as if it were a verb (FTP'ed, FTP'ing): "I FTP'ed that program from Sunsite."

FWIW — Shorthand for "For What It's Worth."

FYI — Shorthand for "For Your Information."

gateway — (n.) An access point between networks or computer systems, a connection that allows computer systems to transfer data between normally incompatible applications or networks.

GIF — (n.) A graphics file specification popularized on the CompuServe network. GIF is an acronym for "Graphics Interchange Format." Widely used on the World Wide Web.

Gopher — (n.) An Internet program that organizes information into menu hierarchies. Gopher puts a uniform interface on network navigation, providing links to varied network resources scattered throughout the world and providing access to search tools for finding that information. Created at the University of Minnesota, where the school mascot is the Golden Gopher. (v.) To use Gopher client access network resources.

Gopher hole — (n.) Nickname given to a Gopher site and the collection of resources accessible from the site. Also called a "burrow."

Gopherspace — (n.) Aggregate of all resources available worldwide through Gopher servers. The cyberspace "places" occupied by Gopher servers and their resources.

home page — (n.) Applied to HTTP documents on the World Wide Web. Originally used to describe the page first loaded by a World Wide Web client program (browser) when it starts up. Has come to refer to the top page (welcome, or index page) of Web sites and to personal pages placed on Web servers by many individuals.

host — (n.) A computer (system) offering network access, disk storage space, and client software to its account holders. Typically, the host is the computer where a person's electronic mail is received, stored, and processed. See also "client" and "site."

HTML — (n.) HyperText Markup Language, an ASCII-based scripting language used to create documents served on the World Wide Web.

HTTP — (n.) HyperText Transfer Protocol, the network data communications specification used on the World Wide Web.

hypertext — (n.) A means of linking information.

IMHO — Shorthand for "In My Humble Opinion."

IMNSHO — Shorthand for "In My Not-So-Humble Opinion."

Internet Relay Chat (IRC) — (n.) Internet software that allows real-time interactive typed "conversations" among many participants.

Internet — (n.) The network of computer networks that use the TCP/IP communications protocol and can communicate with each other. Some people see the Internet as the prototype of the Information Superhighway.

list — (n.) In e-mail, all the people subscribed to a discussion group.

Listproc — (n.) A program for managing an e-mail discussion list. Very much like ListServ software.

ListServ — (n.) Software for managing an e-mail discussion list. ListServ takes messages sent to a list and distributes those messages to all who are subscribed. ListServ is also used to designate the machine on which the software resides.

lurk — (v.) To read, without posting, messages to a newsgroup or an e-mail discussion list. Recommended behavior for people new to a list or group.

mirror — (n.) A computer site that provides the same resources as another, distant one. Set up to redirect network traffic away from especially popular, busy sites.

network — (n., v.) Computers linked in order to transfer information and share other resources. The act of so linking computers.

newbie — (n.) Term applied to persons new to a network or any one of its online communities.

newsgroup — (n.) A discussion forum within the Usenet news system.

node — (n.) Term applied to a host computer (or computer system) for a subnetwork (LAN or WAN). The node is assigned a domain name and all other computers part of the system share that domain name.

OS — (n.) Acronym for computer Operating System, the basic instruction set used to give a computer the routines necessary to communicate with the user and hardware devices. Macs run Mac OS. Other OSes for microcomputers include BeOS, DOS, GEOS, Linux, OS/2, UNIX, and Windows (3.x, 9x, NT, CE).

packet — (n.) A discrete block of data carried over a network. The packet contains all or part of a text message (or a binary file), the addresses of the originating and destination computers, message assembly instructions, and error control information.

PC — (n.) Personal Computer. In this book it may mean a Macintosh, an IBM compatible, or any other machine that is yours to work with and on which you may run programs of your choice.

post — (v., n.) The act of sending a message to a discussion list or a news group. A message so sent.

PPP — (n.) Point-to-Point Protocol. A set of communications parameters that enables a computer to use TCP/IP over a standard voice telephone line and a high-speed modem. PPP provides the computer the functionality of one directly connected to the Internet through a network card and cable.

program — (n.) A set of instructions written in binary code, telling a computer how to perform certain tasks. (v.) The act of writing such instructions.

protocol — (n.) A set of rules and procedures by which computers communicate.

RTFM — Shorthand for "Read the Manual." A curt response when somebody asks a question for which the answer is readily available elsewhere.

server — (n.) A machine on which resides software designed to deliver information across a network in a manner specifically recognized by a client. Also describes the software that delivers the information.

SIG — (n.) Acronym for "Special Interest Group," a virtual community of people who "meet" online to exchange information on a clearly defined topic of interest.

SLIP — (n.) Acronym for Serial Line Internet Protocol. A set of communications parameters that allows a computer to use TCP/IP over a standard voice telephone line using a high-speed modem. PPP provides the computer the functionality of one directly connected to the Internet through a network card and cable.

string — (n.) A series of characters tied together without interruption. A unique sequence of characters used to locate specific text is called a search string.

sysop — (n.) The systems operator, usually the owner, of a computer bulletin board. Sometimes used to identify the person who moderates a SIG on a larger system such as CompuServe or America OnLine.

system prompt — (n.) A character or string of characters that tell the computer user in a command line environment that the machine is waiting for a new command and that all non-system programs have terminated. In DOS, the system prompt is typically a "C:>"; in UNIX it often is "%"; in VMS it frequently is "$."

TCP/IP — (n.) Acronym for Transmission Control Protocol/Internet Protocol, the set of communications rules by which computers connected to the Internet talk to one another.

Telnet — (n.) an Internet application program that allows you to log on to another computer and to use programs available there.

terminal — (n.) A computer work station composed of a monitor (VDT) for viewing computer output and a keyboard for talking to the computer or network. One of the most universally accepted terminals is the DEC VT100. Most personal computer communications programs allow the computer to emulate terminals such as VT100s so that the network host or server can understand what you type at your computer.

UNIX — (n.) A popular operating system used by computers more powerful than PCs. Server software is often based on computers running UNIX and many times people will log on to UNIX-based machines to access the Internet.

username — (n.) A name assigned to an account holder by a system administrator. The username is associated with a password in providing access to network computing resources.

virtual — (adj.) Having the quality of existing in effect, but not in reality. Network newsgroups are said to be virtual communities because they bring together many people who are united by common interests and goals.

virtual community — (n.) A term used to describe the collective presence of people who "come together" in an online setting to "chat" or exchange information on a topic of mutual interest. Used by Howard Rheingold as a title to a book about "life" on computer networks.

WAIS — (n.) Wide Area Information Servers allow for the indexing, identification and retrieval of information located on specific Internet computers. WAIS servers are accessed by WAIS client programs.

World Wide Web — (n.) allows for information located on many different computers to be linked through key terms. This approach is called Hypertext or Hypermedia. The Web is accessed through client programs such as Internet Explorer, Lynx, Mosaic, and Netscape.

Credits

Fig. 3-1: Network Solutions Web site: "Register a Web Address" screen: Copyright © 2000 Network Solutions, Inc. All rights reserved.

Fig. 3-3: Download.com Web site: Copyright © 1995–2000 CNET, Inc. All rights reserved.

Fig. 3-4: FACSNET Web site: Top Issues, Internet Resources, Reporting Tools, Sources Online: Courtesy of the Foundation for American Communications.

Fig. 3-5: FACSNET Web site: Top Issues, Internet Resources, Reporting Tools, Sources Online with pull-down menu: Courtesy of the Foundation for American Communications.

Fig. 3-6: Adding the *New York Times* Web site using Add Favorite to list: Copyright © 2000 The New York Times Company. Reprinted by permission.

Fig. 3-7: Yahoo! Subject Guide: Text and artwork copyright © 2000 by Yahoo! Inc. All rights reserved. *Yahoo!* and the *Yahoo!* logo are trademarks of Yahoo! Inc.

Fig. 4-3: Lycos Network Web site "WhoWhere? People-finder" screen: Copyright © 2000 Lycos, Inc. All rights reserved. Lycos® is a registered trademark of Carnegie Mellon University.

Fig. 5-2: Newhouse Net List #1 Web site by Barbara Croll Fought at Syracuse University: Courtesy of Dr. Barbara Croll Fought, Syracuse University, N.Y.

Fig. 5-5: Deja.com Web site "Let's Get Digital": Copyright © 1995–2000 Deja.com, Inc. All rights reserved.

Fig. 6-1: Direct search Web from Gary Price: Courtesy of Professor Gary Price, George Washington University, Washington, D.C.

Fig. 6-2: Alta Vista Web page: Copyright © 2000 Alta Vista Company. Alta Vista® is a registered trademark and Smart Is Beautiful and the Alta Vista logo are trademarks of the Alta Vista Company. All rights reserved.

Fig. 6-3: Alta Vista Web site searching for items on "immigration policty": Copyright © 2000 Alta Vista Company. Alta Vista® is a registered trademark and Smart Is Beautiful and the Alta Vista logo are trademarks of the Alta Vista Company. All rights reserved.

Fig. 8-1: The U.S. White House home page: Courtesy of the White House, Washington, D.C.

Fig. 9-1: Tripod Web site: Copyright © 2000 Lycos, Inc. Tripod® is a registered service mark of Tripod, Inc., a subsidiary of Lycos, Inc. All rights reserved.

Fig. 9-2: BBC News Web site: Copyright © 2000 BBC. All rights reserved.

Fig. 9-3: HotWired Web site: Copyright © 2000 Wired Ventures, Inc. All rights reserved.

Fig. 9-4: News Unlimited Web site with a photo of the British Prime Minister: Copyright © 2000 Guardian Newspapers, Ltd. All rights reserved.

Fig. 9-5: The *New York Times* Web site with headline "Democrats Abandon Effort to Delay Vote on Test Ban," 13 October 1999: Copyright © 2000 The New York Times Company. Reprinted by permission.

Fig. 9-6: *The Slate* Web site featuring a caricature of Al Gore, 13 October 1999: Copyright © 2000 Microsoft Corporation. All rights reserved.

Fig. 9-7: CNN Web site, 13 October 99: Copyright © 2000 Cable News Network. All rights reserved.

Fig. 9-8: VerticalNet Web site: Copyright © 1996–2000 VerticalNet, Inc. All rights reserved.

Fig. 11-9: CNN Web site with headline "GOP proposes health care legislation for nation's uninsured," 29 September 1999: Copyright © 2000 Cable News Network. All rights reserved.

Fig. 11-10: CNN Web site with Alexa configured vertically: Copyright © 2000 Cable News Network. All rights reserved.

Fig. 11-13: Ft.com Discount Flights Web site: Copyright © 2000 The Financial Times, Ltd. All rights reserved.

Fig. 12-1: Salon.com Web site with old man in hat: Copyright © 2000 Salon Internet, Inc. Katherine Streeter, *Salon Magazine* (http://www.salonmagazine.com)

Fig. 12-2: Philly.com Web site with Jon Benet Ramsey's photo: Copyright © 2000 Philadelphia Newspapers, Inc. All rights reserved.

Index

"About us" information, 147

Access, 3–6, 198–199
  costs of, 31, 255
  country code and, 64
  dial-up, 16, 254
  provider for, 253–256
  to public information sources, 4–5
  speed of, 32
  while traveling, 219–221

Accountability, 243–244

Acrobat Distiller (Adobe), 224

Acrobat Reader (Adobe), 44, 223, 224, 227

ActiveX, 168

Adams, Scott, 80

Addresses. *See also* Web sites
  e-mail, 15, 64–65, 69–70
  e-mail discussion lists, 85
  finding for e-mail, 75–77
  IP, 22
  of portals, 27

Adobe Systems, 44, 223

Advanced Research Projects Agency, 21–22

Advanced search options, 117

Advocacy groups, 159

Agent software, 122–124, 207

Agreement, Internet as, 19

Albert Murrah Federal Building, news on bombing of, 83

Alert services, 126

Alexa, 224–227

AllPolitics, 175–176

AltaVista, 50, 77, 100, 117, 118, 119, 121

Amendments, First, 183–184

America Online (AOL), 6, 15, 26, 102, 103, 150, 233–234, 246, 253
  confidentiality and, 196
  e-mail and, 63
  junk e-mail and, 194
  keyboard shortcuts and, 233–234
  libel and, 187
  Netscape *Navigator* and, 36

Amsterdam Mathematics Center, 34

Andreesen, Marc, 23, 36

Anonymous FTP, 25, 136–137

AOL. See America Online (AOL)

AOL Instant Messenger, 25

Applets, chat rooms and, 101

Applications. *See* Software

Archie, 25, 140–141

Archives
  of discussion lists, 92–94
  Usenet, 100

Arizona Center for Law in the Public Interest, 81

Arizona Daily Star, 171

Arnett, Peter, 237

ARPAnet, 22

ASCII files. *See* Text files

Ask Jeeves, 50

Associated Press, 78

Association for Education in Journalism and Mass Communication (AEJMC), 40

AT&T, 26

Atlantic Monthly, 193

@ sign, in e-mail, 64, 70

Attachments, 71–72, 78, 232

Attribution, of sources, 201

Audiences
  Internet reach and, 239–240
  new media and, 178

Audio. *See* Plug-ins

Baker, Jane, 197

Barry, Robert, 176

BBS. *See* Bulletin board

Beginners Guide to HTML, A, 53

Behavior. *See also* Netiquette
on Usenet, 100–101

Being Digital (Negroponte), 11

Bennett, James Gordon, 235, 245

Bernardo, Paul, 83

Berners-Lee, Tim, 23, 34–35, 112

Bernstein, Leonard, 203

Bitnet, 21

Black Hawk Down (Bowden), 241–242

Blumenthal, Sidney, 181

Bookmarks, 42, 47, 48, 124–125, 210–217
editing site titles and descriptions, 215
grouping in folders, 213–215
multiple files, 216–217

Books, online, 30

Boolean logic, 117–119

Bot. *See* Robot (bot)

Bowden, Mark, 241

Brandeis, Louis, 241

Branzberg v. Hayes, 195

Brill's Content, 211

Brown, Chip, 164

Brown, Douglas, 12

Browsing, 48–51

Bulletin board
First Amendment and, 197
obscenity and, 199

Burgess, Chet, 124, 211

Business, Web and, 37

Cables, linking via, 13

Cable television, 6, 163

Caplan, Richard, 166

Capture, of Telnet session, 135

CARR-L (Computer Assisted Research and Reporting List), 83, 89, 90, 92–93

Catalogs. *See* Directories

CERN, 23, 34, 54

Chao, Rex, 61

Charlab, Sergio, 1

Chasse, Ken, 83

Chat, 23, 25, 29
legal regulation of, 185–186
libel and, 186–187
news and, 102
using, 101–102

Chat rooms, 101–102. *See also* Chat
libel and, 187

CIA World Factbook, 29

Client(s)
defined, 14
distinctions among e-mail, 231–232
location of, 16

Client/server computing, 13, 14, 15, 35. *See also* Gopher
client location and, 16

Client software, mail identity and, 206

Clinton, Bill
crime bill information and, 5
impeachment of, 166–167
investigation of, 239
link about ethics of, 176

CNN, 237, 238

CNN Interactive, 174–175

Codes of use, 78

Cohen, Sarah, 64

Commands, for listservs, 86–87

Commercial hybrid online services, 253–256. *See also* Online services

Communication
online, 28–29
via Web, 11–12

Communication protocols. *See* Protocol

Communications Decency Act (1996), 183, 187

Communicator (Netscape), 206, 208

Communities online. *See* Discussion lists; Usenet; specific communities

Companies
.com addresses of, 150
domain names for, 127
e-mail use at, 77

Compressed files, 138

CompuServe, 6, 26, 150, 233–244, 253, 255
e-mail and, 63
Executive News Service, 126
keyboard shortcuts and, 233–234
libel and, 187

Computer(s), familiarity with, 7

Computer Assisted Research: A Guide to Tapping Online Information (Paul), 51

Computername, 69

Computer terminals
dumb, 16

networks and, 14–15
Confidentiality
    erased files and, 196
    of online material, 194–196
Connection type, network, 16
"Consortium, The," 176
Constitution, free speech and, 183–184
Content, presentation and, 240–241
Convergence, 178–179
Copy-and-paste approach, to obtaining information, 53
Copying text, keyboard shortcuts for, 218–219
Copyright law, 187–188
    fair use and, 190
    implied license and, 189–190
    market value and, 191–192
    misappropriation and, 189
    of online materials, 188–193
    protection of creators by, 193
    and Web sites, 192–193
Costs
    of Internet access, 31, 255
    of Internet use, 20–21
Country code, 64
Court records, 5
Court reporters, 4
Crawlers, 110
Credibility. *See* Information; Information sources; Reliability of data
Crime bill, information about, 5

Crispen, Patrick, 108
Cubby v. CompuServe, 187
Currency, of Web sites, 125–128
Cyberspace
    convergence of, 26
    as network of networks, 16–17
    sourcing material from, 54
Cybersquatting, 151
CyberTimes Navigator, 211

Data. *See* Information; Information sources
Database(s)
    of government agencies, 4
    services for, 27
    Whois, 152–153
Data transmission lines, 17
Dates, searching and, 120
Debate, public, 243–244
Defaults, on search sites, 120–121
Defense Department, Internet origins and, 21–22
Deja.com, 99
Deleted files, 74, 78, 195
Delphi, 253
Delzer, Jeffrey, 77
Design, of Web site, 147
Dial-up access, 16, 254
    shell accounts and, 254
Diaz, Arnold, 243
Digest, for listserv, 87
Digital Equipment Corp. (DEC), 134
Digital News discussion list, 86
Digital Subscriber Line (DSL), 7

Direct connection, 16
Directories. *See also* Search engines; Subject directories
    for e-mail addresses, 76–77
    FTP servers and, 137
    general sites, 247–248
    search, 106
    subject catalogs and, 110–112
Direct search site, 114
Discussion groups, 51–52
Discussion lists, 83–86
    archives of, 92–94
    communicating via, 29
    e-mail and, 157–158
    finding relevant, 89
    legal regulation of, 185–186
    listing of, 90
    posting messages on, 89–91
    quoting from, 91–92
    reliability of, 157–158
    setting parameters of, 86–88
    subscribing and unsubscribing to, 85–86
    two-way vs. one-way, 88
    using, 89–91
Dobbs, Lou, 161, 245
Dr. K's Best of the Internet Tutorials (Klopfenstein), 108
Documentary material, e-mail and, 81
Documents, access to, 4–5
Dogpile, 50
Domain(s)
    checks of, 148
    cybersquatting and, 151

in e-mail address, 69
growth of, 21
naming conventions,
    127–128
registration of names, 37
top level, 41, 148
Whois and, 152–153
Domain Name Server
    (DNS), 46
Donaldson, Sam, 237
Download.com, 45
Downloading, 141
Downs, Hugh, 161, 245
Drag and drop, for
    bookmark
    organization, 212
Drudge, Matt, 162, 181
Drudge Report, 181
DSL. *See* Digital
    Subscriber Line (DSL)
Dumb terminal, 16

Earthlink
    Communications, 63
Economics, of journalism,
    245–246
Editing, of e-mail, 67–68
Educational institutions,
    domain names of, 151
Edward Jones & Co., 194
*Edwards v. Audubon
    Society*, 185
Elections, television and,
    236–237
Electronic mail. *See* E-mail
Ellis, Michael, 243
Ellsberg, Daniel, 201
E-mail, 23, 24, 28–29. *See
    also* Addresses;
    Discussion lists
    address for, 64–65, 68–
    69
    attachments and, 71–72,
    78, 232

automatic signature for,
    210
basics of, 62–64
creating, 66–67
discussion lists and,
    157–158
distinctions among
    clients, 231–232
editing, 67–68
establishing accounts,
    62–63
finding addresses for,
    75–77
free speech and, 193–
    194
getting to destination,
    70
law and, 77–78
mail identity and, 206–
    209
managing incoming, 72
netiquette and, 78
for obtaining files, 53
outside U.S., 64–65
password for, 209
public record and, 80–81
receiving, 71–72
responding to, 72–74
saving, 74
sending, 68
signature file for, 68
software for, 65–66
stationery options, 232
story leads and, 80
as tool, 78–81
uses in legal cases, 61–
    62
viruses and, 74–75
Web-based, 27, 221
on Web site, 15
Emperor's New Mind, The
    (Penrose), 1
Empowerment, 2–3

Endres, Kathleen L., 166
ENS. *See* Executive News
    Service
Entrepreneurial activity,
    245
Erased files, retrieving,
    196
Erlich, Dennis, 192
Error messages, on Web,
    56–58
Etheridge, Jason, free
    providers listing of,
    255
Ethics. *See also* Fair use;
    Law
    Internet and, 181–182,
    200–201
Etiquette. *See* Netiquette
Eudora (Qualcomm), 66,
    69, 73–74, 204, 206–
    207, 210, 232. *See also*
    Web browsers
Eudora Light, 66, 206,
    209–210
Eudora Pro, 206–207
European Internet, 34
Excel, 75
Excite, 27, 111
Excite@Home, 6
Executive News Service,
    126
*Explorer. See Internet
    Explorer* (Microsoft)
Extensions, to file names,
    43, 44, 138, 139
Extraction programs, 138,
    139
E-zines, 166

FACSNET, 45, 46
Factbooks, 29
Fair use
    doctrine of, 190, 191–192
    of quotes, 91–92

FAQs (Frequently Asked Questions)
FTP and, 136
for newsgroups, 99
"Favorites." *See* Bookmarks
Federal Communications Commission, 245
Federal Information News Service (FINS), 198–199
FedWorld, 133–134
Fiber optic cable, 13
FidoNet, 21
Fields, in e-mail header, 66–67
File extensions. *See* Extensions
File names, 43, 44. *See also* Extensions
Files
e-mailing to oneself, 53
moving with FTP, 135–139
saving, 53
File transfer protocol (FTP). *See* FTP (file transfer protocol)
Financial services, 30
First Amendment
free speech and, 183–184
obscenity and, 199
shield laws and, 195
Flaming, 186
Folders, for bookmark groups, 213–215
Forté. *See* Agent software; *Free Agent* (Forté)
Forwarding e-mail, 73
Fought, Barbara Croll, 89, 91, 110
Fram, Alan, 199
Free access, 255

Free Agent (Forté), 207
Freedom of Access to Clinic Entrances Act (1994), 184
Free Republic Web site, 191
Free speech
confidentiality and, 194–196
copyright and, 187–193
e-mail and, 193–194
Internet and, 183–187
libel laws and, 184–186
obscenity and, 199–200
open meetings and, 197–198
speech codes and, 196–197
French National Institute for Research in Information and Automation, 29
FTP (file transfer protocol), 23, 24–25, 38, 40, 129, 130
anonymous, 136–137
data reliability and, 157
moving files with, 135–139
server directories and, 137
Functionality
client location and, 16
network connection type and, 16

Games, online sources of, 30
Gates, Bill, 103
Gateways, 26
GateWay Systems, FedWorld and, 134
GEnie, 253
Gertz v. Robert Welch Inc., 184

.gif graphic files, 43, 55
Gleaning services, 126
Google, 50
Gopher, 1, 23, 25–26, 38, 40, 111, 130, 141–144
reliability of, 156
Gore, Albert, Jr., online conference of, 11, 12
Gorman, Christine, 79
Government
domain names and, 127–128, 149
information from, 4–5, 31
Web sites of, 4
Graphical user interface, 7, 23
Graphic files, 43
Great Scouts (Williams), 112–113
Greeley, Horace, 245
Groupwise, 66
Gulf War, television and, 237

Halifax *Daily News,* 1
Hamilton, Ian, 191
Hard wired connection, 16
Harper & Row v. Nation Inc., 190, 191
Harte-Hanks Communications v. Connaughton, 185
Harwood, Tobert, Jr., 61
Hearst, William Randolph, 189
Help, 135
Helper programs, 204
Hibbs, Mark, 33
Hierarchies, in network news groups, 95–96
Hieros Gamos, 113
High-speed lines, 17
Highway system, Internet as, 18, 19

Hits, *Archie* and, 140

Hobbies, information about, 30

Home page. *See* Web sites

Homulka, Karla, 83, 199

Host computing, 14–15

Host name, 41

Host-terminal computing, 14–15

Hotlists, 42, 109, 212, 248–249

HotMail, 63

HTML, 42, 224
    programming for, 55–56, 243

HTTP, 23, 38–39, 40, 41

Hubbard, L. Ron, 192

Hybrid alert services, 126. *See also* Commercial hybrid online services

Hybrid search engines, 106–107

Hyperlinks, 23
    URLs and, 41

Hypertext, 35

Hypertext markup language. *See* HTML

Hypertext Transfer Protocol (HTTP). *See* HTTP

ICQ, 25, 102

Implied license, 189–190

Indecent speech, 183

Index
    for listserv, 87
    subject catalogs and, 110–112

Inference Find, 77

Information
    evaluating, 145–159
    freedom of, 197–198
    on Internet, 27–28

limitations of online, 201

locating on Web, 48–52

MIDIS for measuring integrity of, 154–155

production qualities of, 146–147

tools for gathering, 2–3

variety on Internet, 37–38

Information sources. *See also* Information
    access to, 4–6
    books and magazines, 30
    human, 28–29
    Internet as, 1
    libraries and special depositories, 29
    proper identification of, 201

Information Superhighway, 10, 17

Infoseek, 50, 111

Infrastructure, online, 31–32

In-line images, 55

Instant messaging, 102–103

Intellectual property rights, 192. *See also* Copyright law; Free speech

Intelligent computer, 16

International News Service v. Associated Press, 189

International organizations, domain names and, 149

International summits, 33

Internet. *See also* Free speech; FTP (file transfer protocol);

Gopher; Telnet; Web browsers
    access provider for, 253–256
    access to, 6
    as agreement, 18–19
    barriers on, 10
    commercial sites, 23
    commercial traffic on, 36
    connecting while traveling, 219–221
    control of, 19–20
    cost structure of, 20–21
    defined, 17–18
    European, 34
    evaluating information from, 145–159
    growth of, 36–38
    history of, 21–23
    increased use of, 8
    information on, 27–28
    interviews on, 3
    journalism and, 235–246
    list of service providers, 256
    military origins of, 21–22
    non-Web resources, 129–144
    researching on, 3
    usage costs, 20–21
    wireless access to, 222

Internet Academy, 108

Internet-based services, 253–256

Internet Explorer (Microsoft), 23, 34, 36, 42, 96, 97, 124, 203, 213, 214, 215. *See also* Web browsers
    compared with other browsers, 228–231
    configuring, 96

Internet Protocol (IP)

addresses, 22, 35
  URLs and, 40
Internet Public Library
  (IPL), 112
Internet Relay Chat
  (IRC), 25
"Internet Roadmap"
  (Crispen), 108
Internet service providers
  (ISPs), 15, 149, 253–256
  connecting while
    traveling and, 221
  e-mail account through,
    63
  home page and, 8
Internet Society (ISOC),
  148
"Internet Tourbus"
  (Crispen), 108
Internetworking, 17, 19
InterNIC, 148, 153
Interviews, 78–79
  online conference and, 11
  via Internet, 3
Intranets, 19
Investor's Business Daily,
  240
IP. *See* Internet Protocol
  (IP) addresses; TCP/IP
  protocol
IPL. *See* Internet Public
  Library (IPL)
IRC. *See* Chat; Internet
  Relay Chat (IRC)
IRE-L (Investigative
  Reporters and Editors
  List), 83, 86, 89
ISPs. *See* Internet service
  providers (ISPs)

Java, 21, 101, 168
Johns Hopkins University,
  shooting at, 61

Johnson, Tom, 52
Jornal do Brasil, 1
Journalism
  economics of, 245–246
  information sources,
    158–159
  Internet and, 1, 235–246
  technology, access, and,
    3–6
  television and, 236–239
Journalists
  access for legitimate,
    198–199
  accountability of, 243–
    244
  hotlists for, 109–110
  multimedia, 241–243
jpeg files, 43, 55, 140
Jughead, 144
Junk e-mail, 194
Juno.com, 63

Kalnoskas, Aimee, 136
Kennedy, John F., 236
Kennedy, John F., Jr., 84
Keyboard shortcuts, 217–
  219, 220
  on AOL and
    CompuServe, 233–234,
  for copying text, 218–
    219, 220
  listing of, 220
  navigating by, 219, 220
  for searching, 218
Keyword, 89
Keyword search sites,
  247–248
Kiefer, Kara, 59
Kinsley, Michael, 161
Klopfenstein, Bruce, 108
"Knock-Knock" feature, of
  Switchboard, 76
Kramer, Staci, 149

LANs. *See* Local area
  networks (LANs)
Laurin, Fredrik, 129
Law. *See also* Copyright law
  e-mail and, 77–78
  Internet and, 181–182
Legal reporter, 5
Leutwyler, Kristin, 11
Lewinsky scandal, 237–
  238
Lexis-Nexis, 27, 193
Libel, 184–186
  flaming and, 186
  service providers and,
    186–187
Libraries
  non-commercial, 112
  online, 29
Library of Congress, 29
Links
  criteria for, 176–177
  with HTML, 55
  on Internet, 17–18
  Web navigation with, 47
  from Web site, 147
Listproc, 85, 86
Lists. *See* Discussion lists
Listservs, 85–86
Listserv software, 85–86,
  92–94
Literals, 117–119
Local area networks
  (LANs), 13
Log utilities, 135
Lotus *Notes*, 66
Lundberg, George, 161
Lycos, 27
Lynx, 130

Macintosh computers, 7
  FTP clients for, 137
  OS of, 19

Telnet and, 130

Macromedia, 44

Magazines
online, 30, 171–174
Web links and, 165–166

Magid, Lawrence, 201

Mail. *See* E-mail

Mailboxes, privacy of, 77

Mailing lists, 72–73

Mailto, 40

Majordomo, 85, 86

Makulowich, John, 109, 113

Manowski, Stefani, 38

Map(s), 29. *See also* Site map

MAPI mail server, 207

Market value, copyright and, 191–192

McGinnis, Joe, 237

Media
challenges of, 176–179
Web as, 34

Meislin, Rich, 211

"Melissa" virus, 75

Menus, in browser, 217

Mercury Center, 170, 171

Messages. *See* Chat; E-mail; Instant messaging

Messenger (Netscape), 66, 69, 73, 74, 204, 209, 210, 231, 232

Metabolife, 243–244

Meta-search sites, 50, 122–124

Michael Lerner Productions, 108

Microsoft. *See also* *Internet Explorer* (Microsoft); *Outlook Express* (Microsoft); Web browsers
anti-trust suit against, 61–62

browser updates from, 45

Excel, 75

HotMail, 63

instant messaging and, 102–103

NetMeeting, 25

NetShow, 103

Outlook, 66, 74

PowerPoint, 72

Word, 75

Microsoft Network (MSN), 6, 26

MIDIS (Miller Internet Data Integrity Scale), 154–155

Military, as Internet origin, 21–22

Milkovich v. Lorain Journal Co., 185

Miller, Stephen, 154, 159

Miller v. California, 199

Milliron, David, 211

MindSpring Communication, 6

Misspellings, 146–147

MIT, Web material at, 54

Modem
as network connection, 16
wireless, 222

Mosaic, 23, 36

Moving files, with FTP, 135–139

Multimedia journalist, 241–243

Murrow, Edward R., 235

Naming conventions, 127–128

Nando Times, 170, 171

NASDAQ-AMEX Web site, 84

National Archives, 28

National Center for Supercomputing Applications, 23, 36

National Science Foundation (NSF), 22

National Security Archives, 80

Navigator (Netscape), 23, 36, 96, 124, 203, 213, 214, 215, 216–217. *See also* Web browsers
Alexa and, 226–227
and other browsers, 228–229

Negroponte, Nicholas, 11

Net Happenings, 112

Netiquette, 78

NetMeeting (Microsoft), 25

Netscape, 36, 42. *See also* *Communicator* (Netscape); *Messenger* (Netscape); *Navigator* (Netscape); Web browsers

Netcenter, 27
WebMail, 63
Web server and, 45
Web site of, 45

NetShow (Microsoft), 103

Network, 13, 19. *See also* E-mail
accessing, 17
connecting to, 14–15
connection type, 16
control of Internet, 19–20
cyberspace and, 16–17
development of large, 17
early, 21
hosting services and, 149
Internet as, 18
Local area (LANs), 13
URLs of, 40

Network computing, 14–15

Network host. *See* Host computing

Network news, 94. *See also* Newsgroups
hierarchies of, 95–96
Web publishing and, 161–162

Network News Transfer Protocol (NNTP), 94

Network Solutions, 37, 153

"Newhouse Net Lists," 110

News. *See also* Publishing online; Usenet
chat and, 102
major categories of, 96

Newsdesk, 88

Newsgroups, 25, 83–84. *See also* Usenet
communicating via, 29
finding right groups, 98–99
flaming on, 186
legal regulation of, 185–186
network news hierarchies, 95–96
newsreader and, 96
organizing, 96–98
reading and responding to messages, 98
reliability of, 157–158

Newspapers
online publishing by, 168–171
television news and, 238–239

News photography, 241

News protocols, 40

News reader, 96

News stories, information about, 83–84

New York Times, on Web, 168–170

New York Times v. Sullivan, 184

Nixon, Richard, 236–237

NNTP. *See* Network News Transfer Protocol (NNTP)

Nonprofit organizations, domain names and, 149–150

Northern Light, 77

Novell *Groupwise*, 66

Object-oriented software, 39

Obscenity, 77, 199–200

Onion, The, 55

Online communication, 28–29

Online conference, by Gore, 11, 12

Online information, 4
legal uses of, 188–193

Online services, 6, 26, 253–256
libel and, 186–187
list of, 256

Online tools, 7. *See also* Tools

Online tutorials, 107–108

Open Meeting laws, 197–198

Open Records Act, 80

Opera browser, 204, 210, 228–231. *See also* Web browsers

Operating systems, 19

Optic cable, 13

Outlook (Microsoft), 66, 74

Outlook Express (Microsoft), 66, 69, 73, 74, 204, 208, 209, 210, 231–232

Pacific Bell, 26

Password, for e-mail, 63–64, 209

Pathfinder site, 172–173

Paul, Nora, 51, 112, 147

.pdf (portable document format) files, 147, 223–224

Penrose, Roger, 1–2

Pentagon Papers, 201

Personal names, spelling of, 146–147

Photography, 241

Pine software, 130, 207, 233

Planned Parenthood of America, free speech and, 184

Plug-ins, 43–45, 103, 222–227
for audio and video, 168
chat rooms and, 101

Point-and-click approach, 66

Pool, Ithiel de Sola, 182

POP mail server, 207, 221

Pornography, 183, 199

Portable document format. *See* .pdf (portable document format) files

Portal sites, 26–27, 255

Posting messages, on discussion lists, 89–91

PowerPoint, 72

Power Search, 117

PPP (Point-to-Point Protocol), 16, 254–255

Presidential debates, 236–237

Press. *See* Journalism; Journalists

Press conference, on Web, 2

Price. *See* Costs

Price, Gary, 114–115

Printing
from browser, 53

of e-mail, 74
Privacy. *See also*
  Confidentiality
company e-mail
  networks and, 77
Prodigy, 26, 63, 77, 187,
  253
Professional
  organizations, 249–250
Programming
  for HTML, 55–56
  tools, 168
Protocol, 17. *See also* TCP/
  IP protocol
  IP, 19
  range of, 40
  transfer, 38–39
  weight and data
    reliability, 155–157
Providers, 6–7
Publications, 29–30, 55.
  See also Publishing
  online; specific
  publications
Public debate, 243–244
Public figure, 185–186
Public record, e-mail and,
  80–81
Publishing online, 161–180
  books about, 55
  economic incentives for,
    164–166
  by magazines, 171–174
  media challenges and,
    176–179
  newspaper ventures
    and, 168–171
  parameters of, 167–168
  readership of, 166–167

Qualcomm. *See Eudora*
  (Qualcomm); *Eudora
  Light; Eudora Pro*

Quoting
  from discussion lists,
    91–92
  of online information, 188

Radio, 251
  Web and, 164–165, 174–
    176
Raleigh *News & Observer*,
  170, 171
Rather, Dan, 219
Raymond, Henry, 245
Real Media plug-in, 44
Real Player (Real
  Networks), 103, 223,
  227
Regan, Tom, 1
Regulation, 182
Reisner, Neil, 62
Reliability of data
  MIDIS and, 154–155
  protocol weight and,
    155–157
Replying, to e-mail, 72–74
Reporters
  e-mail and, 78–81
  Internet and, 3
  television's impact on,
    237
  at White House, 4
Research. *See also*
  Information sources
  Alexa and, 224–227
Retrieval, of files, 195, 196
Reuters News Service,
  online tutorial and,
    107
Riley, Mike, 162
Roadrunner, 6
Robot (bot), 49, 106, 110–
    111
Romer, Roy, 80

Roosevelt, Theodore, 4
Rules. *See also* Codes of use
  Internet and, 18–19

*Salinger v. Random
  House*, 191
Salon, 173–174, 239–240,
  245
San Jose Mercury News,
  online publishing by,
    170, 171
Save, e-mail and, 70, 74
Save As, 53
  e-mail and, 74
Schleifstein, Mark, 211
Schreibman, Vigdor, 198–
    199
Science, FTP and, 138
Scout Report, 112–113
Search capability, on Web
  site, 147
Search engines, 49–51, 106
  hybrid, 106–107
  meta-sites and, 52
  for Usenet postings, 100
Searching. *See also* Search
  engines; Web browsers;
  specific search engines
  bookmarks and, 124–125
  Boolean logic, literals,
    and, 117–119
  current sites and, 125–
    127
  of discussion list
    archives, 93–94
  journalists' hot lists for,
    109–110
  with keyboard
    shortcuts, 218
  keyword sites, 247–248
  meta-searches and, 50,
    122–124

at multiple sites, 121–122

naming conventions, 127–128

online tutorials and, 107–108

productive, 116–122

refinements for, 119–121

Scout sites, 112–113

sites for, 106–107

specialized tools for, 113–116

strategies for, 52, 105–128, 107

subject catalogs, directories, and, 110–112

Selling of the President, The (McGinnis), 237

Servers. *See also* Client/server computing

defined, 14

function of, 15

problems with, 57

Telnet as, 131–132

Usenet, 94

Servers FTP directories, 137

Service providers. *See also* Online services

libel and, 186–187

list of, 256

Sex-discrimination charges, online computer conferences and, 197

Sexually graphic materials, 183

SGML, 42

Shame of the Cities (Steffens), 32

Shell accounts, 254

Shield laws, 195

Shockwave, 43–44

Shortcuts. *See* Keyboard shortcuts

Signature file, 69, 210

Silicon Graphics, 2

Silicon Valley, 36

Site map, 147

Site Ownership Confidence System (SOCS), 149

Slate, 173, 174

SLIP (Serial Line Internet Protocol), 16, 254–255

SLIP/PPP, 254–255

SMTP mail server, 207, 221

Smyth, Michael, 77

Snail mail, 62

SOCS. *See* Site Ownership Confidence System (SOCS)

Software, 110. *See also* Robot (bot); Web browsers; specific programs and types

browser selection and, 227–233

client-server and, 14

for creating HTML, 55

for e-mail, 65–66

for Internet, 23–24

location of client, 16

Source credibility. *See* Domain(s); Information; Information sources

Sources. *See* Information sources

Sourcing material, 54

Special depositories, 29

Speech, freedom of, 183–187

Speech codes, 196–197

Speed

of access, 32

problems with, 56–57

Spelling, 146–147

in e-mail, 68

Spiders, 110

SPJ-L (Society of Professional Journalists List), 83, 89

Squires, Sally, 79

Standard Generalized Markup Language. *See* SGML

Starr, Kenneth, 167

Starr Report, 239

Stationery, 232–233

Statistics, in Web site, 147

Steffens, Lincoln, 32

Sterbakov, Ira, 113

Stone, I. F., 4–5

Stratton Oakmont v. Prodigy, 187

Streaming media, 223

Stuffit, 138

Subject directories, 51–52

catalogs and, 110–112

Sullivan, Danny, 106–107

on major search sites, 120–121

Sulzberger, Arthur, Jr., 168

Summit meetings, 33

Sun Microsystems, 21

Sunshine laws, 197–198

Supercomputing centers, 22–23

Surfing, 14, 53

Switchboard, 76

Tags, 55–56

TCP/IP protocol, 19, 22, 34

Technologies of Freedom (Pool), 182

Technology
  access, journalism, and,
    3–6
  computer networks and,
    13
  content, presentation,
    and, 240–241
  speed of innovation,
    235–236
Telephone lines
  data transmission and
    voice, 17
  Internet access through,
    6–7
  modems and, 16
  network linking
    through, 13
Telephone service, over
  Internet, 21
Television
  cable, 6, 163
  impact on journalism,
    236–239
  impact on reporting, 241
  Web and, 165, 174–176,
    239–240
Telnet, 23, 24, 25–26, 38,
    40, 111–112, 129, 130–
    135, 253
  functioning of, 131–132
  online help for, 135
  reliability of, 156
  sample session with,
    132–134
Telnet log utilities, for
  capturing session, 135
Terminal. See Computer
  terminals
Terminal emulation
  software, 16
Text files, of Gopher, 143
TheStreet.com, 245
Third-party providers, 7

TLDs. See Top level
  domains (TLDs)
Tools
  for information
    gathering, 2–3
  online, 7
  programming, 168
  for searching, 113–116
Top level domains (TLDs),
    41, 148
TotalNews Web site, 189
Tradewave Galaxy, 111–
    112
Transfer protocols, 38
Transmission Control
  Protocol (TCP), 19, 22.
  See also TCP/IP
  protocol
Transmission Control
  Protocol/Internet
  Protocol (TCP/IP). See
  TCP/IP protocol
Transmission facilities, 18
"Trash," 73–74
Travel, Internet
  connections and, 219,
    221
Tutorials, 107–108

Uniform (Universal)
  Resource Locators. See
  URLs
United Kingdom
  domain names in, 151–
    152
  government site
    addresses in, 128
United States Copyright
  Act (1976), 187–188
Universities and colleges,
  domain names for, 127
UNIX, 19
URLs, 39–40, 46–47
  analyzing information

from, 40–42
USA Today, 238
Usenet, 2, 21, 23, 25, 38,
    83–84, 253. See also
    Newsgroups
  archived information,
    100
  behavior on, 100–101
  categories of, 95–96
  configuring news reader
    for, 96
  navigating levels of, 98
  network hierarchies
    and, 96
  newsgroups and, 94–95,
    96–98
User name (ID), 63–64,
    65, 69
Utilities. See Log utilities

Veronica, 144
VerticalNet, 174, 177
Video. See also Plug-ins
  Web links and, 165
Video conferencing, 21
Virtual Library, 112, 113
Viruses, 74–75
Visual Basic, 168
Voice telephone lines, 17
Von Rospach, Chuq, 100

WAIS, 40, 156
  reliability of, 158
Wallace, Mike, 237
Watergate scandal, 237
Web. See World Wide
  Web
Web browsers, 14, 34,
    42–45, 203–204. See
    also E-mail
  bookmarks and, 210–
    217
  chat rooms and, 101

configuring for e-mail, 207

configuring public, 222

distinctions among, 228–231

and file types, 43–45

Gopher and, 1, 130, 141–142

in-line images on, 55

locating information with, 48–52

personalizing, 204–210

plug-ins for, 168, 222–227

printing from, 53

selecting, 227–233

Telnet and, 24

Web navigation with, 47–48

working with, 45–47

Webcasts, 103

WebFerret, 123, 124

Webliography, 112

WebMail, 63

Web page. *See* Web sites

Web publishing. *See* Publishing online

Web servers, 36, 45

Web sites, 8. *See also* Hotlists; Searching; URLs; specific topics

copyright and, 192–193

e-mail and, 66

for finding discussion lists, 89

free space for, 163

FTP and, 136

general directories and, 248

growth of, 36

ideal, 147

of journalism students, 56

journalist hot lists, 109–110

"jumping off" places, 251

keyword search sites, 247–248

ownership of, 148–152

personal, 29, 77

of professional organizations, 249–250

setting up, 205–206

of White House, 4

Weiss, Alan, 101

Wells, Justin, 83

White House, 3–4

White papers, 3

Whois database, 152–153

WhoWhere, 76

Wild cards, 120

Williams, Paul and Margot, 112

Wilson, Duff, 125, 216

Windows computers, 7, 19

FTP clients for, 137

Telnet and, 130

WinZip, 138

Wireless technology, 13, 222

Word, viruses and, 75

Word forms, searching and, 120

Working Group on Intellectual Property Rights, 192

World Wide Web, 24. *See also* Internet

access to, 6, 253

application protocol for, 23

economics of journalism and, 245–246

e-mail services on, 221

enhancing use of, 48

growth of, 8

history, development, and structure of, 34–36

impact of, 236

new journalism on, 176

press conference on, 2

problems with, 56–57

structure of, 38

television and, 239–240

Virtual Library, 112, 113

working on, 33–34

Wright v. Warner Books Inc., 190

www. *See also* World Wide Web

format of, 49

use of, 41

Yahoo!, 27, 50, 52

e-mail and, 63

index, 111

instant messaging and, 102–103

Yahoo! GeoCities, 164

Zicko, Tanya, 48–49

Zines, 166. *See also* Magazines

.zip, 138